2021 | Volume 5

U.P. READER

Bringing Upper Michigan Literature to the World

A publication of the
Upper Peninsula Publishers and Authors Association (UPPAA)
Marquette, Michigan

UPPAA

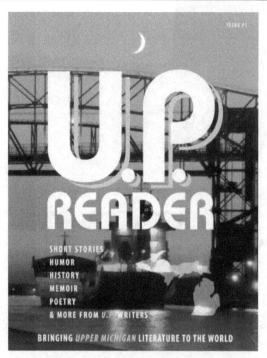

www.UPReader.org

U.P. Reader

Volume 1 is still available!

Michigan's Upper Peninsula is blessed with a treasure chest of writers and poets, all seeking to capture the diverse experiences of Yooper Life. Now U.P. Reader offers a rich collection of their voices that embraces the U.P.'s natural beauty and way of life, along with a few surprises.

The twenty-eight works in this first annual volume take readers on a U.P. Road Trip from the Mackinac Bridge to Menominee. Every page is rich with descriptions of the characters and culture that make the Upper Peninsula worth living in and writing about.

Available in paperback, hardcover, and eBook editions!

ISBN 978-1-61599-336-9

U.P. Reader: Bringing Upper Michigan Literature to the World —Volume #5
Copyright © 2021 by Upper Peninsula Publishers and Authors Association (UPPAA). All Rights Reserved.

Cover Photo: by Mikel B. Classen.

Learn more about the UPPAA at www.UPPAA.org

Latest news on *UP Reader* can be found at www.UPReader.org

ISSN: 2572-0961

ISBN 978-1-61599-571-4 paperback
ISBN 978-1-61599-572-1 hardcover
ISBN 978-1-61599-573-8 eBook (ePub, Kindle, PDF)

Edited by- Deborah K. Frontiera and Mikel B. Classen
Production – Victor Volkman
Cover Photo – Mikel B. Classen
Interior Layout – Michal Splho

Distributed by Ingram (USA/CAN/AU), Bertram's Books (UK/EU)

Published by
Modern History Press
5145 Pontiac Trail
Ann Arbor, MI 48105

www.ModernHistoryPress.com
info@ModernHistoryPress.com

CONTENTS

Your Obit

by Barbara Bartel

I wrote your obituary today. I'll read it to you later. Other than that, my morning was uneventful. Did you know there's an actual formula to writing an obituary? I'd never noticed before reading a handful in the newspaper so I'd know what to write in yours. I think most people only read the entire obit of relatives and friends. Otherwise they read the name, date of birth (to know the real age of the deceased), check for the cause of death to make sure it's nothing they personally are afflicted with, then scan down to the time of the services. That's what I usually do. Who cares if someone was a member of the Daughters of Isabella, taught piano, or loved to knit? What people want to know is which brothers and sisters are still alive, who they married, where they live now and what funeral home or church to send flowers or cards. Most folks know where to bring a casserole.

You'll have to pick a photo to run beside your obit. Please don't defer this chore to me. Just don't choose your graduation picture. Remember your mom insisted on giving you a Toni's Home Permanent with those tight pink hair curlers the night before? I shouldn't laugh but all the girls in our class thought it was so bold of you to wear a hat for your photo shoot. They called you a Feminist. A woman's libber. A rebel. Here your blond natural waves had been fried to brittle clumps. You smelled like ammonia for weeks! I hope you pick a photo of you now or very recent. One that captures the crow's feet and laugh lines you earned.

Oh, in the opening line I wasn't sure how to handle the God issue. I know you spent most of your adult life searching for meaning and with your scientific mind set could not "believe" as they say. All the redundant phrases like "meet her savior", "joined the Lord" or "went home to Jesus" would be insulting to your intellect. I don't like the fragment "passed away". That sounds so trivial. Cars pass. Clouds pass. Gas passes. Also, it implies you went some place. We'd had the 'where do you go when you die' conversation throughout our life together. There was never a conclusion we agreed upon.

So I made a list of ways to describe your, uh, exit, departure, expiration, but none of them fit. I decided to not sugarcoat the fact. I wrote that you died, plain and simple. I can add the date later, when I know. I didn't include your middle name; you hated the aunt you were named after, how when you were little she made you wash your hands before you could play her piano, an upright, for crying out loud.

Knowing how you feel about your father, I left him out of the second paragraph. Wrote you were the daughter of Genevieve Starling, life-long resident of Summit County. Why mention the asshole that molested you as a child and screwed up your entire life? Thank goodness you won't have to be buried next to him.

You're going to have to tell me if you want both your brothers listed. I know that the oldest one is only a half-brother (of a different mother, as the kids say today) but he was always the nicest to you, right? He helped you move several times; you kept in touch over the years. I'm not including Davy. Let him rot. Any brother who steals his sister's car to use when he robs a gas station should automatically not be included in anyone's obit. I figure your mom is going to read this and why cause her more heartache. She'll be dealing with your death and shouldn't have to be reminded that her bad blood son is still in the state pen. Mentioned your sister since she is respectable but I only listed her most current husband.

If people want to know the entire list of husbands they can look them up at the courthouse. Who cares anyway? Some of those guys she married were very good men. We all know she is a nut case. But I put her in because you guys always had a way of forgiving each other and letting go of the past. I listed her kids with all their last names, too. Her kids are her best work, don't you think? They haven't hounded us for any of your tools or other possessions like some of the other insensitive family vultures.

There are too many uncles, aunts, and cousins to list and they know who they are. They don't need their names in the newspaper. Some of them may appreciate not being listed. I am sure Donny wouldn't want any bill collectors to know he's still around. After the family paragraph comes the education and adult life part.

If you read other people's obits they write where they went to high school, college; some people mention places of employment. This one stumped me. Do I really list all the jobs you had? Would you want the world to know you ran away with a draft dodging trucker your first year in college and ended up in that "art" film? Or how you spent that year backpacking in Europe as a "translator"? I really didn't know where the adult part of your life started.

When we first met and hid our relationship from our parents or when years later we started living together as roommates? As I reviewed the decades it became harder and harder to put importance on the rollercoaster ride of life together. Mostly we just got by, lived from check to check, scrambling to take a short vacation here and there, with

and without the kids. How can I ever put all those years into a couple lines that would make sense to anybody but us? Who else would understand how exciting it was for us to open the front door to that shack bungalow we bought for back taxes from that alcoholic book salesman? Or what it was like to stand in the snowbank outside freezing, our teeth chattering, while watching the place go up in smoke two years later after that pretend-to-be electrician left a live wire exposed in the fuse box on the kitchen wall? Remember the good job you got with that non-profit outfit run by the lusty butch Mennonites who kept asking you to lunch? Who would understand how hard it was living in a lower duplex in the inner city when we couldn't let the kids off the porch? Little Ruthie still talks about those days. She wasn't five when we got out of there but she remembers gunshots down the block at the Seven Eleven. No one would believe all we'd survived in those early days. I left it all out. Each thing I thought of just flooded more and more pictures into my mind. I couldn't select any one to represent you. None of them are who you are today, now. But each one made you who you are, now. That's the truth.

After the education and job section comes where people list the person's hobbies and organizations they belonged to. Like if you've been a 4-H leader for eighteen years or a church lady, you'd mention it. What does it matter? If you taught the blind to see, hey, go for it, write it down. Most of us normal folks don't have anything unique or exceptional is how I see it. If you didn't cure cancer or write a bestseller, I can't see including anything. Who cares if you collected salt and pepper shakers to sell on eBay? I can guarantee you that the only person interested in your salt and pepper shakers is the burglar reading the obits to see when your house will be vacant during the funeral services so he can help himself to your collection.

I got to thinking about what I will remember forever about you, not that you were born under the sign of Leo, or that you had the thickest, straight natural blond hair in the world, but that you were extremely generous. I'm going to mention how you spent one whole summer of your junior year painting a barn for old lady Courson. Some senior center program hired teenagers to work for old people for three months. You never missed a day out on a rickety scaffold getting the worst sunburn of your life. When you got paid in mid-August (your mom expected you to buy school clothes and you'd at first wanted to buy that beat up green Firebird at Loco Motors) but you surprised everyone by going over to the courthouse and paying the back taxes on Courson's farm so that the old lady wouldn't have to go into a nursing home.

Also, I'm going to remember what courage you had. Exceptional courage. Like when you were driving to work, taking Fond du Lac Avenue through the dicey part of the north side, passed the chained up liquor stores, boarded store front churches, and dilapidated grocery stores tied up with wrought iron gates, remember that? Friends would tell you a hundred times to not go down Fond du Lac. At a red light, a skinny woman came running into the street hitting her arm and elbow on the hood of your car with a loud "thunk". You thought maybe you hit her cause she bounced some. Then you saw she had a broken nose that was spitting blood. One hand held on to the rose colored chenille bathrobe keeping it half closed. She looked directly at you, in your eyes, and you could tell she was terrified. She looked back from the direction she'd come from and there came this tall dude with a wooden baseball bat in his big hand. I'll never understand how you got out of the car, put your arm around the woman's shoulders then scooted her into the back seat.

The dude came right up on you and you simply looked him in the eyes and said, "Not today, man. Not today." You calmly slid back into the driver's seat and drove off to the hospital with the woman's screams drowning out the morning traffic report. Your generosity and courage. That's what I'm gonna remember. Those things and the private stuff I won't go into.

Following that paragraph, comes the name of the funeral home, date and time of services. I know how you feel about this. You don't want a funeral home involved in any way. I know, I know, I know. You think I can manage getting your body out to your camp and

onto that raised log rack you worked on for the last three years, to offer your body to the elements, returning it to nature. Even with the help of the sons-in-law, I know I cannot grant this last wish. None of us are going to be emotionally capable to conceal your body, load it into the van, then transport it the fifty miles to the camp road and get it on the small trailer behind a four wheeler. I mean, please. Ask me to slit my own wrists, ask me to wear black for the rest of my days. Knowing our family, this final act would turn into a Stooges bungle. There are laws. I cannot fulfill that request. Obviously the obit states, "No service will be held due to the wishes of the deceased." You will need to come up with another plan for your remains. What's wrong with cremation? Other than needing to be transported by a funeral home? We could spread your ashes wherever you'd want. Other people do it all the time. Didn't I tell you that Irv's granddaughter went on a tour of Lambeau Field last summer and sprinkled some of Irv in the end zone of the famed tundra? I could put you on the fifty yard line behind the Packers bench. Think about it. You'd be there for every home game for the rest of time. Best seat in the house for eternity.

At the very end I'll suggest in lieu of flowers to send memorials to organizations closest to your heart, like the Sherpa Widows Fund of Bhaktapua, Nepal, the Up In Smoke Medical Research Project at the Veteran's Hospital, Portland, WA., the Roswell Historical Society, or the Sundance Committee, Lakota Nation, Pine Ridge, South Dakota.

Now that I know how to write an obituary I think I'll do mine. Or maybe if you're feeling good enough tonight you can write mine.

Barbara Bartel has been Library Director of the West Iron District Library in Iron River for 27 years, Barbara Bartel earned her B.A. in writing from Mount Mary College in Milwaukee, WI. She enjoys talking about writing and books with friends and patrons, hosting author visits at the library, and cherishes her time with family. She is knee-deep in writing a novel.

A Little Magic

by Binnie Besch

"She's back in my life and once again she wants to ruin it," I almost screamed to my friend, Pam. She had called to ask me about a New Year's party I had attended the day before.

"The party was okay but she's back!" I knew Pam could hear the upset and anger in my voice as it traveled over the phone.

"Then you better do something quick to stop that." I could almost picture her shaking her head as she answered me.

"Hear me? Do it now or you might be sorry."

The day before, that fateful New Year's Day, had started out innocently enough. Two friends had asked me to join them at a 10 a.m. church service. Chrissy is younger than me by about ten years, has masses of red hair and is a gifted musician. She is also irreverent, bubbling with life, and addicted to knitting. Sarah, who drives a delivery van for a florist shop, is ten years older than me and is my guiding light.

It was New Year's Day, the start of a new year and a new beginning, and I was feeling optimistic. I would face the New Year with a song in my heart and the Lord in my bosom. I am not overly religious or holier than thou but the offer to attend a church service had been made with an additional lure.

"We'll go to brunch afterwards at Jerry and Lisa's and drink Bloody Mary's and Mimosas," my friends told me in their efforts to lure me to attend.

The service was lovely. The priest—witty, urbane and a bit of an intellectual rebel who had come to the Upper Peninsula from Con-necticut by way of Oklahoma—blessed us with his usual grace during the service and added just enough humor to keep us from taking ourselves too seriously. He dismissed us with the expected farewell blessing, "Go in peace."

I shivered and pulled my long coat around me even tighter as I left the church and walked towards my car. My 15-year-old beater was cold after being parked outdoors in zero-degree weather for over an hour but it soon warmed up as I drove down back roads deep into the woods several miles north of town. The county snowplows had been out earlier that day to plow even these deserted roads. They'd done their job well and now towering, icy drifts of white disguised local landmarks. Driving was hazardous and it took me almost half an hour to reach my destination. I managed to find a cleared space on the side of the road and parked my car.

"Brrr," I muttered under my breath as I rushed indoors. I was struggling to remove my coat when a stranger approached me.

"Hi, Franny, don't I know you?"

The stranger appeared to be in her late 50's, was at least three inches shorter than me and wore a beige shirt tucked into black formfitting slacks. Brown hair hung to her shoulders and she wore a light application of pancake makeup. It was when she smiled that I noticed her protruding front teeth. Her smile seemed familiar.

"I'm Lexi, Lexi from college," she said. She paused and a flood of memories tumbled through me.

"Ann Arbor Lexi?" I asked like some kind of idiot.

"Yes," she said laughing.

"Oh, my gosh, it's been forty years since I last saw you," I said. "What are you doing here?"

"We retired and moved here a few years ago to live in my Grandma Irma's house. Remember it?"

Irma's house was the site of many beer parties in our youth. Lexi had been infamous for being a good-time girl. If some guys showed up with a few six-packs, Lexi would climb into the back seat of their car with one of them. I was always the one left behind as they'd take off.

At that point our host joined our conversation and offered us drinks. I asked for a Mimosa and Lexi asked for orange juice, plain. Seeing the startled look on my face, she said, "Yeah, I don't drink anymore."

She told me that after she'd graduated from the University of Michigan-Ann Arbor she had moved to Phoenix, AZ where she'd worked as an editor for various government agencies. She was proud of having taken out a $10,000 loan to purchase a computer in the late 1970s. She'd done freelance software design to pay off the loan. The years passed and she continued working as an editor on the east coast where she met her husband. Lexi then introduced him, a friendly guy of sixty or so with a nice smile.

Together they told me of the first, then second, and recently, the third addition they'd put on Irma's house. Childless, they've filled the house with cats. I am a proud single parent of two grown sons. When asked, I will speak in glowing terms of their accomplishments. But that day these two out-talked me with tales of their cats. One is called "Oky" because they'd adopted him after a visit to Oklahoma. He was their favorite.

I gave them a shortened version of my life during the past forty years. Two unhappy marriages ending in divorce and a broken engagement to a medicine man/shaman. I added my recent downsizing from a teaching job of fifteen years on a nearby Indian reservation. They both asked me a few questions about teaching there. We chatted a few minutes more and then I left the party.

Two days later, shopping at our local supermarket, I stood in line behind Lexi in the checkout lane as she was bagging her groceries. We walked to our cars together but conversation was forced.

"I looked your address up on the internet. Can you see the lake from your apartment?" she asked.

"Only from one room and that's if you stand in front of the window and twist your head in the right direction to face the lake," I replied. Our apartment building was the epitome of elegance when it was built seventy years ago but it's sadly outdated now. We lack a lot of the amenities like air conditioning, microwaves and elevators in favor of one priceless luxury—a lake setting. As tenants we can walk outside and within a few hundred steps we are facing Lake Michigan.

I'd been shopping for bandages that day at the supermarket. I needed Band-Aids, extra-large ones, to cover a burn on my arm.

Hours after I had returned home from the New Year's Day brunch I was determined to cook a complete meal for myself instead of settling for canned soup or Lean Cuisine. I'd assembled the ingredients for One-Pot Chicken and Brown Rice. I was at the step where instructions directed, "Pour off all but one tablespoon of fat from pot." I'd picked up the pot and as I attempted to pour the grease into a small can I use for that purpose, the grease splattered up and ran down the length of my right arm burning it badly. I immediately ran cold running water over the burned area for about five minutes and then sat down with a bowl of ice water, ice cubes and a terry towel to ice my arm at regular intervals for the next several hours.

When Pam called me later that evening I told her what had happened.

"How did you know to use cold water and not butter?" she asked.

"Because when I was in college I had a similar accident. I was living with some girls in an old house a few miles off campus. One day I decided to make a casserole but after I lit the gas oven it exploded. I had second-degree burns covering both my arms and burned off my eyebrows and some of my hair. And you know the worst of it? The girls

I was living with were mad because I had gone next door to get help from the medical students living there."

"They don't sound like very good friends to me," Pam said. "Who were they?"

"Well, Lexi and Candy and Sue," I replied. "But once they saw how badly I was burned and that I had to go to Student Health every day for a month to get the dressings changed they forgave me. But Lexi was really mad and didn't speak to me for days after that because she thought I was hitting on one of the guys. I'd shared my food with her and I know she stole from me and I never said anything to her about it. Worst of all, she hid a shoebox of marijuana under my bed. After I found it she told me it was because she didn't want to get caught."

"Caught?" Pam asked.

"She had a regular stream of guys coming in to buy. She didn't want them to know where it was so she hid it my bedroom and not hers," I explained.

"Isn't it funny how you haven't seen this woman for forty years and the day you see her you burn yourself again. You better take your power—and your life—back from her," Pam told me.

"How?" I asked her.

"I don't know but you better figure it out."

After I hung up the phone I recalled my horoscope for that day. It instructed me to repeat the mantra, "This is my day, this is my year, and this is my decade." I repeated it several times each time using a stronger voice and emphasizing the words with more meaning.

I learned a lot from my years working on the reservation. I smudged my apartment using sweetgrass and sage. I lit a fragrant braid of sweetgrass and used my hands to waft the smoke throughout each room. It's better to use a feather but I didn't have one so I relied on my hands. I had gathered cedar a few months ago and it was now dried. I lit the cedar and repeated the smudging. I spread the smudge smoke throughout my apartment. Then I removed my glasses and "bathed" myself in the fragrant smoke.

I asked the Creator to remove all negativity from my surroundings and from me. I repeated my new mantra, "This is my day, this

is my year, this is my decade." I also asked the Creator to send back to Lexi all the good or all the bad she had created. I asked for the good that she had done to come back to her in increased measure as would the bad. Some might call this a version of that saying, "You shall reap what you sow." I had learned more from my former lover, the medicine man/shaman, but I had done enough.

During the next several days my burns started to heal and aside from feeling more tired than usual I seemed to be healthy. I was surprised at how New Year's Day had morphed from a meaningful church service to brunch with friends, where I was reacquainted with someone from my past, to a thorough cleansing (via smudging) of myself and my apartment.

After not seeing her for forty years I was surprised when I encountered Lexi at the supermarket only two days later. But maybe I passed her regularly during the past several years and hadn't recognized her? She had changed. People always recognize me and tell me that I look the same as I did in high school. I thank them, cross my fingers, and hope that it's meant as a compliment. We all age differently, that's how life works.

I often do my best thinking when driving. Pulling up in front of a local shop after I left the supermarket, this thought hit me.

"She now wants your life. You're single, you have a great apartment, you're managing financially and you have your freedom. She's going home to make lunch for her husband. She loves him but feels trapped. Lexi was never one to be tied down."

"Well," I added to myself, "this time she can't hurt me." I parked my car and entered the shop where I bought myself a few pink roses.

My trusty feng shui book recommended starting the new year by putting in a small pouch dried fruit and nuts to represent a healthy harvest, coins to represent easy abundance, seeds to symbolize fertility, and mistletoe for protection, healing, and a splendid love life.

I thought to myself, "Why not? It couldn't hurt and it might help."

It's now been ten years and I haven't seen Lexi since.

Deal Me Out

by Don Bodey

The little round guy who used to pastor down the road was selling sweepers now. He had left a business card in the door, and Doug recalled him while he used the card to pry dog shit from the tread of his boots. Familiar dog shit, from the neighbor's runt-ass mutt. The old lady next door let the dog out at daybreak, and it shit on his mother's side of the property line every day. He used it for slingshot practice, sent it yelping, but it never quit. It seemed like an insult to his mother.

He hadn't touched a gun in twenty years, but when he lifted the rifle from the back-door closet, it felt familiar, comfortable. A gun was a gun; this one might have been his dad's. He found its balance, put a spot of the linoleum floor in the sights and dry-fired, then leaned it in the corner. No moon. Beyond the short range of the weak kitchen light was a profound blackness that beckoned him to disappear into nothing. He considered it. There was one round in the buckle of the rifle sling, his only chance at shooting his mother a birthday present when it got light.

They had made a deal last night. She was old and ill and trying to die. She had grown up eating rabbit and squirrel and quail, and she wanted one more meal of wild game. Unless the dog was there, squirrels came to the feeder, an easy shot. His part of the deal was to give her that last taste and leave. Her part was to starve to death.

•••

His cigarette smell. Fifty-eight years of living in this house, she could smell every corner of it. He was by the orchard door. No, orchard *doors*. Until thirty years ago there was a heavy wooden Dutch door there, where their burro hung out, looking in. Ears like upside-down garden spades, voice like a bagpipe. Then D.D. put in them sliding glass doors. The next day she saw the burro walking down the road and never saw him again. Nobody did. But the doors opened a postcard view of the hills from her sink.

D.D. died when Doug was seven and by the time he went into the Army for twenty years, the orchard was giving out too. Now the doors stared out at 25 dead fruit trees that used to make 90 bushels of apples. Ghosts, every one of them.

Still not light, or barely. Like an old picture, darks and grays, no white. She wanted to get sitting up, her birthday. Sit and recollect. She can remember seventy years. River traffic, barges coupled together to make an acre floating down. Bottom farmers at the squat town grocery. Music out of jugs and fiddles. Turtle bakes and harvest carnival. Playing cards with half a deck of cardboard slivers.

Doubledoug is whistling. Like that bagpipe burro, he whistles through his teeth and his nose both so it sounds like two whistlers. Truth is she isn't sure about the whistling because she often had a whistle between her ears, that goddamn ringing like a hundred thimbles bouncing on a tin pie pan. Sometimes wrapping her pillow around her head and crying sent the ringing away.

But he was whistling.

She meant to listen but she got the peppermint farts. Three months ago, a new medicine made her fart, and they smelled like peppermint, like walking downwind of a green ditch full of wild mint, and after a few soundless ones, she fell asleep in one of those ditches, hearing a calf cry in the distance.

•••

He left a door open an inch and lighted a cigarette, cupping its glow out of habit. From half a mile away he could feel the concussive hypnosis of a long train on the trestle over the river. The birds were warming up in trills; no squirrel chatter yet. He liked sitting here, looking out at where he grew up and left thirty-five years ago. He knew that when light came, that what was left of the orchard would walk out of the black all at once.

Maybe she was awake now. Mornings were the hardest for both of them. She'd need a diaper change and a butt wipe. Two weeks before she had lost all control, and she lost her pride and dignity with it. She had been crying most of the time since, off and on. He almost ran away then; tomorrow he'd go, but it wasn't running away.

It seemed so light now he wondered if he had fallen asleep. He leaned the rifle in the corner and went to the landing, where he could hear her bird clock chirping off seconds. Except for the clock, there was no sound in her room. The only light came under the drawn shade, which she insisted be five inches above the sill.

•••

She saw the first light and watched a swath come into the room and land on her bed in the shape of a big butcher knife. Now, awake for about the last time, she wanted to remember being a pig-tailed girl farting into the dust of the playground at that dinky school she went to. Maybe she would come back as

that girl in her next life. Maybe as squirrel. She felt herself beginning to fart again. She sniffed and couldn't smell cigarettes. She wondered if he had left.

•••

Mama. Mama.

He couldn't tell if her covers were moving. When he looked around the room again, it looked full. Her whole frugal life here: cluttered shelves full of pictures of all sizes, some framed and hung on the wall. Many more in piles on the shelves. He found the oldest one of his mom, in pigtails, and one of his dad, and pocketed them. The biggest frame was a bunch of pictures she had taken her scissors to, so it looked like a crowd and she had filled between them with wallpaper snippets; his graduation picture, his wallet-sized boot camp, his mom and dad, dogs and a burro, shoats in the water trough, and his dad's obituary.

The room was chilly. The wind chimed outside her window tinkled, and the floor board squeaked. He heard her breathe and was turning to go when she called him in a tinkling voice, so weak. There was a vague smell, like candy, when he turned back.

Mama?

I hope breakfast isn't ready. I want to lie here awhile first.

I haven't even seen a squirrel; it's barely daybreak.

Oh Lord, that's good. I want another of them red-striped pills. Golly, but sunrise is a happy red.

Then he saw what she did. A red, pulsing light came under the parchment shade.

That's cops, mama.

She felt she was about to die or play dead.

Next door, ambulance, Mama. I'll watch.

•••

An ambulance was backed up to the porch, but the old dog had already been let out, and was shitting on his mom's side of the property line. The ambulance beacon made its eyes red, evil-looking. Some inside lights were on. He couldn't see anyone but some-body was turning lights on in other rooms. The dog hardly moved. Old dog: droop-faced and skinny. He couldn't tell if it had a tail.

•••

She pulled herself almost to the top of her pillow. Maybe she could make it to the win-dow. Maybe not. So weak. Her muscles have no thickness; feel like binder twine, about to break. All she can do is lie here, listen, pray. She didn't hear anything from the rest of the house, or from God.

Probably a year ago when she first couldn't put what she heard together with her brain. So she faked it. She got along that way until Doug came back; then she began to hear again, like a miracle. They had a conversation last night. She felt im-portant and it was the best she could hear for a long time. Now she heard him come to her door. His hand slapped the door cas-ing. His voice sounded like he was the one under covers.

No cops, mama. Downhill neighbor. Ambu-lance. Some volunteer firemen on the road. Sort of ruins my plan for getting a daybreak squirrel. If you can sleep, we'll eat in a cou-ple hours. Squirrel and biscuits, but I can't make the gravy like you. Okay, mama? Want to take a pill?

He looked foggy. Everything looked foggy. She just couldn't see good enough. But when he sat on the bed, it was real weight, no angel nor devil. Her son. She could feel his hand on her arm, big enough to go around it twice. So opposite of when he was in a crib in this room. She was strong and able and he was like she is now. Except she can think and reason and make decisions, and it is time to give that up. Her part of the deal was not to die before he left. She promised him she would eat again, and he promised she could die where she was.

She thanked him when he brought the pill then watched the slit of light under the shade until the throbbing red slices quit and the familiar yellow of morning emptied into the room. She thought of the neighbor, a woman her age who once stole her clothespin bag.

The pill was working. She was remember-ing a toboggan ride through an icy field, then into a creek bed breached by winter tree limbs. The remembering switched to a dream, like there was a switch in her pillow, to a hot air balloon at the end of the tobog-gan run, waiting on her.

•••

The ambulance light quit and two men wheeled a gurney to its back door. A small black car came and both vehicles left af-ter a few minutes. The dog stayed on the property line. No squirrels around the feeder or on the ground. He shot the dog. Head shot.

He started the biscuits. Couldn't help but whistle. Felt light, less burdened than he'd been feeling. Didn't know where he'd go, but he would leave today.

Six biscuits underneath foil over the pilot lights. Made him think of a sow's belly when they butchered. His mom did all the work. Harvest the meat, cure it, eat it. Today he has to gut that dog, dress it, fry it up. His part of the deal. He'd not figured on hav-ing to lie to his mother. She wouldn't eat much anyway. He would if she would, but he wasn't hungry right now. He changed his whistle to loud and blew *Rawhide*, which he'd learned from TV, in this house. A hap-py song.

Mama?

Now the light in her room was pleasing, cool like inside refrigerator light. She was grunting or snoring. The edge of the bed he sat on was damp and wrinkled. Her cover was two quilts sewn together; the bottom one was made from feed sacks from when feed came in colorful bags.

You're not an angel. They don't whistle.

Biscuits are raising, getting ready to fry him up. He's an old rascal. I'll try some gra-vy.

She was rolled in the blankets, facing away from him. She didn't have any hair left on the back of her head. This room had gotten smaller since the last sunrise. Crazy—when he looked at the picture shelf, it seemed like the pictures were looking at him. He looked his dad in the eyes and his dad was here for an instant.

Mama?

One little yellow onion left, boy. Slice it thin. Sautee it till it's soft and put it in when the gravy bubbles. When the leg muscles will come off the bone easy, put him in the pan, put a tin lid over it on low for ten minutes. Squirrel taste like shrimp. Remember... remember that time? Took a basket to the river fair. Cuts of squirrel on pointed sticks, squirrel-kabobs we said but you called them shrimp cabbage so we sold it that way. Sold out. 'member?

He couldn't tell if she was sighing or sobbing. She had told him not to touch her anymore and he was grateful now that she looked like a discarded doll. Over with. They both wanted it over with.

•••

Nothing changed next door. No other cars came. No lights changed.

The dog was a male, sort of. No nuts. Nothing but dog-food-looking-stuff in his gut. His back legs were disproportionately bigger than his front ones and whatever muscles he'd had was now sinew; he broke them into squirrel-size; once he dressed it and put it in salt water, it could pass for a squirrel, except it was pinker.

He found the yellow onion. Her flour was in the same canister, rusty on the bottom, that had held her flour for fifty years. It was one shelf lower than it used to be. He had never made gravy, but it was his part of the deal. He knew where the skillet was. He cleaned the counter, whistled, watched outside, and listened for sounds from her room.

Three cars went down the road, each raising a small dusty cloud and these floated toward the river like three ducklings in a column. The next car slowed until its dust caught up, then turned into the yard and stopped. Panic crept up his back. The rifle was leaning against a porch post, in plain sight. The preacher got out, sort of rolling from underneath the steering wheel. He saw Doug just as he got to the rifle, and raised his arm. He waved back and lit a cigarette. He'd tossed the skin and guts into the weeds, was relieved to see its only trace was a swarm of flies.

Pastor? Hello young man. How's your ma?

Weak. I'm getting ready to feed her.

Would she be wanting to pray?

She won't want you in her room. Go around back, to her window, and I'll tell her you're here.

Mama?

I been listening. I like your whistling. I hear you rattling pans on the stove, I heard you talking to somebody in the yard.

The preacher, mama, come to talk.

No.

He'll come around to the window.

No.

From her doorway, the preacher's belly showed in the slit between the shade and sill but his mom didn't know he was there until he rapped on the window.

Honey?

The preacher, mama.

When he rapped again, she saw Doug raise the window to even with the shade. Like a cartoon frame, she could see an open coat, the end of a twisted black tie, and a zipper only half way up. He could have had a basketball under his white shirt. The rest of him was a shadow on the window shade. His shoulders weaved like he was trying to balance on a log.

I came because Widow Smith died this morning, but there's no one there. His voice was soothing; there was some pulpit to it, but it sounded like something from an earlier time.

And since I was next door, I stopped to offer my goodwill. Are you well?

Are you nuts?

Ma'am?

Well, hell, mister. I'm tired. I'm about dead. And I don't want you peeping in my window when I die. Go on about your business.

Ma'am?

Pastor?

Honey?

Right here. I'm flouring the meat. Seeing the preacher out of here. Need any—

A pill. One of...
Peppermints. Here, mama.

He wasn't surprised the guy was on the path toward his car, but he didn't expect to see him smiling so big. When he saw Doug at the doors he cleared his throat.

Never blessed anybody through a window shade. And her... spirit. Makes me feel worthy, son.

Makes selling vacuum cleaners worthy, Pastor. She's not religious, wouldn't pray for herself, but if you want to pray for her, that's your business. I'm making us a meal and I need to tend some biscuits. That's my business.

•••

The dog was old but lean. He tore off a piece of meat. Chewy. At least it wasn't a cat or a rat. He put the biscuits in and found a gravy pan; then he didn't know what to do.

Mama?

I been lying here smelling you cooking. It's wonderful. Wonderful.

How you make gravy?

I told you.

You told me how to add an onion, but I don't know how to start. Just tell me like I was a little kid, okay?

She saw him at six years old, standing on a three-legged milk stool at the stove, and told him how to make gravy. In the back of her vision stood his father who would be dead in a year. She tried to hold as much of that as she could. Without touching her, he used the sheets to flip her and clean her then somehow changed the sheets. She kept focused on that vision of him, them.

He had a quick smoke and saw there was nothing going next door, then started the gravy, did it like she told him to. He cut wedges of the meat and added it, then cream and pepper and a tin lid on the skillet. He had done it, done the deal. He tasted it, ladled two scoops over two biscuits.

Ready, mama.

Before he said that, she had been trying to focus on the slit of light but she saw several slits; she knew she hadn't died because the smell of the squirrel cooking was in the room. But, why so many slits of light? She tried once more to focus. Then he was on the window side of the room, but he was all broken up like a jigsaw puzzle. She tried. She wanted to see him once more. But she failed, and it made her cry.

His instinct was to touch her but he had promised not to. After half a minute her sobs got further apart; then she sniffled.

Honey? Right here.

I am blind. I can only see, I don't know, like I'm looking at an empty bed with buttons spilled on it.

I'll feed you.

She wrestled her cover and elbowed her head onto the pillow, opened her eyes when she felt the spoon on her bottom lip, but what she saw looked like the sun reflecting off a pile of broken windshields. The smell of the spoon was so familiar she breathed deep through her nose before she opened her mouth enough to suck the gravy in. Divine. She accepted a few more spoonfuls. Perfect. She could taste it all the way to her stomach. Decades ago, now, the river people gathered for dozens of squirrels cooked in a big kettle over a fire. Everybody danced.

When he came back, he had read her mind.

One more big spoonful, Mama, with a peppermint pill in it.

She felt him looking at her, at her face.

Honey. We did a deal and I'm very happy. Fifty-three dollars under the paper on the bottom of the silverware drawer. Gas money, deal?

Deal.

She opened one eye. Not to see, not to blink. She opened it to close it. She knew he'd see her wink.

How to Hunt Fox Squirrels

by Don Bodey

Many people, especially big-city women, think squirrel hunting is nothing short of cruel, that it consists of carrying some powerful weapon into the woods and looking into the trees until a squirrel pops up like a Pac-Man bug, then *bloweee*, shoot 'em dead.

Ain't no way.

This is how you hunt squirrel. I know, because I've been doing it since I was old enough to crap by squatting over a log. Of course, in those days when I first started hunting and shitting over logs I was a boy, and my part of the hunt might only be to carry the squirrels home from the woods. But, nonetheless, I sat many mornings by my old man's side, us leaning against the same tree, blowing bubble-gum (*don't pop them bubbles, or you'll have to face the old man's face, see it turn hard as a hickory knot*) I hated bubble gum. In, say, 1955, he was a struggling carpenter and a· struggling carpenter's diversions were things like hunting. And I was nine years old and so it made perfect sense for the carpenter to take his son into the woods with him, teach him a few things.

He taught me to be quiet. By example. Taciturn might be euphemistic in describing his character, and being in a squirrel woods must have been the logical extension of his withdrawal from society. And in a squirrel woods it was acceptable—nay—necessary, to tell your nine-year-old to shut up, to stay shut up. But he taught me other things, important basics of hunting squirrels, and I'm going to teach you.

Get outa the bed. It's August when the season comes in, and it gets light about 4:30 and squirrels get up at 4:29, so you gotta get out of bed, first off. Usually there is heavy dew down, and that is an important asset to a would-be hunter, because after you get out o' bed the next step in the scientific system of squirrel hunting is natural, but you must do it in a TOTALLY natural way.

Piss. Be barefooted. Stand, barefooted, in the dewy grass and piss. The reason for being barefooted is to allow the chill of the dew to wake you up (4:30 is not a natural hour), and the reason for pissing is to check the direction of the wind. Look down and you will discover why you don't need a weatherman to tell which way the wind blows. Your stream may bend to the right or left or it may bend away from you. If it bends towards you, you are likely pissing on your feet, and you are not awake enough yet. When you see which way the wind is blowing you will know which end of the woods to come in from. Enter the woods downwind. If there is no wind, you have struck a perfect morning to hunt because you will be more able to see every movement of the treetops which is caused by the squirrels.

A shot of cheap whiskey is a good idea for starting the day off. Coffee makes you have to piss more, and besides takes too long to brew; it is high time to head to the woods. If you're blond or bald, wear a hat. Squirrels have good eyes and there are no blond or bald animals nor are there blond colored or shiny-pink leaves or sticks, which is what squirrels see from the trees. If you have brown or black hair, you needn't wear a cap.

Walk to the woods. The important thing is to be quiet, very quiet. Squirrels begin feeding at daylight, and when they have their bellies full, they ride the motion of the tree limbs to digest their breakfast. (Later, when you cut them open, you'll see that they've already eaten a dozen nuts this morning). One thing I forgot to tell you is to know the woods you're hunting. It isn't too late now, though, if you are carrying this set of instructions with you on your first hunt (the reason it is written on brown paper should be obvious if you've been following along: camouflage) to scope the woods.

Look for big trees that are partially decayed. These trees may be den trees. Look too for the pattern of the nut trees. Hickories and oaks usually grow in fairly straight lines, probably because squirrels, who seed more trees than the wind does, generally feed along the same routes their grandfathers did, either because of the location of their den tree, or possibly a water supply. Actually, I don't know why hickories and oaks grow so linearly, but they do. Trust me. There are very few chestnut trees left anymore because the wood of chestnut trees became valuable to furniture builders in the 1930's, as Osage orange trees became scarce when fence-builders discovered the wood is so hard it can be used between a dump truck and a loaded trailer in place of an iron pin; thus the Osage orange trees made good fence posts.

I digress, but these are facts told me by my father on squirrel hunts, whispered around the mouth of a whiskey bottle if, say, maybe there's too much wind and we had to wait it out or, say, it would be raining and we would wait that out too, because after a rain is the perfect time to hunt if they are moving, because every move they make shakes water off the branches and betrays their position. Whispered around the whiskey bottle, a pint, yes: I can see him now, leaning back against the shaggy trunk of a hickory and looking into treetops, like we will be doing shortly, as soon as I get us to the woods.

Enter downwind. Remember that. Chamber a round and check your safety and walk very quietly. Avoid every stick on the ground. Even the small ones that look like they would break silently if you step on them won't. Step on one, and the sound will be as loud as if you snapped the brassiere of the girl in front of you during the minister's silent prayer. Squirrels listen. Squirrels look cute and stupid but are in fact smart and bucktoothed. Step on a stick and they will hear it. Move too quickly and they will see it. When they see you, you won't see them: They will lie among the leaves and outwait you or dash away from limb to limb and tree to tree,' moving like, say, your last dime skips down the subway stairs, and if you shoot at one moving away from you like that you might as well be watching TV, whether it's on or not.

Soak yourself with mosquito repellent now. If you had done it before this, it would be losing its effectiveness. The writers who describe this product on mosquito-repellent bottles or tubes are all unemployed used-car salesmen and take a test to ascertain their lie-ability; only those who could tell their mother she never had bad breath are hired. If you wait any longer to apply the repellent, you'll have as many welts as Chicago has manholes. Mosquitoes that live in woods are always hungry.

Examine the ground. Look for cow shit. If you find cow shit, determine how fresh it is. If it is very fresh, you're in the wrong woods. You don't want to be hunting in a woods full of cows because the farmer whose cows they are is likely to hunt you, and I've never met a farmer in his woods who was glad to see me. Also look for nut hulls to discover what the squirrels are feeding on. If there are a great many hickory hulls, then you should stake out hickory trees; if there are a great many acorns down, then watch the oaks.

Look up now, for clumps of dried leaves in the trees; usually these clumps are a little higher than halfway up the tree and usually will be closer to the trunk of the tree than to the wind-blown outer end. These clumps are the squirrel's nests. A squirrel will never die in its nest. When I was a boy and my old man had his limit, or had had enough whiskey, or for some other reason was ready to quit for the morning, he would allow me to shoot at the nests. I think he knew I wouldn't hit one, or that there weren't any squirrels at home, because shooting up nests is poor sportsmanship. But, I learned how to aim a shotgun, then a rifle, by shooting at nests and knots.

One foggy morning we were ready to leave the woods and I shot at a nest. I don't know if I hit the nest or not, but there was a squirrel close enough to be frightened by the blast and it dashed, fast as a Hershey squirt, to safety inside a den tree. My father laughed and laughed and laughed, I know now that he was laughing at himself for not having seen the squirrel through the fog. I only knew then that he laughed for a change, and that was rare enough to make me feel big and strong and I carried the squirrels home by their tails, as if my single shot was responsible for the upcoming meal.

Keep looking at the ground and keep being quiet. Keep in mind the advice of Don Juan, that you will see your power spot. You will. Somewhere in the woods you will see a spot that looks like the only thing missing is your nervous ass; sit there. The spot will afford you a look at the oaks or hickories or—if you're in a chump woods—the sweet gums. Know where the nests and den trees are in relation to your spot.

There is a good chance you'll now feel like taking your morning shit. I leave the decision to you; I caution you to be damn sure not to wipe with any poisonous plant; even if you've never had weed poisoning before, your tender asshole doesn't know that. I am assuming you are male; if you are not, you likely have a spare Kleenex with you. Kleenex is curiously ubiquitous for women. I suggest you exercise your sphincter muscle; shut it down to f/22. (I am a hunter and a photographer, not an anatomist, so I may have the wrong muscle here).

When you have found your spot, sit. Begin looking up again. Look for movement in the trees. Listen intently for dropping nut hulls. Look for red-blond color amongst the green leaves. No matter how quiet you've been, since you are a novice, you've not been quiet enough, so the squirrels will be sitting tight for a while, looking for you. Sit still and look for them. Ignore the mosquitoes that are buzzing around you; they won't land and bite unless you did a poor job of applying the repellent. Your breath will come fast once you think you have spotted a squirrel. Be sure it is not a knot or a dead leaf. Wait. Make the knot move, and if it does, it's not a knot. One of my old man's favorite teases was this, "See that hole there?" "Yes." "What is it?" "A knot hole." "If it's *not* a hole, what is it?" I have perpetuated that fun pun; I use it many times on first dates and with bar drunks. No one ever thinks it is funny but me. I'm the one who counts.

Count. Count to one hundred to still your impatience. Maybe at number seventy-four, you will hear something hit the leaves of a tree. It may be the tree you've been watching intently for the past ten minutes and have decided is void of squirrels. Listen again, still your breathing. There. Hear it again. See a particular leaf move. Listen again and watch directly above that leaf you saw move. There. You see it hit up higher in the tree. You are seeing a squirrel· litter the ground with nut hulls. These are no city squirrels who are friends with pigeons and old men. These squirrels are jealous of birds and enemies of raccoons. These squirrels have never been spoiled by popcorn or bread crumbs; they have been eating nuts all their life. Mother squirrels put their children to sleep at night by telling stories of dumb hunters. Dumb hunters are impatient. If you were bred in, say, Chicago, chances are overwhelming that you are a dumb hunter because Chicagoans feed on impatience as surely as squirrels feed on nuts. So, count, but don't take your eyes off the imaginary perpendicular line between where you saw the hull shake a leaf and a point directly upward. Somewhere you have a squirrel who doesn't know where you are, or a squirrel that somehow migrated from a Chicago park to these woods, a dumb squirrel. Dumb or not, he's tasty.

Breathe slowly and close one eye at a time. Eventually the squirrel will move a few feet and you'll see the movement, or you'll see him sitting on a limb and reaching out for a nut. They eat like Chinamen talk: fast and choppy and they spit a lot. They spin the nut in their small hands and chop away the hulls to get the fruit. These hulls are your allies.

See it? Right there in the spot you'd looked at five times before, his tail as plain now as a roll of toilet paper in a cornfield. Quit counting. Raise your gun and put the end sight on his earlobe. (You won't be able to see his ears, and if you could, they don't have lobes, but pretend; if you're that close to the mark he'll die). Breathe deep and squeeze—DO NOT JERK—the trigger. Forgot to take the safety off, didn't you? And you probably jerked anyway. If you had fired, that squirrel would be sitting around with his pals tonight telling them you missed him by so much he had time to get a nut to go, while you squinted and watched only leaves fall out of the tree, while brother squirrel would chatter-laugh and scoot out of your life forever.

But let's say you had forgotten to put the safety on anyway, and let's say you squeezed the trigger after all, and let's say you hit him. He'll fall fast and turn like a slow boomerang and hit the ground with a thump. (They never thud and never splot; maybe it is their full belly that hits and makes the thump). Now, just as you are exercising the muscle around your asshole, you must now exercise self-denial. You must not move, must not get up and go retrieve the game, or you'll give your position away. You are in the woods for more than one squirrel and, unless you have your son with you—in which case it would be his job to mark the spot—you are compelled to remember where he landed, and remember surely. Innumerable squirrel carcasses lie until the worms come because a hunter thought he knew where it fell, only to discover that looking for a squirrel on the ground in the woods is like hunting a golf ball in a field full of dandelions gone to seed.

If you brought the whiskey with you, buddy, have a drink.

There are more squirrels in the woods but the shot of which you are the proud Papa is now working against you. Time for more patience. [What you have to kill *now* is time.] Of course, if you were an experienced hunter you would have, say, two or maybe three

feeding squirrels located and could now concentrate on finding the others. But, since you're a new guy in the woods, chances are you'll have to wait for the squirrels to get more hungry than afraid. Keep looking up into the trees but don't wear your eyes out. Recite poetry; think about the last time you got laid, or the next. Pretend you don't want to get up and go over there, see did you really kill yourself a squirrel. Me, I never remember poetry and during certain summers I get more squirrels than I do ass, so I would probably be thinking backwards to days when, after I'd napped a couple times, the old man's pint of whiskey would be half gone and there would be a smell of cigarettes on his breath as he flipped his false teeth out with his tongue,' then snapped them back in, the way a dollar-bill changer rolls your bill inside. There might be the sound of a tractor in the distance and there might be the crack of another hunter's rifle too. If he didn't have another squirrel half-located, then I'd be allowed to retrieve the last one he dropped, to practice walking ever-so-quietly through the woods that when I'd take my bubble gum out of my mouth, like he took his false teeth out, and stick it on the squirrel's mouth, give it a pink beard, or a Halloween mask.

The possession limit of fox squirrel is five. Let's make a quantum leap of our imagination and say you've got your limit. Or, more probably, let's say you're bored or that you've missed three in a row or seen one too far away to get a shot at so tried to sneak up on (you know he's laughing at you now) or for some other reason are done hunting for the day. Empty your gun's chamber and take the squirrels by their tails. Carry them proudly; somebody is likely to see you. Go to some running water and dress them. Dressing squirrel is a skill all its own, one I'll teach you in Chapter Two. Tell you what: get some help this time. Find somebody like me and offer a meal for a lesson on how to dress squirrel. It's probably unlikely that you have a knife sharp enough to split the skin on the squirrel's back anyway.

There are two steps left. One is cooking. Be sure to separate the young squirrels from the old ones because they have to be cooked two different ways. Cooking squirrel is nothing like frying a hamburger nor baking a chicken; it is some kind of amalgamated knowledge that isn't written down anywhere, and I will not write it down here. It is a knowledge passed from one woman to another, usually when the women are sharing the task of preparing lard for making soap. You must find one of those women and beg her. Not much begging will be needed because they all know the cooking is worth the eating. A good place to look for a woman with this knowledge is on a construction site. She won't be there, but her husband or son will. He will be a sheet-rocker. The vast majority of sheet-rockers are hillbillies; sheet-rocking hillbillies all come from some mythical place, called "down home." If they are working "up north", they have the satanic ability to get into a car on Friday after work and drive who-knows-how-many-miles to "down home," get in a day, maybe two, of hunting, drive back up north (usually four men to a car, and four bottles) in time to be at work Monday morning. They spend a week of days hanging board, sanding, taping, whistling and singing hillbilly songs, and dreaming of their woods.

So, go to the nearest pile of sheetrock and ask for somebody who knows how to cook fox squirrel. Wear a hat, at least touch the brim when you ask; don't try to act smart and don't try to act dumb; be honest. Tell them I sent you. If I'm not down home, I might be the one you ask.

The last step is managing to get the correct proportions of gravy, biscuits, peas and potatoes onto a normal-sized plate.

Don Bodey was a draftee mortarman in Vietnam. The idea for *F.N.G,* his award-winning novel about the war, took root when he was washing dishes in a restaurant in Florida. Then, he earned a MFA in the writing program at University of Oregon. For the next few years he built houses in Oregon, taught university classes and bought a bar in Chicago. Afterwards, he worked as a carpenter until his retirement. Learn more about him at www.DonBodey.com

St. Ignace and Mackinaw Island

The Fairy in a Berry Can

Craig A. Brockman

"Stay away from there, Scotty. If Dee's drunk, ya never know if some bull in a rut is shackin' up over there with her, again," Grandma called, standing on the porch, her fists thrust in her waist, elbows flaring. My two favorite remembrances of her are either wearing that stained apron with the little pink and blue flowers or sitting by the Christmas tree with a glass of brandy, a slice of fruit cake balanced on her knee, and a big grin.

"I'm just going to see if Duanes's around, then I'm riding into town," I answered.

"Get back before supper 'cause I need help with that damn sink in Cabin 3," she said, "And watch out on the highway!"

She was not a mean grandma. Quite the opposite. It's only that she had no setting for idle on her engine or throttle on her tongue. I tried to sweep from my memory those last years as she shuffled, oxygen strapped to her walker, smoking her Camels, and tending the cabins.

Duane was Dee's kid—smart and bust-a-gut funny for his age. According to Grandma they'd landed here from the Potawatomi rez in Wisconsin. I didn't care where they came from; I only knew that there were no other kids around and we always figured out some silly way to have fun despite our age difference. I was older, but not old enough to understand the silent torment that he endured while living with a mother who spent her days in a fog of alcohol and weed, while entertaining a cavalcade of crude and abusive men. She yelled at Duane whenever he called her Ma. She said that she was too damn young to be called some kid's Ma—probably true. So he had always called her Dee.

Grandma's place was called Shirley's Cabins and it stood along the shimmering shores of Lake Superior just a couple miles south of Paradise in Michigan's Upper Peninsula. It seemed as though I had spent every summer of a divine childhood there. However, knowing how memory works, it was probably only a couple years and only a few weeks each year helping with cabins, then fishing or tearing around on my bike.

Near her wooden dock, lined with bobbing row boats, stood six clean, yellow cabins with log siding. Connected to the property before my grandparents bought it, had been three cabins further to the north. In the sixties the land had been divided and those three cabins were stranded along a sandy driveway that curved back around to the highway amid scrubby pines, berry bushes, and trash. The largest of the three had been maintained as a shoddy year-round rental and the other two were used as sheds to store junk. Duane and Dee lived in the ramshackle larger cabin.

I pumped my bike around the bend, weaving in the soft dirt, and hopped off in front of the cabin. Behind Dee's dingy Ford stood a beat up red pickup. Set above the gray, broken down wooden steps, the front door was wide open, even though the mosquitoes back here could flay flesh and the deer flies circled nearby with fork and knife ready to finish off the scraps.

Before my foot creaked on the first step, I heard a man's voice from inside the dim cabin mumbling a string of curses followed by, "Hey girl, we gonna smoke this thing?"

Out of the darkness Dee emerged at the open door giggling and slurring. Older looking and more haggard than the last time I'd seen her, wearing only a thin tank top and a pair of short denim cut-offs, her vacant eyes downcast. "Duane went out back by the berry patch. Go on," she said flicking back her long, black hair and slamming the door.

At my age I knew four types of females: First there were family, which speaks for itself; then there were girls-who-might-talk-to-me—which were few; next there were outta-my-league, which included all high school girls and especially the cheerleaders; then finally there were women. Dee was a woman, though she was not much taller than me and she was probably only a couple years ahead of my older brother, Seth. Despite my limited point of view, I was pre-adolescent enough to notice this young Native woman. But she was definitely a woman, and besides, she was somebody's mother.

I circled past car parts, an old toilet, rotting lumber and all of the other debris that had been scattered among pine trees and birches, and I found the path leading to the beach. The path split left toward a blackberry patch that lay in a clearing about as wide as a kid could throw a stone. That's why we came back here to play. It was far away, we could throw stuff, and it was the only open area near Duanes's house where we could shoot my BB gun.

Across the middle of the clearing, like a great snow drift, the berry patch lay with canes of white blossoms reaching twice as high as Grandma. By late summer the branches would bow with fat berries that were prized by the few neighbors nearby, especially those lumbering, surly neighbors that lived in the woods—the black bears—who were desperate to fatten up for their winter nap.

"Duane?" I called. He didn't answer so I skirted to the other side of the patch. "Hey, Duane!"

"Back here." I heard from inside the berry patch. "Find the tunnel."

Curious, I walked a few steps farther, bent at the waist, until I saw the small arch that receded under the white ceiling of flowers. At the end of the tunnel, far in the middle of the berry patch, I saw Duane kneeling in a clearing no bigger than a camp tent. Duane's fine, black hair usually stuck out like a bunch of marsh grass, making him look like a surprised otter, but Dee had given him his summer buzz so now he was uniformly fuzzy.

He beckoned me with a finger, "C'mon." His face was sullen and unreadable. He did not have his usual big smile as he would rattle off two or three eager plans for us to do. He was quiet.

Before I reached the end of the tunnel, he laid on his stomach, looking pensively into the tiny room canopied with blossoms. I crawled beside him and saw the dried gulches of silent sadness that traced his dirty cheeks. I was twelve. I didn't know the words to say, or how to manage the brief awkward silence.

"What are you doing?" I blurted. Of course I knew he was probably hiding, but I wanted to change the subject.

"Look," his face brightened immeasurably into a crooked grin, "It's under here."

He pointed with a stick toward an old, blue porcelain camp kettle, overturned and partly buried, dappled with moss. He slowly edged the end of the stick forward until I grabbed his arm. I imagined anything from a nest of hornets to a badger living under there. He looked at me, shook his head, and made a wan smile. I slowly let go. Resting the stick on the top of the pot he carefully pushed. The stick slid off the slick surface and again the kettle fell back. I flinched. He tried again. This time the kettle tilted. At first I saw nothing, only darkness and gray sand.

"See? There she is," he said

I cautiously scuttled a little closer but still saw only darkness.

"Back there. It's Rosy," His smile broadened, "Rosy the Fairy."

Following the boy's colorful imagination, we had played some strange games together so I never knew what to expect. As he tilted the pot further back, there it was. Delicate and mysterious as a Luna moth, a small, white figure stood as though newly unfurled only for us.

My older, jaded brain soon realized that it was no more than an errant weed or black-berry shoot that had produced a fan of white leaves while it struggled to grow under the darkness of the old kettle. But I loyally played along.

"Hi Rosy, posey, how's it hangin'?" I said.

"No, dummy. You have to ask her for a wish. One wish a day, that's all ya get."

"Oh, that's how it works. So what did you ask her for?" I said looking at him with a goofy grin.

Looking serious he pursed his lips, looked down, and quickly shook his head. I should have known better than to ask.

"Ok, I'll ask for a wish, or did you use them all up already?"

Brightening, he nodded while pushing the top of the kettle further back, bringing the stunted plant into full view. "Go ahead. Ask her!"

"Um...let's see. I wish, I wish that Duane's farts didn't stink so bad."

"No. A real wish." He laughed.

I rested my chin on my hands, peering at the sad sprout, and made a wish. I hoped that two boys asking for the same wish did not cancel each other out.

On the way back, he tapped a stick on the trail and smacked trees and said matter-of-factly, "I'm gonna see if Dee wants to ask Rosy for a wish."

"Are you sure? I mean, do you think she's going to want to crawl all the way back there?" Knowing that he was probably set-ting himself up for severe disappointment.

He shrugged.

"Um," I stopped. I was stalling for time, "So, why did you name her Rosy? It doesn't sound much like a Fairy's name. Shouldn't it be like Tinkerbell or Dingleberry or some-thing?"

"It's Ma...I mean Dee's name: Rose De-light White Bird," He stared at me confused for a moment as though her name should have been obvious, as though I should have

known, then he meandered ahead to the cabin.

Dee was milling around behind the house looking dazed, smoking a cigarette, and humming to herself. She had pulled on a long sleeved shirt and shabby sweatpants. Seeing us, she folded her arms, smiling crookedly. The red pickup was gone.

"So where you boys been?" she said in a weird giddy tone.

"The berry patch. Wanna see?" Duane said hopefully.

"What's in the berry patch? A little early for berries, ain't it?" she said, weaving as she tried to focus on her son.

I was silent, waiting for the mortification.

"The berries are all blossoms and there's a surprise." Duane smiled.

She shrugged and waved her hand, "Let's go."

I was worried as I trailed behind; Duane waving his stick and Dee shuffling along dis-tracted.

It took more than a little coaxing to get her to crawl into the tunnel, though it was obvi-ous that she was as impressed as any moth-er with the array of white blossoms arching above her.

I told them that I would hang back by the woods to watch for bears, sensing that this was a private moment for Duane or maybe I just wanted to avoid the scene.

Before I'd taken a few steps I heard Dee in-side the berry patch. "There's my berry can. Well, dammit, Duane why didn't you just bring it home? I had to drag my ass all the way back here just to get an old kettle?"

A metallic thunk preceded a wail from Duane.

"Well get your damn big head out of the way. The kettle was stuck and it just came loose. Jeez, sorry!" She scolded.

Soon Dee scuttled out of the berry patch, kettle in hand, and stumbled back to the cabin.

I leaned over to crawl into the tunnel, but Duane was already scrambling out, crying, his hand covering his eye. He pushed past me, heading for the beach leaving me stand-ing stupidly for a time until I wandered back, skirting the junk around the cabin to get my bike. Thankfully Dee was nowhere to be seen.

Later in the afternoon, I returned from town. Out of curiosity, I turned down the sandy road past the old cabins. As I came closer, I slowed. Dee sat on the broken front steps, face downturned, washed hair framing the scrubbed and cleaned blue kettle. Her hands spread on each side as she looked helplessly into the depths of the empty Fairy can. Sad and broken she looked up, then using her pursed lips to point toward the cabin, she nodded a tiny salute as I rode past. Wanting to avoid another scene, I shook my head quickly and rode to Grandma's.

A week later the cabin was locked up and "Dee and the kid" had left, according to Grandma. It seemed I had spent most of the summer with Grandma until I had to reluctantly go home for a couple weeks to have my dreaded sports physical, a haircut, and an even more dreaded dentist appointment. When I got back, I figured that Duane's cabin would still be empty.

It was getting on in August, nearing that time when every kid wakes up in the morning gasping for air amid nightmares of getting up for school, being late for the bus or being forced to eat pea soup in the cafeteria. I was back at Grandma's cabins and I was going to make this final week of summer count.

Grandma hardly had time to say hello before I hopped on my bike, spinning my tires while steering for town along a sandy driveway that seemed lonely without Duane. My head was down while navigating ruts, looking for the hard pack dirt.

"Hey champ!" I nearly toppled, startled by a friendly voice as I passed the old cabin. A Native man with a gray pony tail and blue shirt stood on the neat, new landing that had been added to the cabin. He held a hammer in one hand and a carpenter's level in the other. A shiny black Chevy pickup was parked along the short two-track next to the cabin.

I slid to a stop.

"Are you Scotty?" he said.

"Uh, yeah," I said, wary that he knew my name. I had seen too many strange men lurking around Dee's cabin.

"Duane told me all about you. Your little friend in need..." He waved me toward the cabin.

I laid down my bike and cautiously stepped forward. Before I made it to the cabin, Duane came skipping around the corner. His hair was once more in full, black bristle from a summer's growth.

"Scotty!" He dropped his stick and ran to me. "Papa, this is Scotty."

Now I could see that the whole place had been spruced up almost like a real house and much of the junk had been hauled away.

Duane beckoned me around back with a conspiratorially curled finger and a big smile.

In the shade of a tall white pine, a card table had been set up, strewn with empty pans and other utensils. In the center of the table, stood the blue porcelain kettle, brimming with glistening blackberries.

"Hey. Scotty, our boy." I turned to see Dee coming from the cabin. Radiant. Her engaging black eyes nearly made me blush, looking very much like one of those outta-my-league girls. Her hair was a little shorter but shiny and full; she wore a pink tee shirt, black jeans, and stepped smartly over to us in new brown sandals.

Her appearance rendered me speechless, for so many reasons.

"Yeah, Ma. Scotty, our boy. Our little boy. So cute, eh?" Duane mocked.

I punched him on the shoulder.

"Hey, why don't you guys get me another pan of berries so I can top off this batch," she said, waving us on with a cake pan.

It was fun to hear his chatter as we tripped down the path. I had missed him.

"I like your Papa," I said.

"Yeah, I know, he's fixing up the cabin while Ma's in school." He busted a rotten stick across a tree trunk. "I stayed with him while she was in the hospital." He paused, smiling at me, "That's when Rosy helped us."

"What do ya mean?"

He looked at me incredulously, "Rosy the Fairy, crazy head. I made a wish. Remember? Then she got freed from the berry can.

She couldn't answer my wishes when she was stuck in the dark under that old kettle." He reached for a wrinkled puff ball at the side of the trail. "You have to uncover them fairies so they can see the light and be free. That's how Ma was saved." He pitched the dry fungus in the air and hit it like a slugger, thrusting a fist in the air and cheering after it exploded in a brown cloud.

Those big, bumbling forest neighbors, scooping paws full of berries while resting on their broad haunches, had crushed the north edge of the blackberry patch in their clumsy feast. The tunnel had been undisturbed as Duane led me under swaying canes wafting a fragrance of sweet, fermenting berries that squished under our knees and stained our hands. Arriving at the center, he hurriedly waved me forward. I eased my way ahead trying to avoid thorns and berries.

"Look Scotty. She's here. She's all free now."

I approached with a puzzled look, prepared to oblige his hungry imagination once more.

There she stood. Proudly unfurled in bronze late day sun was an apparition that had escaped the bruised imagination of this hopeful child. Clothed in pink blossoms with moss green leaves, grew a proud, radi-ant wild rose with fragrance that rivaled the wine-scented berries.

Duane beamed a smile that is burned in my memory.

The Fairy under the berry can that had dwelt in darkness was free.

Craig A. Brockman released *Dead of November: A Novel of Lake Superior* in 2020. He lived in the U.P. for nearly 20 years while employed by the Indian Health Service, Lake Superior State University and other facilities.

In 2017, an article in the *Ontonagon Herald* chronicled the final 140-mile leg of his meandering 450-mile hike across the entire U.P. from the Drummond Island Ferry Dock in De Tour Village to a sandbar at the mouth of the Montreal River on the Wisconsin border.

Craig currently lives with his wife in Tecumseh, Michigan. In 2007, he published *Marty and the Far Woodchuck*, a middle grade novel. You can visit craigabrockman. com for more information or contact craig@craigabrockman.com.

St Ignace waterfront railroad

The Walk

by Stephanie Brule

Her soft nose brushes my calf. Her hot breath is wet on my skin. Her brown eyes are filled with the black pools of her pupils. Her light eyelashes seem out of place. My husband used to joke that she looked like Boris Becker. I crouch down, rub the velvety fur on her ear between my fingers.

"We're going. I just have to get my shoes."

She tips her head to one side when I talk to her, searching for a familiar word. She lets out a whine when I backtrack into the kitchen for my phone. She follows me, her toenails clicking on the wood floor. She shakes her head, her ears flapping like a blackjack dealer shuffling cards.

"Okay, okay. We're going."

I put a handful of small dog treats in my pocket and grab a little plastic bag. She usually finds tall grass or a wooded area to go, but sometimes she picks a neighbor's yard. I clip the leash to her collar. It's one with a lead that extends and contracts as she wanders ahead along the road. The dog trainer we hired when she was a puppy had recommended it. I can stop her short with the lever under my thumb, but she's strong and sometimes jerks my hand painfully. The metal tags on her collar jangle as she runs ahead, a sound that terrified me as a child when I was afraid of dogs. I give her slack to walk and stop at random, nose to the ground, fascinated by the smell of another creature, long gone.

"Sweet girl."

She looks up at me, walks by my side for a moment. I give her one of the treats from my pocket. She's gentle when she takes it, hardly touching my fingers with her lips. She chomps it quickly, chewing with her mouth open. Her tail is upright with happiness, spinning and flicking back and forth. I can't help but smile.

The walk is my routine after dinner now. I am alone and it helps to fill the time before bed. It's a circular route, beginning and ending at the bottom of the driveway. I go in almost any weather. When it's dark, I use a headlamp to see patches of ice on the shoulder of the road. We used to take the same walk together. We would get a chance to talk. Sometimes we'd hold hands for a few minutes. In the winter months, we used to shuffle our boots down the driveway, checking to see how icy it was. He'd warn me, "Careful, it's slick." We would laugh when the dog dove headlong into a fresh pile of snow and rolled on her back like a delighted child making snow angels. I loved how the snow muffled everything but the sound of our boots squeaking as we walked, mine leaving footprints that turned out slightly.

Most of the houses in the neighborhood have deep, grassy front yards. White pines with their feathery branches spread like wings, old oaks and white birch trees filling the spaces between lots. We moved here from the city when our oldest was a toddler. I can still remember the relief, the burden lifting as my bare feet sunk into the grass that first afternoon the house was ours. Our son had run around the yard calling it a park. There aren't as many children in the neighborhood now. They left for college and their own lives. The pine trees that had been planted in row along the side of the house had looked small and spaced too far apart, like a new Christmas tree farm. Now, they grow in a canopy of shade, dropping brown needles that kill the grass.

"Come!"

A car roars past. The noise interrupts my trance of thoughts; the moments of forgetting. I pull her leash, jerking her away from the road. The slack keeps me from being able to move her as fast as I want. We are walking against traffic along a curve in the road, but it's hard for cars to see us. Usually the sound of an engine gives me warning, a chance to make sure she's not wandering too far onto the pavement. I had reacted in time, but the car had not moved to avoid us at all. My heart beats faster; a sudden cold sweat chills me.

"A little too close, wasn't it?" She's busy sniffing again, unaware.

We are on the busier road that borders the neighborhood. It's a bit of a throughway from one side of town to the other, with no stop signs for over a half mile. There's a gravel shoulder in the road where we walk, especially along the curve. High school students and parents picking up younger ones race by in the late afternoon. It's the same stretch of road where the neighbor boys had shot an AirSoft gun from the cover of trees, sending pellets whizzing past me, laughing at the danger as only teenagers can. Often, as I walk, I construct fantasies about passing cars; the redhead woman is meeting a man from work, excited about their illicit affair; the teenager with glasses has a pistol in the trunk and is plotting how to get it inside the school.

I walk, lost in these stories. I don't know where the thoughts come from, but as strange as they are, it's better than remembering what happened.

She stops in the spot almost every time we pass it. It's been well over a year, but it's like she can still smell him. She pushes the ground with her nose, wagging her tail. She stands, unmoving, then lowers her nose to the same spot again. Smell is her memory. The first time she did it, I broke apart with grief. For her, and for me. At least I know

what happened to him. For her, he is just gone. Now, I wait while she sniffs. I can feel him sometimes in the stillness. Other times, I can hear the screeching tires, the sickening impact of metal and human flesh.

"It's okay girl," I kneel next to her for a moment. "I know."

After a few more moments I pull on the leash. "Let's go." She walks beside me for a moment then trots ahead, tail up, ears alert. She pauses at the corner, smelling tall grass around the post of the street sign. We turn back into the neighborhood, to finish the walk.

Stephanie Brule grew up in Illinois, went to college in Massachusetts, law school in California, then came to her senses and returned to the Midwest. She and husband Dave settled in his hometown of Iron Mountain in 1997 and raised three children to appreciate pasties, winter and hard work. Stephanie worked as a prosecuting attorney for Dickinson County for over thirteen years. She loves spending time outdoors and with the family's yellow labs.

Captain on the bridge · S.S. Harvester

A.S.S. for State Slug

by Larry Buege

◆❖◆

It had been a long time since the old neighborhood had seen such excitement. The vacant lot, which had been home to the We Energy power plant on the north side of Marquette, was now crawling with every form of humanity. An insufficient assortment of police officers was gallantly trying to bring order to the chaos, but they were quick to admit their shortcomings. Flashing lights beamed from their squad cars in a vain attempt to magnify their presence.

In the center of activity, three bulldozers, engines in idle, sat helplessly while their operators and other construction workers conversed in small groups. Their frustration was palpable. Over a hundred highly vociferous protesters waving large posters and chanting a farrago of provocative pabulum surrounded the helpless construction workers. Although unnecessary, a provocateur with megaphone egged on the demonstrators.

Ethyl Higgenbottom, standing at the edge of the protesters, surveyed the chaos with pride. They had stopped them, at least for the moment. It would be sufficient to obtain a court order, and that was what mattered. There would be no further development here. With environmental impact studies and frivolous lawsuits, she could keep them tied up for years.

It didn't take long for the media to arrive (they had been alerted in advance). Helicopters armed with telephoto lenses circled above as camera crews set up satellite dishes to provide live feed to the eagerly waiting world. They would be just in time for the six o'clock news. A TV newscaster thrust a microphone into Ethyl's face.

"Mrs. Higgenbottom, I'm Rob Carter from the Channel 6 News in Negaunee. Can you tell us what this protest is about?"

Ethyl smiled at the man with the camera on his shoulders. Form is everything, she told herself. "I'm glad you asked, Rob. We are concerned citizens who are fighting to save the Amorous Spotted Slug."

"Did you say spotted slug?"

"Yes, Rob. But this is not just any slug. The Amorous Spotted Slug is currently on the endangered species list and is normally found only in Marquette's Presque Isle Park. Many felt they could not thrive anywhere else."

"Are you saying they are now propagating on the grounds of this old power plant?"

"That's correct, Rob. Two days ago several of these extremely rare slugs were found right here in the remnants of this old coal pile. That's why it is so important we leave the land in its pristine beauty."

The newscaster looked around at the scattered lumps of coal, old tires, and other trash. Only in minds of the visually impaired could such a pigsty be considered pristine beauty. "Amorous Spotted Slug, that's a strange name for a slug. What makes it so important?"

"Rob, most people are unaware of this wonderful creature's natural beauty. I recently talked with Toivo Rantamaki, Professor Emeritus of Finlandia University, on the phone who describes the sex life of the Amorous Spotted Slug as unique within the animal kingdom. Professor Rantamaki says before the Amorous Spotted Slugs copulate, they perform this ritualistic mating dance, which is quite intricate. Each subspecies has a slightly different cadence. Professor Rantamaki says the choreography is unbelievable."

"Have you seen this mating dance?"

"No, Rob, I haven't. Unfortunately, the A.S.S. is nocturnal and is seen best with night-vision goggles. The A.S.S. tends to be very slow, which is why they're so rare. The mating dance can take hours, and often one of the A.S.S. will fall asleep before they copulate. The mating dance is quite meaningful when seen in time-lapse photography."

"And these slugs are normally found only at Presque Isle Park? That's just a ways down the road."

"That's right, Rob. Professor Rantamaki believes they originated in the Amazon Jungle and migrated to Michigan's Upper Peninsula on drifting coconuts during the Great Biblical Flood. As you know, the unicorns were less fortunate. Professor Rantamaki says the A.S.S. can't propagate below the bridge, because Trolls carry a virus that is often lethal to the A.S.S. We hope to make the Amorous Spotted Slug the official state slug. The Petoskey Stone is our official state stone and the Kalkaska Soil is our official state soil, but we have nothing unique to the U.P. The A.S.S. would make the perfect state slug."

"Mrs. Higgenbottom, are you aware there are plans to build a school for blind paraplegics on the site of the old power plant?"

"Rob, sometimes we have to make sacrifices for the good of this planet we live on. I'm sure, when all of those blind paraplegic kids see what we've done, they'll leap with joy."

"How did you happen to find these slugs?"

"That's rather weird, Rob. Someone phoned in an anonymous tip, which is strange since few people would recognize an Amorous Spotted Slug."

"I see not everyone is enthralled with the A.S.S. You have some counter protesters."

"Rob, I believe that would be protester, in the singular. Wally gets some strange ideas, especially when he's been drinking."

"Let me get his take on the Amorous Spotted Slug."

The TV 6 reporter worked his way through the crowd toward a long protester holding up a *Deport the A.S.S.* sign.

"Excuse me, sir. I'm Rob from the TV 6 News. Are you Wally? Can you tell me why you're protesting against this loveable slug?"

"They stole my pasty."

"They stole your pasty?"

"Yep. Two years ago I was hunting deer on Presque Isle, and one of those **&#%#** slugs stole my pasty. Then last year they infested my attic—wild parties every night—couldn't get any sleep. They're a public nuisance. Now Ethyl wants to make them the state slug. Those Amorous Spotted Slugs are an invasive species, illegal aliens. They should be deported back to the Amazon Jungle."

"How do you feel about making the Amorous Spotted Slug the official state slug?"

"Over my dead body! Ethyl spends way too much time on Facebook with those environmental groups. Those lascivious slugs are destroying our marriage. Half the time, Ethyl doesn't even have time to fix dinner."

"You're married to the protest leader?"

"Yeah, but don't print that. It could ruin my credibility."

•••

Officers Koski and Beaudry were patrolling the donut shops in north Marquette when they received the call: "Hostile protesters blocking traffic at the Presque Isle Park entrance. Officers on the scene requesting backup." It was not a welcomed assignment this close to the end of their shift, but Koski and Beaudry were the only officers on duty with riot training. Koski took a bite from his nut-covered donut and brushed the crumbs from his uniform. With everybody armed with cell-phone cameras, it never hurt to look his best.

"Hit the siren and lights," Beaudry suggested. A flashy arrival with a modicum of police brutality often defused tense conflicts, at least that was the lie Beaudry told himself.

"It must be that women's lib group again," Koski said, referring to a small group of women advocating the removal of Father Marquette's statue. It was a flagrant sexist symbol of male domination, at least from their viewpoint. Why Father Marquette and not Mother Marquette? They normally protested early in the day to ensure coverage by the evening news.

Koski turned the police cruiser onto Lake Shore Drive and headed toward Presque Isle. Residents called it an island, but in reality it was a small peninsula jutting into Lake Superior. All the land and adjacent marina were part of the city park system. It was a popular spot for boaters, bikers, and star gazers. Presque Isle came into view as they crossed the Dead River Bridge.

"Holy Wah!" Koski dropped his donut mid bite. "There must be several hundred people in that mob."

"Should we request additional backup?" Beaudry asked as his trembling hands reached for the mike. "Maybe National Guard?"

"Let's check it out first," Koski replied. "They seem peaceful." He had a new can of pepper spray he was itching to try out. Koski was several years senior to Beaudry and activating the National Guard would show signs of weakness.

Koski stepped out of the car and stretched out his five-foot, six-inch frame. A CNN helicopter was hovering overhead. Down below hundreds of energetic protesters were waving protest signs that stated, "A.S.S for State Slug." Koski assumed they were referring to the Amorous Spotted Slug. Koski had encountered them several times in the past—never with a good outcome.

Several officers were trying to usher the protesters away from the road. They would have had better luck transporting a load of frogs in a wheelbarrow. A long line of cars filled with irate occupants hoping to spend the day at Presque Isle waited impatiently for the protesters to clear a path. That was not about to happen.

"We need to find the ring leader," Koski said.

The leader was not hard to find. Ethyl was waving her "A.S.S. For State Slug" sign and working up the crowd with her megaphone. Wally was equally energetic as he waved his "Deport the A.S.S." Koski and Beaudry had encountered the couple several times in the past. They changed any minor disturbance into a disaster. The two officers weaved their way toward the center of the crowd.

"Officers Koski and Beaudry, it is so nice of you to join our protest," Ethyl said when she saw the officers approaching.

"We're not here to join your protest. You're blocking traffic. Unless you have a parade permit, you have to disperse."

"Are you going to deport those A.S.S.," Wally asked. "They're illegal aliens, ya know."

"Can I borrow you megaphone for minute," Koski asked. Assuming Koski was, indeed joining her cause, Ethel passed over the megaphone.

"Listen up, everyone. The pasty shop on Presque Isle Avenue is giving away free pasties to the first one hundred customers."

"Is that true?" Beaudry asked. He was thinking a pasty would go well with the donuts.

"Heck if I know," Koski replied, but within five minutes, only officers Koski and Beaudry remained next to the lingering lumps of coal from the old power plant.

Larry Buege's short stories have received regional and international (English speaking) awards. He has also authored nine novels including the ever-popular Chogan Native American series. More information about his novels can be found at www.Gastropodpublishing.com or by contacting the author directly at LSBuege@aol.com. For a tongue in cheek look at the campaign to make the Amorous Spotted Slug our state slug, please visit www.AmorousSpottedSlug.com/

A Matter of Time

by Tricia Carr

Mrs. Willet came into the small store jauntily, smiling her lopsided mute smile at Mrs. Jarple and the store clerk and giving the bulb of the kadooka horn on the front of her walker a little squeeze.

"Dolly, how nice to see you out and about on this beautiful day!" Mrs. Jarple exclaimed. "Kay, do you have a chair?" Mrs. Willet lowered herself carefully.

She was a very old lady but flamboyant still. Her hair was a determined red, worn long and wavy in the back. A soft gray fedora, its front brim pinned up with an enameled butterfly, hid the thinning top hair; feathery earrings dangled. Bicycle streamers flapped from the sides of her walker and a small rear-view mirror was clamped next to the kadooka on the front. The two women with her had none of her style. "One as plain as a mud fence and about as talkative, and the other one of those big-grinned chirpy women in loud checked pants," Kay said afterward to Mrs. Jarple. "You could hear those pants all the way to Marquette."

The quiet woman went down a side aisle. The chirpy woman looked around and smiled. "Not a bad place. Carry a little bit of everything?"

Kay laughed. "Goodness, no. Mostly stationary, school supplies, craft stuff. Chips and candy for the kids. Mrs. Willet loves crafts. We used to sell a lot of the pillows and quilts she made, hey Dolly?" Dolly Willet smiled and squeezed the kadooka bulb. They all laughed.

The quiet woman came back. "Mrs. Willet will need a good pen," she said to Kay. "Where would they be?" She put two DIY will forms down on the counter.

There was a sudden silence. The chirpy woman moved a shade closer to the old woman's chair, smiling brightly. Kay looked quickly from Mrs. Jarple to Dolly Willet. Mrs. Willet looked steadily back at them and then turned her head a fraction and glanced toward one of the aisles.

After a moment Mrs. Jarple said, "I can help with that, I think. Dolly has some special ways of coping since her stroke."

She went down an aisle to the fabric section and came back. "She likes to use these felt pens now. They're easier to control. I'll take them out of the packages for you, shall I, Dolly? Do you still like purple?" She touched the older woman's shoulder gently. Mrs. Willet looked at the pens and smiled up at her friend.

Kay took the opened packages to scan them and paused; then she nodded to herself and printed out the receipt. There was a small mischievous glint in Dolly Willet's eye.

Mame Jarple, Mrs. Willet, and her two new companions stopped next at the Korner Kafe for lunch. To the customers who greeted Dolly, the women told stories about Mrs. Willett's childhood friendship with their grandmother, and that they had promised to see how she was doing when they came through the Upper Peninsula. "Close as sisters, they were!" Mrs. Willet sat nodding agreeably. This news flashed through

Dolly's circle of friends before dinner, and a few of them arrived at the Senior Center to discuss things.

"So, what do you think, Mame?" Peg Maki asked, pouring herself a cup of coffee. She was a small chronically worried woman who got around the island on her fat-tired bicycle in all but the very worst of U.P. weather. "Should we talk to someone when the state police make their rounds? Fraud! Coercion!" Her short sandy-red hair was bristling.

Mrs. Jarple blinked. "Well, maybe, if they carry through. Smooth your hair down Peg, you look like a rooster! The thing is that these women might not go through with what we think they're planning. But can you imagine! Coming into a little community like this and assuming no one would notice or be concerned!"

"*Not* bright," Peg agreed. She frowned. "Well, I know Dolly's caregiver is there now and will be overnight. But still, let's switch the meeting of The Pieceables to Dolly's house tonight. I'll call everyone."

"How do you think it's going?" The quiet woman asked later. The Pieceables quilting group had finally left, Dolly had been helped to bed, and her caregiver had retired to the room she used. The two women had spent the last half hour with the will forms and Dolly's ancient typewriter.

The chirpy woman shrugged. "Well, of course they're wondering. That's why all those silly women came here tonight. The important thing is that people saw us with her, and she was comfortable. She certainly has gone along with everything! I don't think she minds at all. After all, we're nice to her. And you can see she's pretty out of it. Never says a word, just smiles and nods all the time! Now – the form is all filled out; we'll just cover up the typed part, ask her for her autograph as a memento, and then it will just be a matter of time."

Mrs. Willet lay in her bedroom off the living room listening to this. She was very tired. She had been tired very often lately, as she had written her old friend Lucy just before her stroke. So impossible to connect Lucy with those two out there. But then, Lucy's daughter had married a man who skated

pretty close to the law. Apparently his daughters had learned from him.

Dear Mame Jarple. So clever of her to remember that Dolly had always used purple ink, in case those two knew about that. It was good to live in a community where you were really known.

"Just a matter of time," the chirpy woman repeated. Dolly nodded to herself and closed her eyes, nestling her papery cheek against the quilt, one of the many she had made. A matter of time. Exactly. She was smiling a little mischievously to herself as she drifted off to sleep.

"I really don't think you need be worrying yet," Mrs. Jarple said firmly.

It was ten days later. Dolly Willet had been hospitalized temporarily with one of her 'pesky infections', as she called them; and Mame Jarple had received an anxious phone call from two of Dolly's relatives that morning. They had come over on the morning ferry and she had gone to Dolly's house to meet them.

"But Mrs. Jarple, we've actually received photos of the will on our phones! It's signed and everything!"

"Yes, so I see." Mrs. Jarple looked with interest over her glasses at the color printout they handed her. Dolly's quavery signature was plain. "And the original is where?"

"Their text said they sent it to our cousin Tom. He's been out of town, but he's a lawyer, he does all the family business. He'll be here in a few minutes. Who *are* these people? Why should auntie suddenly leave them everything? I mean if she really wants to – but right out of the blue? This is just crazy!"

"Well, apparently these women are related to Dolly's closest childhood friend," Mrs. Jarple said. "They were visiting her a couple of weeks ago. I suppose they heard she was in the hospital and thought it was serious, and so they sent you this picture they had taken before they mailed the will off."

She hesitated a moment. "I really do think, you know, that you may be worrying prematurely. Whatever Dolly has done she did deliberately and with full understanding. I promise you that. So, you see – no worries." She nodded emphatically and smiled at them. They stared at her and then at each other.

The doorbell rang and Karen went to answer it. She came back in a moment with a tall middle-aged man. "Mrs. Jarple, this is our cousin Tom."

"I don't understand this at all," he was saying. "Let me see that print out – yes, you see, it's signed, and I *know* this form was signed when I received it! It's been locked in a folder in my safe this whole time. But now – see? No signature! I don't understand this."

Mrs. Jarple sat down suddenly. "Oh Dolly," she said softly. "You did pull it off! Good for you."

Tom looked at her. "You know something about this?"

Mrs. Jarple nodded, a little flustered. "Well, I remembered about the pens. And so The Pieceables, our quilting group, we all decided to meet here at Dolly's house. It's a small community on this island, and we do know each other!"

They blinked. "Mrs. Jarple," Anna said after a moment. "We don't have a clue what you're talking about."

Mame Jarple looked around at them. "Oh, I'm sorry! It was the pens, you see. Felt ones like ones your aunt has used since her stroke. And purple because she always used purple ink. And so, she went ahead and signed the will they made up with that pen. And of course her signature disappeared."

She paused at their bewildered faces and tried again. "Oh, I'm telling this badly. What I mean is, we switched her regular felt pens for quilting pens. They have special ink for marking material, and the ink just disappears after a while. Forty-eight, seventy-two hours."

And then, at their dawning comprehension, she nodded with satisfaction. "It's just a matter of time."

Tricia Carr is now a long-time Gwinn resident. She grew up downstate on stories from her mother and grandparents about life in the Upper Peninsula of Michigan, and especially life on the little island where they lived. She has edited newsletters and co-published a regional magazine, but her first love in writing is the traditional mystery and especially short stories. Her three cats, her Pomeranian Sir-Trips-A-Lot, and her human family cheer her on.

Escanaba smelt fishing

The Lunch Kit

by Deborah K. Frontiera

Alice's voice floated up the stairs. "Joe, Sophie forgot her lunch kit again. I've got my hands in a mess down here. Would you take it up to the school office? Please?"

"Humph … I suppose," Joe responded to his wife. Sophie was just like her mother—and looked just like her, too. *That girl would have forgotten her head … just like she forgot about us, leaving home like that, taking up with that no good … promised Alice I wouldn't say such things.*

Joe tromped down the stairs, pulled on his boots, gloves, heavy coat and scarf, picked up the forgotten "Barbie" lunch kit, with one cracked edge plastered with duct tape, and headed out into the snow. *We were supposed to be in Arizona this winter with all our snow-bird friends, not freezing our butts off again after saving so long that we wouldn't have to, stuck with a child we didn't even know existed until …*

Joe's eyes fell on the brand new fifth-wheel parked at the far end of the driveway, covered in snow. He and Alice had such a good time shopping for it, planning a year long trip all over the country, north to south and east to west, to see as many national parks as possible.

Probably should shovel again when I get back. The school was only five blocks down the street, too short to bother with the car but long on a windy winter day. Half way, Joe stopped in the middle of a bridge over a creek, a bridge he had engineered years back. Out of habit, he looked down into the trickle of open water, the rest running beneath a deceiving layer of ice. He leaned over to look underneath at the bridge's structure, checking it as he always had, along with other bridges in the area, for any signs of structural wear. *Maybe I should see if I can get my job back with another kid to take care of. Crap! At my age! Just when we thought we were finally free.* Joe hung his head at his own thoughts. *But not to take in Sophie? No way! Like Alice said, "Over my dead body will she stay in foster care!"*

That day just after Thanksgiving flooded Joe's mind. The knock on their door. The sheriff standing there … that look in his eye. "Hey, Joe, can I come in?"

"Sure. Want some coffee?"

"Yeah, that'd be fine. Alice home?"

"Yeah. Hey, Alice, Rick's here."

Rick often stopped in during deer season on his way out into the woods to help the game warden make sure that a couple of county residents, with a reputation for having more deer tied to their vehicles than their licenses allowed, weren't at it again. But a knot formed in Joe's gut with the look in his friend's eyes.

Alice came in with a tray of steaming mugs, cream and sugar. "How's everything?" Alice asked, setting a mug on the coffee table in front of Rick.

A long sigh and then Rick said, "Might as well come right out with it. Got a message from Wayne County Sheriff's office. Your daughter … well, she OD'd on crack … I'm so sorry."

Alice's hand went to her mouth. Joe scooted over on the couch and put his arms around her, biting his lip.

"I know how you two have grieved over the years with no news of Ronda after she lit out at eighteen. You know I notified every sheriff's office in the state, and beyond when I could, to be on the lookout."

Joe nodded. Alice's head was buried in his chest; his shirt was getting soggy.

Rick continued. "The thing is, Ronda had a child, and she's seven now. She's the one who called 911, saying her mommy wouldn't wake up."

Alice's red face rose from Joe's chest. "We have a granddaughter?"

"Her name's Sophie. She's in emergency foster care downstate. Email along with the notice said you can retrieve Rhonda's body from the morgue and I've got a number for you to call child services to get Sophie back. God, I'm so sorry! Anything you need ... just let me know."

The week after that had been a nightmare whirl of travel, paperwork, grilling by child services, lists of documents they had to produce, what family court would be like, requirements for guardianship (which they wouldn't have permanently until the child's father's rights had been severed), arranging for their daughter's body to be shipped home, planning a funeral, meeting a thin bewildered child, whose only possessions were a paper sack of clothes and that lunch kit with Barbie on it, and taking her home, home to a place she'd never seen before.

Sophie seemed happy to be with them in the beginning. Christmas had been delightful—a child in the house to open a stocking again, new toys and books, a fresh look to their daughter's old bedroom ... Sophie had seemed to settle right in to school. Then about mid-January ...

Joe looked up from the icy water into the sky. *Why is Sophie such a mess now? Forgetting her lunch almost every day, arguing with her teacher, then hitting that other girl. Why me? Why us? Where is that deadbeat jerk who ran out on his responsibilities? They better find him before I do. I swear, I'll*

strangle him! Joe stomped his feet, clapped the numbness out of his hands, left the bridge, and picked up his pace toward the school.

He stomped the snow off his boots on the mat and removed his fogged-up glasses at the office front desk. "Hi, I've brought Sophie's lunch—again—sorry."

"Oh, don't worry about it," the clerk said, taking the kit, which now had two seams covered with duct tape, from Joe's outstretched hand. "Better yet, in a minute or two, her class will be walking down that hall on the way to the cafeteria. You can give it to her yourself."

Then there she was, jumping out of her class line. "Grandpa! It's you this time." Sophie nearly knocked him over with a totally unexpected bear hug. Joe bit the inside of his cheek. *Where's this coming from after all the nasty faces lately? Oh, Lord, she's the image of her mother—my little princess is back.*

"Sophie, come back to our line now."

Joe detected a twinge of grit in the teacher's ever-gentle voice. Sophie let loose her grandpa, accepted the lunch kit and skipped back into line. Joe stared after her.

Another came voice from the office behind him. "Hello, Mr. Maki. Have you got a few minutes?" It was the school district's one-and-only counselor.

"Sure." Joe followed her into a cubicle-sized conference room in the front office complex. She closed the door behind them and pointed to a chair.

Joe shook his head. "Christmas was magical. Then boom! Yesterday she's yelling that she hates us. Today I get tackled with love. What's going on?"

"I was actually watching for you today—I never know when I'm going to be here at the elementary, up to the middle school or wherever," the counselor admitted. "There's a lot to explain here. Your first several weeks are what we sometimes call 'The Honeymoon', and you were lucky to have that last as long as it did."

"Honeymoon?"

"When a child loses his or her parents and goes to live in foster care, or with another family member, at first they are on their best behavior. Your granddaughter went through a severe trauma, losing her mother that way, having to be the grownup. We may never know exactly what it was like for her, but judging from how thin she was and how she's gained weight, there was at least a great deal of poverty and neglect."

Joe shifted in the chair. "She eats like there's no tomorrow, so why keep forgetting her lunch?"

"Well, I think it could be to see if you or your wife will still come with it—sort of testing you. She found acceptance and love with you on her best behavior, and now, she wants to see if you'll still keep her when she acts out."

Joe shifted in his chair. "She plans these things?"

"No, not consciously." The counselor opened her folder and checked a couple of notes. "But she is testing to see if you will abandon her like her father did, and then her mother left her, too, or at least that's how she sees it. She's starting to open up to me in our sessions. Of course, I can't tell you everything she says—confidentiality and all, plus I want her trust in me to grow—but her acting out is typical of children her age who have lost family for whatever reasons. Even kids who've been abused still want their parents and are traumatized at their loss—even when removed from terrible circumstances."

Joe stared at the floor. "What do we do?"

"Keep bringing that lunch kit. It lets her know you're there for her. I've filled her teacher in on the basics of Sophie's circumstances and given her advice about how to head off outbursts in class when she sees tension mounting in Sophie. Talk to Sophie about her mother. Show her any photos you have; let her get to know her mother as a child. Yes, she has to face consequences when she hits somebody, but let her know you love her in spite of it. It will take time, but she'll come around. I'll try to get in a session with her at least once a week."

She reached into her pocket and handed Joe a business card. "This is the name of a family counselor. I think you should call and make an appointment for all three of you. I know that's a bit of a drive from here, but it's the closest. I've heard many good reports about Dr. Hill."

"Thanks." Joe put the card in his pocket. "Guess I better head home. Alice will wonder what took so long."

They shook hands and Joe pulled his coat back on. He kept his pace quicker this time but his mind still rambled. *What if I'd been more patient with Ronda? She went from princess to monster at about fifteen. What if someone had suggested family counseling then? Would we have gone? Or would I have just done what I did—told her to shape up? How am I going to explain all this to Alice? Will she go? Will I go?*

Alice was more willing than Joe expected. Over the next several weeks, they took turns working with Sophie on her homework, reading to her at night, telling her stories about her mother—trying not to cry—and working through the anger and confusion they felt, and that Sophie felt, too. The family counselor set up weekly appointments after school hours—it was important, she said, for Sophie to have a consistent routine. She talked with Sophie first, then Joe and Alice, and then all three of them. They worked out a plan with the school that if Sophie remembered her lunch for four days, one grandparent could come and eat lunch with her on Friday. Small steps here, sometimes backward, then more forward; soon there were more good days than tough ones.

The Barbie lunch kit had duct tape on every seam by that time. Alice found a new one just like it, but Sophie threw it aside and grabbed the old one out of the trash. She sat on the floor next to the kitchen trash bin; tears streamed down her face. Alice wrapped her arms around the sobbing child. "Sophie, what's wrong?"

Joe came in, hands in the air. Alice waved him away soundlessly mouthing, "I'll tell you later."

Joe stood there, hands in his pockets, looking at the ceiling.

Several minutes passed before Sophie's sobs turned into hiccups and then a few more minutes before she could talk over the sniffling. "My lunch kit ... Mama got it for me at Goodwill. It was the last thing she gave me before . . ." sobbing took over again.

Joe sat down on the floor with his arms around both of them. For the first time, all three of them cried together.

• • •

At supper toward the end of April, Sophie asked, "Grandpa, will you read to me tonight?"

"But it's Grandma's turn," Joe replied.

"Well, can't you take two turns and then Grandma two?"

Joe raised his eyebrows at Alice.

"Sure," Alice said. "I'll do tomorrow."

Once Sophie was in her pajamas, Joe picked up the latest in a popular children's chapter book series and sat down on Sophie's bed. "How about we change it up a little? You read a paragraph and then I'll read one."

"Okay."

Sophie read a few words, hesitated, started again. Joe put his arm around her. "You're doing great."

She smiled up at him. "I love you, Grandpa."

"I love you, too." This time, the tears Joe bit back were those of joy.

• • •

When school ended in June, Joe, Alice, and Sophie opened the door of the fifth-wheel trailer, loaded clothes and groceries into storage compartments, checked out the other equipment Joe and Alice had bought the fall before, and headed out on a camping trip close to home—a shake-down cruise. Longer trips followed, cementing the bonds between them.

A few weeks before school would start again, Alice spoke up at dinner. "Sophie, what would you think about us traveling more?"

"But school's starting."

"Yes, it is, but I was a teacher many years, you know. I could teach you. Would you like to give it a try?"

Sophie beamed and nodded.

"I'll go up to the school tomorrow and talk to the principal, see about getting materials, and ask what internet programs we should use."

"We can plan our route together," Joe said.

Author's note: This work of fiction was inspired by a photo prompt during the 2020 Fall Fiction Workshop with Doug and Bethany Leonard sponsored by UPPAA. According to the AARP website, over a million grandparents in the United States find themselves parenting grandchildren for a variety of reasons. If you Google AARP, and then put "raising grandchildren" in the site search box, you'll find a long list of helps, tips, resources and conferences offering support for these grandparents. Those mixed feelings of resentment/guilt/love are very common. The author had personal experience with that in 2007-8 when her daughter and son-in-law were wrongfully accused of child abuse and had to spend thirteen months proving their innocence, during which time Grandma and Grandpa had temporary custody.

Deborah K. Frontiera grew up in Michigan's Upper Peninsula. From 1985 through 2008, she taught in Houston public schools, followed by several years teaching in Houston's Writers In The Schools program. A "migratory creature", she spends spring, summer, and fall in her beloved U.P. and the dead of winter in Houston, Texas, with her daughters and grandchildren. Four of her books have been honor or award winners. She has published fiction, nonfiction, poetry, and children's books, and is the current newsletter editor for the Upper Peninsula Publishers and Authors Association. For details about her many books and accomplishments, visit her web site: www.authorsden.com/deborahkfrontiera

Alphabet Soup

by Elizabeth Fust

This (ths) is the story (stry) of how (hw) I was taught (tght) to use abbreviations (abbrs).

You (u) see (c), it all started (strd) when (whn) the chief (Chief) asked (akd) (actually [actly] told [tld]) me to take (tk) dictation (dction) of a letter (ltr). Chief said (s-d), while (whl) dictating (dcttng) and (&) reading (rdng) over (o'r) my shoulder (shlr), "No (n!), we must (mst) save (sv) space (spc)! Abbr. everything (evytng) after (aftr) its first (1st) use!"

We spent (spt) all day (dy) working (wkng) on the ltr.

"Can (cn) we tk a break (brk) for lunch (lch)?"

"N!, just (jst) keep (kp) wkng on the ltr!" S-d Chief.

So we kept (k-t), wkng. & k-t wkng, & k-t wkng...

"Cn we tk a brk for dinner (dnr)?"

"N!, jst kp wkng on the ltr!" S-d Chief.

My stomach (stmch) grumbled (gmbd). I k-t thinking (tnkng) about (abt) food (fd).

Chief made (md) me go back (bck) again (agn) & agn to abbr wds I had (hd) missed (msd).

My stmch gmbd louder (ldr) & ldr. I k-t misrdng wds as fd.

'Tonight' (tngt) became (bcm) 'taco' (tco) 'night' (nt).

'Bcm' bcm 'bacon' (bcn).

'Chesapeake' (Chspk) bcm 'cheese' (chs).

Mmm (mm), tcos with (w/) bcn & chs.

The wds began (bgn) to swim (swm) in the ltr before (b4) my eyes (eys).

Visions (vsns) of tcos danced (dncd) in my head (hd).

Chief jst kpt dcttng.

I blinked (blkd) & the ltr was gone (gn)! It was replaced (rplcd) by a bowl (bwl) of alphabet (alphbt) soup (s-p)!

Well, I dug (dg) right (rt) in.

Chief stopped (stpd) dcttng.

The s-p wasn't (wsn't) very (vy) good (gd). The vowels (vwls) were soggy (sgy) & the consonants (cnsnts) totally (ttly) raw (rw). For s-p, it tasted (tstd) vy dry (dy).

Aftr eating (etng) the s-p I fell (fl) asleep (aslp).

Whn I woke (wk) at (@) my desk (dk) the next (nxt) morning (mrng), there was a ltr from Chief. He was sending (sndng) me on vacation (vctn)!

So, dear (dr) friends (frnds) & family (fmly), that (tht) is hw I ended (endd) up in Michigan's (MI) Upper Peninsula (U.P.)!

Elizabeth Fust has been writing since she was a little girl and plans to still be writing when she is a little old lady. Elizabeth is the author of *Wooly and the Good Shepherd* and *The Hungry Kitten's Tale* picture books. She has a lso written and had many short stories and feature articles published. Elizabeth's writing is greatly inspired by the beauty surrounding her home between Lake Superior and the mountains of Michigan's Upper Peninsula.

The Rescue of the L.C. Waldo

by Robert Grede

One
November 9, 1913
Near Gull Rock, Lake Superior

Henry King saw it first. There appeared a black hole where there should have been blowing snow amid the pallid gray of the roiling water. He rubbed at the window to clear it. "There, sir."

Captain Eddmann lifted his seaman's cap and pressed his face to the glass. He had an old man's eyes and an old man's mouth set in an old man's face lined by the years as the rings of a tree. The 400-foot steamer, *George Stephenson*, westbound for Duluth, was his ship. He had been her master for over ten years, knew every nook and cranny of her just as a woman knows her pantry. The Great Lakes were his home, the ship his mistress. It was not an easy life.

The water had shown a healthy chop as they made the run through the Sault, but by midday, rising wind had whipped the lake into a lashing frenzy; the sea ran so high the ship's propeller would breach with a whining roar. So Eddmann had ordered a heading for the lee of the Keweenaw Peninsula and Henry King had set the course.

"Off the port bow, sir. There's a ship."

Sea spray coated the pilothouse windows and quickly froze. Henry kicked open the portside door and, holding to the frame, reached around to scrape away the ice. "There, sir. It's a ship, and a big one."

Captain Eddmann peered into the gray. Blowing snow and distance played vision tricks – a boat, as if some child's play toy, splashed in the waves like a skipping stone just three hundred yards off the port bow.

"Hard a-starboard," he shouted. A wave lifted the *Stephenson* to give another view. "Good Lord, she's huge."

"Looks to be stuck on Gull Rock," said Henry.

"Hard a-starboard! Damn, this wind is blowing us straight at her."

Henry rolled the wheel as far as she would swing, willing the mighty steamer to skim past the floundering vessel, but waves pitched her more than any rudder could hope to counter. The *Stephenson* rolled through a set of swells cresting at angles and she fell into a trough that carried her past the wounded boat.

"Look at that," Henry said. "She's covered in ice." The big steamer hung on the rocks while the sea mocked her, slapping her sides and icing her decks as if frosting a cake.

The captain said, "There are people aboard that boat," and Henry King suddenly knew what he must do.

The world had done its best to subdue and humble Henry King. As a child, Henry had nearly drowned when he fell through the frozen surface of Lake Medora, and he forever feared the ice. At 15, playing in an abandoned mine, he had survived a cave-in, but gained a fear of small places. He had ridden with Teddy Roosevelt at Las Guasimas when the jungle exploded, and found excuse to fall out when they charged the San Juan Heights.

Fear had proved a merciless disease. It stained all other endeavors for him. It had darkened all ambition, all hope. Henry King lived for the opportunity to demonstrate he was not the coward he had been. To prove it, he had gone to sea. It had been an easy choice. Growing up in Manistee, Henry watched ships. Over an hour horizon to horizon, they made their way from Duluth to the locks at Sault St. Marie. At night, he would fall to sleep as their lights floated in the darkness. He wondered what this one carried in its hold. What special mission did that one follow? What adventures could be told in their wakes? As he rose from ship's mate to first mate, he had confronted lesser episodes of dramatic possibility – rough weather, common maladies, close calls – but nothing of import.

Then the captain said: "There are people aboard that boat." And Henry King heard opportunity.

"I could lead a lifeboat to see if there are any survivors," he said.

"We can't launch a boat in this gale. I won't risk it," said the captain.

"But we must report this."

"Yes, when we get to Bete Grise. We can launch the boat there, find a telephone, alert the Life Saving Service."

An immense wave burst over the stern quarter and sloughed the *Stephenson* off her southerly course. Henry countered with a sweep of the wheel and rode the trough past Keweenaw Point. When he searched the port quarter for the stranded ship, he could see no trace.

The leeward side of the Keweenaw Peninsula provided protection from the gale and Henry piloted the *Stephenson* through the narrow channel at Bete Grise before the gray skies had turned full dark. Several vessels lay at anchor in the shadows of Mount Bohemia. Lights lined the north shore of the bay.

As the anchor line swept through the hawse, Henry donned his warmest anorak, laced on his thickest mittens, snugged into his deepest boots, and leapt to the lifeboat. Two crewmen levered him over the side and he began to row to the nearest quay. At a small, battered house with plank walls and a roof that held two feet of snow, Henry climbed the front stoop and slapped his mitten hard on the wooden door. "Shipwreck!" he shouted. "Shipwreck! Please help."

A wispy-haired man with stubble cheeks opened the door, a blanket over his narrow shoulders. He had a long thin face that bore the years like vague memories. He wore no shoes. The cabin had a homey feel, warm and dry, a faint odor of soured milk. Henry stomped his boots to free the snow before entering.

As he asked his questions, the old man replied in a voice high and thin as the wind. The nearest lifesaving station lay at Eagle Harbor. About thirty miles. No, there's no telephone here. No lines been run out this far yet. Nearest telephone would be Delaware, eight mile up the road there. Got no horse. Snow is too deep no how. Walk it? No, that's crazy talk. Better maybe to set, wait it out. Yep, them snowshoes is Coureur des Bois style, made them my own self. Come in, set a spell, have some coffee. Shipwreck you say? Not surprised. Heck of a storm, eh? Been blowing hard the better part of two day now, enna? How about that coffee? Hey there, don't go out in this weather. Well, all right. Good luck then. And them snowshoes is mine, remember.

Two
November 10, 1913,
Eagle Harbor, Michigan

The distress call came in the early afternoon. Tom Bennetts was on the second lookout at Eagle Harbor when he saw the signal flags at the lifesaving station. He bundled his coat about his throat and snapped his boot clasps. When he opened the door, the wind pelted his face with sleet and sea spray. His boots broke the ice layer to sink into the snow as he trudged to the main station.

Cold pushed through the open door and he hurried to shut it, then shrugged off his coat and hung it with the other anoraks that lined the clapboard wall. A small fire in the potbelly stove warmed the boat room where the men gathered. Tony Glaza was there, as were the two Swedes, Padberg and Anderson – or was it Anderson and Padberg? They were both new and Tom had yet to work with their shift. Surfmen George Halpainen and Charlie Kumpula arrived, and more snow burst through the door before they could slam it tight.

Tom leaned into his friend's ear. "Hey, Tony," he said. "What have we got?"

Glaza hunched over the tiny stove and spread his fingers. "Don't know," he said. "But the town's all up. They seen the flags, too."

"We got no lifeboat." Tom looked toward the keeper's office door. "I worked on it most of the morning, but the motor still's not right. We'll have to go with the surfboat."

"Might as well swim," said Glaza. "Surfboat is no good in this."

As if on cue, another gust shook the thin boathouse walls. The windows rattled and sparks flew from the stove damper. The stationkeeper's door opened and a hush fell over the men; even the wind died. Captain Charles Tucker stood lean and leathered, a sturdy man with a short neck and dusty black hair. Taskmaster, teacher, and occasional father to his rowdy boys, the Captain held equal regard for people as the weather.

"All right then," he began, "Here's what we got. Sometime early this morning, a ship ran aground at Gull Rock. It's a steamer, a big one. Name unknown. Registry unknown. Cargo unknown. Souls aboard unknown." He paused and stared at their faces. "But by the size of her, she has to have a crew of at least twenty."

"Oh, Jesus," Tom muttered.

"Mr. Tucker, what about Portage?" said Glaza. The next station lay on the canal that cut through the lower part of the Keweenaw Peninsula. "They might have an easier time going up the bay side. Wind here is up near sixty and the lifeboat motor still isn't working."

"Portage has been notified, but they're another 30 miles away. And going up the bay side adds 20 more," said Tucker. "So we're it, lifeboat or not."

The surfboat was small, designed for near-shore rescues of swimmers and the occasional fisherman who ventured too far into the waves. A heavy lifeboat carried a crew of eight and a 40-horsepower motor that battered through heavy seas. While the surfboat was nimble, it was powered by a feeble eight-horsepower motor, virtually useless in rough weather. With a crew of just six at the oars, Tom knew it would be rough going.

"What about the survivors?" said Glaza. "Not much room in a surfboat."

Tom cinched his oilskins and buckled his heavy boots. First they had to reach the stranded ship. Worry about where to put survivors when they get there. If they get there.

"We got snow. We got sleet. We got freezing rain. Hell, I betcha we even got icebergs on the Lake," said Glaza.

Tom wrapped a knitted scarf about his throat and pulled on a woolen forager's cap. "It's twenty degrees out there."

George Halpainen said, "Big wind, too, it about blowed us down when we was coming here, eh."

"That can't take much," said Glaza. "Not for a skinny runt like you."

"No, we saw the cups on the wind vane there," said Halpainen. "It got up to seventy, eh Kumpy?"

"Yeah, hey," said Niko Kumpula.

"Never seen it go so high, eh?" said Halpainen.

"Yeah, hey."

"Everybody up!" Captain Tucker shouted.

Tom tucked his head into his hood and cinched the straps, then slid his hands into his rubberized gloves. Glaza wrapped a knit scarf around his neck and pulled it up over his mouth. The men steeled themselves to a fate of wind and sleet and frost over deep water. Tom Bennetts made a small sign-of-the-cross with his gloved fingers. The Life Saver's motto said they had to go out. It said nothing about coming back.

"Come on, boys," Tucker said. "This is what we live for. The whole town is watching. Let's show them what we do, eh? You are the Life Saving Service!"

"Hoo-Rah!" The men yelled and the boatroom doors were flung wide. A blast of cold nearly knocked him down, but Tom hunched into the wind and held to the gunwale as the slender surfboat slid on its carriage across the sand. Families and neighbors huddled nearby, wind buffeting their collars and fitting their trousers to their legs.

The surfboat slammed into the pounding sea and Tom leapt for his bench when they pulled away the carriage. Captain Tucker shouted orders and the surfmen began to pull. The tiny motor coughed once before settling into a steady buzz, lost beneath the wind noise and the slapping of the surf. The men dragged at the oars and the surfboat slid through the icy water.

Captain Tucker used the long steering oar to maneuver the buoyant craft through the surf with masterly skill. "Stay steady!" he screamed over the din of wind and waves and the grinding of the oars in the oarlocks. "Pull, damn you, pull!"

The boat surged past the second lookout, the tiny building where Tom had stood his watch, warm and dry, just an hour before. More town folk stood outside shivering, too numb to wave. He pulled harder, careful to keep his balance as another blast of wind pitched the boat. When he looked once more, the people had faded to gray where the frosty broth pummeled the shoreline.

They struggled past Grand Marais Bay as darkness fell. Twice his oar slipped through a wave and sent him sprawling. Captain Tucker stood above him, hauling against the rudder, first one way then another, hanging on as much as steering. Tom saw the man shouting, "Pull!" his lips moving, but the words just spilled into the wind to mix with all the noise that clamored in Tom's head.

Nearing Copper Harbor, waves heaved in all direction and it became impossible to meet the heaviest breakers head on. The surfboat yawed, sliding between crests and Tom strained at his oar. Water poured over the gunnels and filled the boat to his boot tops. Were it not for the air chambers fore and aft, the tiny vessel would have capsized.

Tom's ears began to freeze as spray and blowing bits of snow pelted his face, stinging as smartly as any wasp. Icicles formed below his nose and when he went to brush them aside with his fist, his glove stuck fast to the oar. Ice that caked in the oarlocks prevented a full stroke. He kicked at it with his boot and nearly pitched over the side, but an arm arrested his headlong plunge and Tom clamored back onto his bench. Tony Glaza shouted something through his scarf, but Tom just wriggled his frozen fingers back into his glove and once more took to the oar.

Even amid the frost and spray, Tom felt warmed by the effort. Grip on, brace the legs and pull. There became a certain pleasure in the process. The months of training, the discipline, the fitness of mind, the growing awareness that comfort and tranquility were small sacrifice for the rescue. Grip on, brace the legs and pull. You are the Life Saving Service! Honed and burnished to crystalline precision. Grip on, brace the legs and pull. A stinging pain floods your arms, but still you pull. For the community, for the man beside you, you pull. You save lives. You make a difference. You suffer because you are a hero!

And you pull.

Three
November 11, 1913,
Bete Grise, Michigan

It was late afternoon when Henry King arrived once more at the tiny shack on the edge of Bete Grise. At first, the old man didn't recognize him. His watery eyes peered without understanding, until Henry held out the snowshoes. The man ran a hand through his thin hair and a smile broke through the cracked parchment of his features.

Walked that whole way, did ya? Eight mile and some just to make a telephone call. Must have been important. Oh, that's right, a shipwreck. Say, is everybody all right? No, haven't heard a thing about it either. We only get the *Gazette* here once a week, and it's overdue. Can't say as I blame 'em with that blizzard and all. Hey there, how about that coffee? Oh, is that right? One of them ships there, eh? Well, all right then. You take care. Come around any time. I'll be here.

Henry King baled the snow from the lifeboat and rowed the half mile to where the *George Stephenson* lay at anchor.

"Halloo, Henry," Captain Eddmann called as he approached. "Did you telephone the Life Saving Service?"

"Permission to come aboard, captain?"

"Permission granted. So, what's the good word?"

"I was able to find a telephone, sir. I'm sorry it took so long."

"Wind has let up some. We'll be getting underway soon." Captain Eddmann laid his arm across the young man's shoulder. "Glad you're back, Henry," he said. "We feared the worst for you."

"Aye-aye, sir. And thank you, sir." He followed the captain to the pilothouse. The windows had been cleared of frost, the rails had been scraped, the deck swept of frozen chunks of snow and ice. The storm had passed on; order had returned to the ship.

Yet Henry could not bring his mind back to the way things were. He had been a different person then. From the moment he had left to the moment of his return, Henry had not allowed himself to be afraid, had simply refused to allow fear to creep into his thinking. It was a useful device. If you keep such things in the front of your mind, they will eat at you like a wolf chomping on a dead rabbit. Throw your fears in the cellar and keep them there as long as you can. Later, the mere act of stirring them around will allow you to shuffle the elements in a new order, confront them in new ways. Henry King had stirred and shuffled until he could no longer find that which had paralyzed him on the San Juan Heights.

The chain rattled through the hawse and the anchor lifted from the lakebed. The engine chuffed and sent up a pillow of smoke before settling into a deep throaty throb. Captain Eddmann called the course and Henry spun the wheel, and the *Stephenson* slowly moved toward open water.

Along the shoreline, a lone man walked over the deep snow. He wore no hat, and his thin hair floated behind him. His snowshoes were Coureur des Bois style, Henry was sure. He thought to wave to the old man, but the distance was far, and the man's eyes were not so good. Henry waved anyway.

The captain asked where he had found the telephone. Henry told him about the walk in the blizzard, the eight miles in darkness over a snow-covered road, wind buffeting the trees and burning his face. Gusts knocked snowfall from the towering pines that fell in great chunks and several times nearly buried him. Every step had seemed uphill and he had stopped often simply to breathe.

It was nearly dawn before Henry banged on the door of the first dwelling he had seen. Told the only telephone in the tiny town was in a tavern, Henry awakened the proprietor by rapping a stick on the timber siding of the cabin that squatted near the roadside inn.

"We're closed, for godsake!" a voice shouted. "Go away!"

"I don't want a drink, damn you, I need your telephone," Henry shouted back.

Captain Eddmann laughed. It was not something he did easily. He was a man of the sea, so he often took upon himself more dignity.

"The barkeep thought I was out in that blizzard because I needed my pint of beer," said Henry.

"Sounds like quite an adventure, young man, quite an adventure."

And it was. Henry had waited out the storm at the tavern, sleeping on the floor. The next day, when at last the snow had ceased falling, and what little wind remained was deadened by the tall pines, he had made the long walk back to Bete Grise over fallen trees and drifts of snow higher than two men. Yet each step was lighter than the one before, his Coureur du Bois snowshoes seeming to glide across all obstacles. When wolves began to follow, Henry raised his fist in the air and shouted, and they abandoned him.

Yes, it was an adventure. And Henry King had played his part. But no one would ever know his name. Oh, he had told the man when he called the lighthouse station at Eagle Harbor, but it was not something you would write down. So no record would be made of his adventure. In legends and folklore, the hero always receives his recognition, his reward – the love of a beautiful maiden, the adoration of the townspeople, or even great wealth. There were none of these for Henry King. No, Henry would not make the history books.

The *Stephenson* passed Keweenaw Point into open water. Off the starboard bow, the *Waldo* still hung on Gull Rock. Ice crawled up her sides from the earth as if scar tissue had healed her over. The great steamer seemed a small and pathetic thing, a piece of broken litter, jetsam on the rocks.

"Look at her," said Captain Eddmann. "She hardly looks like a ship anymore. There is no way she will ever sail again. They will have to tow her in for scrap."

"At least the people are no longer aboard," said Henry.

"And you to thank for it," said the captain.

Yes, thought Henry. You know it and I know it, and that will have to be good enough. Henry King was but a single oar on the great flagship of life, immaterial, of no consequence in the grand scheme. Jetsam on the rocks. This actually mattered to him less than he thought it might. He had somewhere, sometime, slowly come to an awareness that he had not walked all night through a blizzard for fame or glory or the fair maiden. He had done it for the fear of ice and small places, and for Colonel Roosevelt at Las Guasimas.

At last, the sun melted into the deep purple of the lake. The night sky was large and dark, wide as a country and high as the stars. Duluth lay six hours west southwest. Henry King said goodnight, doffed his anorak, kicked off his boots and fell asleep eight inches above his bunk, tumbling toward the canvas ticking, deep in the restful slumber of contentment long before he landed.

Robert Grede is the author of the best-selling *Naked Marketing – The Bare Essentials* (Prentice Hall) as well as other non-fiction books, short stories, and a novel, *The Spur & The Sash*. His ties to the Upper Peninsula include a family cottage on Spread Eagle Lake and many years on the Board of Trustees of Finlandia University. He resides in suburban Milwaukee and can be reached at rg@TheGredeCompany.com. This story is part of a work-in-progress called *Copper Country*.

VIEW OF THE TOWN OF MACKINAW.

City of Mackinaw engraving · 1850

A Night to Remember

by Charles Hand

Between 1958 and 1962, I attended Michigan College of Mining and Technology (Michigan Technological University since 1964) in Houghton Michigan. The university is located on the frozen southern shore of Lake Superior in the far northwest Upper Peninsula (UP). At the time my hometown was Tecumseh, in the southeast corner of the Lower Peninsula, near the Ohio border and Lake Erie. The college environment was inspiring! My hometown was fantastic! The commute between the two, in the middle of winter, was a bummer!

The only economical, convenient, and direct mode of transportation between Tecumseh and Houghton, a distance of 575 miles, was via private dilapidated automobile. Starving Tech students further controlled their transportation costs by carpooling. Cramming four smelly, irritable Tech students into a cramped old jalopy in the middle of winter, for this monotonous, wearisome journey does not exactly describe an evening of frivolity. It wasn't! Generally, after winter break, our car pool would leave Tecumseh around seven in the evening, drive through the moonless unforgiving night, and reach Houghton just in time to attend our first morning class. This meant we were crossing the new majestic Straits of Mackinac Bridge (Mighty Mac), connecting the Lower and Upper Peninsulas, at about one in the morning. At the straits, we always filled our gas tank at the only all-night station open for hundreds of miles around.

Houghton was still 275 miles and six-hours ahead of us.

To understand the Upper Peninsula in winter, imagine a vast frozen, forested and rocky frontier, with a climate and topography not inviting to a large concentrated population. At its maximum dimensions, the peninsula is about 310 miles east to west (1) and 230 miles north to south (2). The population of this entire area hovers around 311,000 hearty, deep freeze loving people (3). Between the Straits of Mackinac and Houghton on one trip after a winter holiday break, during the middle of the night, we did not meet a single car heading in the opposite direction. A traffic jam would consist of meeting two cars. Meeting one car was just heavy traffic. The words "frozen desolation" come to mind when discussing a winter night in the UP. In comparison, Orange County, California, my current home, has a population of about 3,010,000 people (4) in a concentrated area approximately six percent of the geographical size of the Upper Peninsula and most of these people live within a few miles of the Pacific Ocean coast. (3)(4)

In addition to the frigid temperatures, there was the added dimension of colossal Paul Bunyan size snowfalls. For native Southern Californians, snow is cold, fluffy white stuff, produced by God, which falls from the sky. It is not the stuff that someone pays to have trucked in for children to play in, nor is it manufactured by man. In the Upper Peninsula in late fifties and early sixties, seasonal snow falls of fifteen feet with a ten-foot accumulation on the ground were common, all courtesy of the atmospheric lake effect produced by the cold winds from Canada. We have never forgiven the Canadians. Each winter, snow blanketed the ground from October until April. Minus ten below zero temperatures were expected during the day. Generally, nights were significantly colder.

Returning to college from our winter holiday, three other male Tech students and I were not expecting to spend part of the night slumbering in free lodging, courtesy of the local government. Having crossed the Mighty Mac, we were traveling west along the south shore of Gitche Gumee, by the shining Big-Sea-Waters, under a starless and moonless sky. One of the areas we had just traversed was a 25 mile, straight as Hiawatha's arrow, stretch of highway between Seney and Shingleton. The state had only plowed one lane through this area, not one lane in each direction. The snow depth was a minimum of ten feet. Snow thrown from the plows added significantly more in places. We had just experienced a practical lesson about what the "deer in the headlights" cliché meant when we met a large herd crossing the road directly in front of us. We missed, just barely. We were now driving on a more civilized road where a lane was plowed in each direction. We were more than halfway to Houghton from the bridge, approaching the two small towns of Negaunee and Ishpeming. About fifteen miles east of these two small towns, the car sputtered its contempt, decided that it had taken enough abuse, and died. We had filled our tank at the straits so we knew we had sufficient gas. We were stranded. The frigid temperatures threatened trouble. While we had winter clothing, we didn't dare go to sleep to wait for morning and rescue, because our clothes were insufficient to keep us warm during an outdoor winter slumber. People don't wake up from slumber under those conditions. We also judged that it was way too far to walk to the nearest town. Plus, there was virtually no light, either natural or manmade. This pre-historic era was before cell phones and credit cards. Even if they had been available, we were typical starving college students with no money. There weren't even any emergency telephone booths along this stretch of barren, deserted highway. The Wigwam of Nokomis would have been very welcome (5) (6).

We could see taillights a long distance in front of us and headlights an equally long distance behind us, probably other crazy Tech students returning to school. The taillights would be of no help, but probably the headlights were on a car owned by some compassionate person who could help. The Good Samaritan code prevailing in this forbidden frozen wasteland was to always help friends and strangers during times of distress. It took about 20 minutes for the first car exhibiting headlights to reach us which, of course, contained four Tech students. This lapse of time gave us a chance to take care of some bodily functions. In this sub-zero frigid atmosphere, water never hits the ground, just yellow ice. After they arrived and some discussion, our group decided that all eight of us needed to pile into the functioning car and head for the next town where we could be safely dropped off. The four of us were now stuffed into the car that already held its maximum load of four. Two were crammed onto the back seats which now held four and two sat on the floor boards between the legs of two others. It wasn't comfortable, but it was warm. One of the students from the rescuing car confidently suggested that we drive to the nearest police station and ask to stay overnight in the jail. From experience, he believed that this would be a reasonable request, and the police would be accommodating.

Arriving at the station, we told the night policeman, an older understanding gentleman, of our predicament, and he readily offered:

"We don't have any prisoners tonight, so go find a comfy cell in the back and have a good night's sleep. We won't lock the doors."

The cells were warm with no wind chill, but comfy was not exactly a correct description. That is unless sleeping on welded steel bars with no mattress was a description of comfy. At least we wouldn't freeze to death during the night and would wake up reasonably refreshed in the morning. Also, the price was right. The rescuing car and its passengers left us and proceeded on to Houghton.

Long after dawn, I finally awoke, refreshed and ready to help conquer our misbehaving car and complete our journey. After a big stretch and a healthy yawn, I looked around our Spartan accommodations and noticed my three companions were still peacefully asleep. There were no new inhabitants, and the cell doors were unlocked as promised. At the end of a long hallway, I could see the jailer's office where the day policeman was leaning back on his desk chair apparently sound asleep. I even detected low volume peaceful snoring. Apparently, it was a slow day. I was about to change his day. I walked out to the front desk to say hello and offer a great big thank you. It sure would have been nice if the older understanding night policeman had informed the young excitable day policeman, the only one on duty that morning, that he had guests in the cell block. Was the practical joke being perpetrated on us or him?

Hearing my footsteps approaching from the cell block, the day policeman was instantly awake. Startled is probably an understatement as he leaped up and reached for his gun.

"Don't shoot! Last night, the policeman on duty said that we could stay here! We're not criminals!" I pleaded with both hands on my head. I was exhibiting my most docile submissive personality, judged a necessity at this time and place. Fast sudden moves, aggressive arguments, and angry outbursts would not have been appropriate and could have been potentially fatal.

"Where did you come from? How did you get here?" were the first words he screamed at me.

"From your cell block. The doors are unlocked." I calmly answered.

"Are there any more of you back there?" he frantically continued.

"Yes, three more. They are still asleep." I again calmly answered.

He started to hyperventilate as he became aware that he was outnumbered.

"Why are you here?" he continued to excitedly scream with his hand still nervously fondling his sidearm.

I continued to serenely and calmly explain the situation of the broken-down car, and he seemed to understand. His voice started to become a little softer and less panicky. He even offered me a cup of coffee.

By now my other three comrades, awakened by all the screaming, were standing in the hallway in plain view. Apparently, we didn't look very threatening.

After the four of us had become friends with the day policemen, even sharing some jokes, we walked to the local garage he suggested, which was now open, had the car towed in and repaired.

Whatever was wrong was readily fixed and we were on our way before noon. It was probably something as simple as a broken distributor cap. Although we had missed our morning classes, we had survived our unforgettable adventure of spending a night in jail. It had been much better than freezing.

Footnotes

(1.) Michigan State Transportation Map, Menominee to Copper Harbor

(2.) Michigan State Transportation Map, Sault Ste. Marie to Ironwood

(3.) Wikipedia, Upper Peninsula of Michigan, 2010 US Census

(4.) Wikipedia, Orange County, California, 2010 US Census

(5.) All references to Gitchee Gumee, by the shining Big Sea Waters, the wigwam of Nokomis, and Hiawatha are from "The Song of Hiawatha" by Henry Wadsworth Longfellow.

(6.) Gordon Lightfoot used the name Gitche Gumee to refer to Lake Superior in his song "The Wreck of the Edmund Fitzgerald."

Charles Hand was born in Michigan and lived the first eighteen years in Tecumseh. The next four years, including two delightful summers, he attended Michigan College of Mining and Technology, where in 1962, he earned a Bachelor of Science. His electrical power career took him to companies in Milwaukee, Chicago, and Southern California, plus business trips to Europe, Asia, and throughout United States and Canada. Vacations frequently involved visits to the land of his birth, including the Upper Peninsula.

Feeling Important

by Kathy Johnson

Lines of white steel vertical blinds split the light behind Otto. The examining room was a cubicle of standard white cabinets and stainless steel instruments, set in perfect order. Otto looked awkward amidst this sanitized environment, dressed in old work pants and a faded flannel shirt. Otto was a large man with a bald head and hands that looked like tree stumps. He was entering his 75th year and had come to the doctor because he had developed a cough that would not go away. He had come to the doctor after multiple requests by the wife to take care of the cough.

Adjusting his flannel over his undershirt when his wife was asked to step into the examining room, he was fumbling with buttons on one of his sleeves. Helmi's first reaction when she saw him was to help him fix the problem cuff. But she held back and remained standing on a green square of checked tile positioned to the left of the doctor. Otto was sitting on the examining table with a nervous look on his face.

The doctor began with a long list of technical words to convey the diagnoses to the husband and wife. The medical language frightened and alarmed them both. The doctor rattled off numbers that were to show the dire medical situation Otto was in. His blood pressure, lung capacity, his blood count. There was no appreciation for this medical diatribe, this laundry list of symptoms brought on by his lifestyle. The only phase that Otto understood was, "NO SMOKING."

"No Smoking," Otto said under his breath. Since he was twelve and at his second cousin's wedding in Minnesota, a cigar pushed between his lips, he had used tobacco in one form or another. "I'm suppose to quit that." Otto knew this was going to be hard. He looked at Helmi, and she at him, "Going to be very hard," he repeated to himself under his breath.

On his birthday, one of his four sons had sent him a cartoon of his favorite smokes. It was whisked away by Helmi, and she had declared, "No smoking in the House."

"OK," he thought; the house was her territory. She now dictated that there would be no smoking in the basement (where he kept a few beers and often smoked, in the comfort of the downstairs solitude). She furthered proclaimed that there would be no smoking in his shop, the other refuge of manly contentment.

"I can't smoke in my own house,"

"I can't smoke in my basement,"

"I can't smoke in my shop."

He separated these places as if into some cards in an important cribbage match. He was adding up the points, and it all added up to **female aggravation.**

"What am I a child?" he mumbled to himself. Helmi had challenged his manhood. He started to lace his boots and pull at his socks, the tying and tugging on his boots had deeper cosmic significance. Scandinavian stubbornness with limitations was symbolized in this humble human effort.

As fall evening descended, the smell of leaves and wind and moisture was evident in the twilight. His wife came out on the porch. She was ending the evening by beating several carpets. She called to Otto, "You go town." Otto heard that aggravating female pitched voice. She repeated in a higher octave, "Otto, you go town for me?'

She intoned the request several more times. Otto did not want to answer too quickly. He was hard of hearing; that had never been proven by a medical diagnosis; his hesitation was one way he could protest his "No smoking ban." Finally, he answered. "OK, OK, I go town for you, "

Otto knew that town was one cigarette away and one cigarette back home.

"Yah, Yah, I go town."

With deep satisfaction, he climbed into his rusted red pickup truck. He slammed the door shut, put the key in the ignition, and then punched the cigarette lighter on the dash. As he drove to town, contentment flowed over his being. He had his rifle on a rack behind his head and a cigarette in his lips.

His mind drifted to the hunting camp. It was here that Helmi's rules did not apply. It was here that he could do as he pleased. It was here that he could smoke. The camp loomed large and pleasing from the wood stove's smells to the taste of the venison stew and the likable male companionship. He could be himself. At the pinochle table, he could slowly puff perfect smoke rings like halos around his head and glory in just being male.

The evening was fading; snow cropped up in some dark clouds to the west. Golden and orange leaves fell dramatically on each side of the road. The possibility of snow lingered in the air. Fresh snow would be good for the boys so they could track the deer better.

Otto went to town on female command. Helmi was his better half for the last forty-five years. He thought this as he was returning to the house with bread and milk. Turning into his drive way he looked at his little house glowing with light in the dark and thought, "I want Helmi to feel important."

He said out loud, "Yah, I want Helmi to feel important."

Kathleen Carlton Johnson's work has appeared in *Rattle*, *MacGuffin*, *The Diner*, and *Barely South*. Both poet and visual artist, she lives on the shores of Lake Superior.

Historical Marquette lower harbor 1861-01

Blew: Incarnation

by Sharon Kennedy

"'yes' he says, setting there bolt upright with jest the tears running down his face, at peace now, with nothing nowhere in the world any more to anguish or grieve him."
William Faulkner, *The Mansion*

The water was over my head and I knew it was cold, but it didn't feel cold, not after the first shock of falling in was over. I felt myself sinking and tried to grab a piece of ice, but it slipped away and my hands held only more water. Underneath the surface, down where the suckers live, the river was beautiful—clear and peaceful and inviting. I thought I heard you calling my name and I remember surfacing at least once, but the will to return wasn't as strong as the desire to see what lay beyond. The hard current became gentle the farther I fell. Even more gentle than your words of comfort when I told you I was a bastard. Remember that day? It was August of last year on my 11th birthday. We were in the pea patch. We picked until we filled our pails, and then we went down to the river's edge. I ate like a pig at a trough. Remember the salt shaker you brought with you? I watched as you split the pods and sprinkled white grains over each pea, taking your time as if you had all the time in the world and as if that task were the most important in all of life. As I gobbled the peas, pulling the pods against my bottom teeth, I watched you patiently at your work and wondered why some of that pa-tience didn't run through my veins. We're cousins. Some of our blood is the same, yet you got patience and I got what? Wildness like Ma and the daddy I never knew? When I realized I had a choice, I could struggle to save my physical life or I could surrender it, I realized I had more power beneath the water than any of you had on dry land. In that in-stant I knew I would follow Pops. I would dis-appear and no one would ever find me and then nothing would matter—not patience or impatience or living or dying or bastard or claimed. I drifted down, down. I saw an old tire rooted in the muddy bottom. Next to it was Grandpa's lost canoe, grass waving through its holes. I saw a baby's skeleton. It was intact. I picked it up and held it next to my jacket but soon it scattered. A hand reached for me and as it held mine, my body released its spirit and gave up its ghost. Re-member the nuns telling us something about Jesus giving up his ghost? We laughed so hard you wet yourself. My ghost just gave up its pee, you said, as you pulled off your pant-ies and twirled them around your finger. You weren't ashamed, not then. You believed in God then. You hung your underwear on a fencepost to dry in the sun while we contin-ued picking strawberries. You kept your skirt wrapped tightly around your legs, tucking it underneath your bottom as you squatted be-fore a new patch. No peeking, you said. No peeking or you'll burn in hell. I told you I didn't believe in hell, that I figured it was just a place the pope or Father Gray made up to scare us into being good. You told me not to say such awful things, that God would strike me dead on the spot, and you were afraid I'd burn in hell. But I kept it up, kept telling you there was no hell, no limbo, no purgatory. That the priests and nuns were liars. That there probably wasn't even a heaven. I asked you where these places were. Were they under the earth? Then why didn't we see them when we dug graves and threw dead people in? Were they in the sky? Then why didn't airplanes fly into them? Were they in space? Then why hadn't Sputnik reported them? You told me being Catholic meant we had to believe because Father Gray and Pope Pious XII would throw us out of the church if we didn't. I told you I wanted to be thrown out the back door of our church right through to the front door of the Mennonites' on M-28. I didn't know what they believed, but I knew the McRay boys were Mennonites and they liked to shoot bullets into the metal Jesus sign on top of our hill. I figured if those boys weren't afraid of going to hell for filling Jesus full of holes, then their church was the one for me. Remember? You started to cry. You told me I was wrong. There was a heaven as well as a hell, and it didn't matter where they were. That was God's business, you said, not ours. You spilled your berries all over yourself and wouldn't let me help you put them back in your glass. They stained your fingers red and left red marks on your clothes. You gave up and threw down your glass, snatched your panties, and headed home. I picked up what you left. You always picked clean, but I just picked, throwing stems and leaves and green berries and rotten ones into my container. I told you I cleaned them when I got home, but I lied. I dumped them into a bowl, stirred in lots of sugar, and spun everything around until the milk turned pink. The berries tasted just as good as your spotless ones. I didn't often lie to you. When my spirit left my body I was near you. I followed you down the road as you ran for help. Couldn't you feel me beside you? I tried to tell you I wasn't in the river, but you wouldn't listen. When the grown-ups found the flesh that had once housed me and washed it off and dressed it in its Sunday clothes and laid that clean-clothed flesh in the coffin, I tried to tell Mr. Kelsey I wasn't in the box, but standing next to him, admiring the corpse, just as he was. When people came and looked at the skin I'd lived in and cried over it—saying it was too bad, he was too young to die—I tried to tell them nobody had died. That what they were looking at was just a doll. I was alive and near them. I heard people crying for the dead thing in the coffin but when my flesh had walked among them, sometimes lonely, sometimes afraid, always restless, there had been no tears. Why did people now cry over the empty thing? Father Gray and the nuns cried too, but I don't think they were crying for me. I think they were crying because they knew they'd have to find another boy to pick on and that might not be so easy now I was gone. When Mr. Kelsey drove the corpse to the church in his fancy black car and they wheeled the dead thing down the aisle, Father Gray covered the coffin with smoke from the incense burner, and I watched his eyes. He was afraid, much more afraid than he was the Sunday I caught him doing something sinful to Larry, the thing he had wanted to do to me until I threatened to kill him and he threatened to kill me if I ever told a living soul. I put my invisible eyes next to his and stared at him until his eyes watered. Remember? He almost dropped the burner. He was scared by something his physical eyes couldn't see but his spirit knew was more real than the empty things surrounding him.

Don't cry for me, Katie. I'm in a strange place. I can't describe it to you because I didn't learn words on earth to tell you what it's like here. It's different is the best I can say. It's not what I expected. I haven't found our idea of *God* yet or maybe I have and just haven't recognized it. I'm sorry I left you, but I'm not unhappy where I am, and I'll wait for you. Don't hurry, though. I'll wait as long as it takes for you to join me because I love you and waiting is easy now that I'm free of my flesh.

* (Quote used with the permission of the Faulkner Literary Estate.)

Thomas: Fortitude

by Sharon Kennedy

Wednesday, August 12, 1959, 5:30 a.m.

Almost six o'clock. Thomas awakens before the alarm clock rings. Eva's back is to him and he longs to stroke the shapely curve of her spine and hold her in his arms, but he doesn't. Instead, he reaches underneath the bed for the bottle of peppermint schnapps. He sits upright and unscrews the top. His throat burns as the clear liquid makes its way to his stomach. For a moment he wonders if every man starts his day the same way, wanting to be loved by his wife, but settling for the mistress in a bottle. The booze never says no. It's always agreeable. It neither questions nor torments. It isn't much of a substitute for a loving wife, but he can't get through the day without it. He takes another slug, shoves the bottle back, feels around the floor for his clothes and gets dressed.

Before he leaves the room, he glances once more at his wife. Her hair is messy. Her left leg carelessly tossed over the covers. Her nightgown has ridden up, exposing her shapely thigh. He would give anything to love her now, but not many people get what they want. He walks to the window and pulls down the green shade. Eva likes a cool room, and now the sun's rays will be blocked for another hour. She moves slightly. As her left hand slides over her rump, he notices her gold wedding band. One day he hopes to have enough money to buy a diamond ring. Maybe that will make her happy. He turns, pushes aside the curtain that acts as a door and heads for the stairs.

He thinks of the work awaiting him. There's always plenty of it which makes this day no different from the thousands that have gone before it or the thousands yet to come. The downed chestnut tree in the back forty must be hauled home and buzzed up for the winter woodpile. He'll ask Johnny for help, although he doesn't like to bother anyone and only asks his brother-in-law when a job requires two men. A fence needs mending that runs along the bush leading to the river. The clutch on his tractor is going.

Thomas hears Granny's voice as he reaches the first step. "Coffee's hot and strong," she calls from the kitchen. "Bacon's ready and fried potatoes are keepin' warm in the oven. How many eggs you want? Two? Three?" His mother chatters as she busies herself at the stove, cracking fresh eggs into the hot cast iron skillet, watching as they sizzle and the whites turn brown and crispy around the edges. She wraps the hem of her apron around the handle of the coffee pot, moves from the stove to the table, fills Thomas' cup, and sets a plate of food at his place.

"You just missed the farm report," she says. "Hog's up. Beef's down. Maybe we should hold off sellin' the calves 'till the price goes up." She runs a wet dishrag over the red checked oilcloth and picks up tiny breadcrumbs as she goes. She rinses the rag in the pan of hot dishwater on the woodstove then pours coffee into her white cup. "I heard Katie cryin' again last night," she says as she stirs cream and sugar into her coffee. "Must have been around midnight." Her voice trails off. "Seems like she cries 'most every night since the accident." Granny puts her head down, intent upon stirring every grain of sugar until it dissolves into the hot liquid, willing herself to avoid the eyes of her son, swirling the spoon round and round as if by making a tempest in her cup she can avoid the one in her house.

Thomas shakes his head, ignoring her words and the probing, delicate sound of her voice. "I'll have a refill," he says, pointing to his cup. "And a few more pieces of bacon. Potatoes and eggs are good, too," he says, desperate to talk about food or cattle prices or anything other than Katie because talk-

ing does not help, does not lessen the pain of his child or bring back Blew, the dead cousin she loved.

"It's the green onions that flavor everything," Granny says, knowing even before she mentioned Katie's name or the plaintive sound of her crying in the night that Thomas would not respond because he never responds because to do so would only sharpen the pain of his helplessness. "I don't mean to pry," she continues. "But I'm worried about her. 'Course, it ain't none of my business." She leaves the spoon in her cup and with both hands shoves herself from the table. "I'll get the bacon," she says because that's always been her answer to troubles—a plate of good food cooked on a woodstove, cooked by a woman whose only remaining purpose in life is to nourish those she loves.

Granny moves slowly across the kitchen. Her back is bent and her neck lurches forward like the crook of a cane. There's an odd odor about her, a mixture of liniment and barn and age. It isn't a repulsive scent, merely one nobody noticed before Blew died. Her flowered housedress needs mending. The stains on her green apron are obvious. Her pink slippers are frayed. She glances at Thomas as she shuffles to the stove and gone is the cheerful face that greeted him only moments ago. Gone, too, is the smile, replaced with a look of indescribable sorrow. Thomas wants to comfort her but doesn't know how. He wonders how he missed her growing old before his eyes. When she refills his cup and sets more bacon on his plate, he brushes her arm with his big, rough hand. "Katie'll be okay," he says in the softest, most gentle voice he can muster. "It's the same dream, Blew and those damn dead kittens she found. We have to give her time to heal."

"Sometimes we ain't got no time," she says. "Sometimes it's gone before we know it." There's a strange look in her pale blue eyes, a look Thomas has seen many times. A look that tells him she's searching for something she can't find. Something she misplaced years ago but never quite forgot. The first time he recalled seeing that look was the day they buried Pa, on Thomas' 10th birthday, 43 years ago. It was a beautiful September morning, and his sisters—Zelly, Rene, and Mags—had forced him to wear Pa's clothes. Although they rolled up the shirt sleeves and pant legs, they hung on him like rags on a clothesline. Nobody cried at the funeral except Thomas. When the girls called him a sissy, he lied and said he wasn't crying for Pa. He was crying because he looked like a scarecrow, a child lost in a dead man's clothes. Somehow the lie helped him get through that awful day. He brings himself back to the present.

"It's okay," he says. "Everything will be okay." Granny doesn't answer. She's in the pantry getting things ready for the blueberry pies she'll bake today. He can hear the everyday movements of a woman engrossed in her kitchen duties, the rummaging for the right sized pie dish, the search for the rolling pin, the squeak of the hinge on the flour bin as she pulls it open. Common, comforting sounds he's heard all his life letting him know as long as things remain as they are, everything *will* be okay. The routine will continue from sunrise to sundown with a steady, familiar rhythm as constant as the flow of the river. He finishes his meal in silence and pushes his chair from the table. He reaches for his gray striped cap hanging on a nail behind the stove. "I'm going to the barn," he says, but there is no response. The screen door slams just missing Lard's tail as the dog runs after his master.

Like every farmer, the first thing Thomas does is look at the sky when he steps off the front porch. What signal does it give today? Nothing in particular he notes. Streaks of red are just beginning to appear on the horizon. That's not a good sign. Thomas hopes the weather will hold until most of the day's chores are done. He stops at the well house to get the milk utensils, some water and clean rags to wipe the cows' bags. As he leaves the building, a squirrel crosses a few feet in front of him. Lard chases it until his attention turns to a barn cat, but the cat outsmarts him, stands his ground and hisses instead of running. Thomas laughs.

Nine cows are gathered around the pasture gate, waiting to be let in. Thomas unhooks the latch and watches them sashay to the barn. Their heavy bags sway as they walk, dripping warm milk on the ground. Silver is the lead. The bell around her neck clanks, breaking the quiet of the morning. Dairy cows have been part of his life since he was born, giving him purpose and a feeling of satisfaction. They greet him much as the schnapps does—without question or accusation. He follows them into the barn, chains each one and starts milking.

When the pail is full, he empties it into the tall, galvanized can by the door and pushes the lid down, then goes on to the next cow. He takes care that no burrs, pieces of dung or hair fall into the pail. Katie always enjoyed getting up early during the summer and currying the cows, but since Blew's death in April she hasn't come near the barn. Thomas misses her help as well as her company. "Our girl's sad," he says to Old Tom. "She's not the same as she was. I don't know what will become of her. She rides her bike to the river every morning and is gone for hours. You miss her, too, don't you?"

The cat turns his head to one side as though hanging on every word and understanding its importance. He lifts a paw and rests it on Thomas' thigh. Then he opens his mouth to receive one last squirt of warm milk, meows his thanks and wanders away. The barn is quiet, and smells of milk and dusty hay. The other cats disappear into empty mangers, empty stalls, or run up the haymow ladder. Heat from the cows chases the chill from the air, and the barn is warm and inviting.

Thomas has been around a farm all his life. Milking and planting and harvesting are all he knows. Eva wants him to work off the farm, although he figures it would just about kill him to get a job in town. A steady paycheck would be nice, but he isn't interested in working for another man. He's always been his own boss and doesn't like the idea of taking orders from a stranger. Taking them from Eva is bad enough. He knows that, eventually, she'll demand the milk cows go and after them, the Herefords, and the farm will be one in name only with a few cats and maybe a chicken or two.

Always the dreamer, Eva thinks life will be easier if Thomas gets steady work at the Soo Locks. She'll spend her days at her easel, painting anything that takes her fancy. Sometimes when he's working in a field, he sees her roaming the woods and open pastures, searching for wildflowers or red maple leaves as she escapes the monotonous routine of her life. She despises the mundane things. Cooking and cleaning, chopping wood and hauling water, praying for good weather during haying—the stuff that life is made of is meaningless to her. She wants to live in town. Living on a farm is too hard and economically unpredictable. Everything depends upon the weather.

When the milking is done, Thomas unchains the cows and watches as they walk the well-trodden path. They're a polite bunch. They take their time and wait their turn for a lick at the salt block before heading to the south pasture where the grass is lush and still glistening with morning dew. In the afternoon, they'll seek shade in the bush. At six o'clock, they'll head back to the gate and wait for their master to open it for the second milking. They're as constant as the rising of the sun. Thomas closes the gate when the last cow walks through. Then he calls to Lard.

"C'mon old boy," he says and Lard comes running to the well house. Thomas strains the milk and rinses the empty cans with cold water. Soon MayBeth and Katie will give them a proper washing. He closes the door, heads for the tractor, and hitches a cart to it. Then he puts his chainsaw, a full can of gas, and a couple of sharp axes in it. He mounts the Case and it springs to life with a rat-a-tat-tat. Now the real work begins. Before he drives down the field and crosses the road to Johnny's house, his thoughts turn to Katie. He reaches for the schnapps.

Lard runs ahead, chasing a wild rabbit. In the distance, Thomas hears the bray of a donkey and the answering neigh of a neighbor's horse. "It's going to be a good day," he says as Lard abandons the chase and runs alongside him. Away from the house, away from a sad daughter, a discontented wife, and an aging mother, Thomas will soon be lost in his work and the whirl of a chainsaw. He drives the tractor a little slower than usual and breathes deeply of the fresh morning air that carries the scent of hope. Perhaps it's only the peppermint schnapps parading as hope, but it blurs the vision of his daughter's sorrow and that's enough to get him through today.

Sharon Kennedy continues to write her weekly newspaper columns that run in the *Sault News* and the *Cheboygan Tribune*. She can be reached at sharonkennedy1947@gmail.com.

Historical St Ignace car ferry dock

The Spearing Shack

by Chris Kent

Traversing Iron County via US-2 takes you through what is truly some of Michigan's great outdoors. The black-top ribbon of two-lane road is only halted once by a stoplight, the only such signal in 6000 square miles which just operates twelve hours a day. Along this scenic artery you pass a plethora of outdoor beauty and opportunity from cascading waterfalls, meandering streams, to hundreds of lakes and miles of trails for hiking, snowshoeing, snowmobiling and ATV riding. Each season brings a new checklist of open-air adventures. In winter, nature redesigns the lakes from a place of swimming and boating to a frozen panorama stretching from spruce lined shore to shore. The sun-drenched waters become an ice-covered landscape for daring adventurers.

As the gelid December temperatures thicken the ice covering the lakes, anglers push over the frozen surface toward their ultimate fishing spot. The lure of the fish draws some to venture onto thin ice, risking peril.

The more cautious are patient, as inches of ice turn to feet, eventually thick enough for trucks to ply. Pop up fishing shacks dot the lakes. Some anglers however, the bravest of the bunch, crouch in the open over holes in the ice defying blowing snow and falling temperatures in search of elusive crappie, bluegill or walleye. But of the winter anglers, a band of solitary souls, sit sequestered in a "Spearing Shack." The shack is generally built of repurposed materials found out back in a barn or pole building. Those items leftover from construction projects conducted by generations of Yoopers before them. The old screen door from the back porch, excess lumber from building a sugar shack, or maybe an old pair of skis from the rafters, all secured with a random collection of nails, screws, duct tape and wire.

As I trudge across the frozen lake toward such a spearing shack, my thoughts are on ancestors who participated in similar adventures in decades past. Traditions, customs, rituals, values—those inherited actions that bind us together. The behaviors passed down from generation to generation. A superstition honored. A solemn ceremony consisting of actions performed in a prescribed order. The stories told of fish taken or of the one that got away.

When I finally reach the destination, a hasp latch with a padlock hanging open keeps the entrance closed but not locked. Trust is an accepted virtue in the U.P. I push open the access, a repurposed door covered with blue board insulation. Light floods into the tiny space. The floor of the shack is half open to the ice and the remaining space a platform, just large enough for a brown metal folding chair, a Mr. Buddy propane heater and me. The ice has been cut and chipped away to create a two by three foot opening, a window to the eight-foot-deep lake below. Weeds gracefully sway in the current and tiny fish swim past. The currents forming intricate patterns on the marrow bottom. Nature's own aquarium or fifty-inch TV.

I light the heater, hang my coat from one of the random hooks and rusty nails protruding from the wall. Slush has formed overnight in the hole. I scoop the ice with a long handled sieve. Quietly, I sit in the tiny metal chair, shifting my weight to steady the seat. A ghastly looking weapon, a nine tine barbed spear, most closely resembling an armament suited to be carried by Poseidon, is propped in the corner of the shack. A long cord, attached to the end of the wooden handle of the spear, is connected to a ring on the ceiling so it won't be lost when thrown at a fish. Spears are generally handmade, passed on for generations, a keepsake from father to son or daughter.

Above the water, a fish decoy is suspended from a long piece of stout ice fishing line. The lure is brightly colored, neon chartreuse blended to cherry red. A glass eye sparkles. When lowered into the water, a rudder or spinner guides the decoy as I jerk the line creating life-like movement from the bait. An opportunistic pike sees what it thinks is a wounded prey and comes to take a look. The enticement is often so strong it overcomes the better judgment of the fish.

A thin stream of sun light is spilling in under the door creating a ghostly apparition on the floor. The wind howls across the open lake, whistling spookily as it makes its way through the cracks in the shack. Strips of duct tape cover seams and chinks in the walls unsuccessfully applied to keep out the bone-chilling elements. The shifting ice under the shack creaks and moans, as a ghostly haunted house. Daylight reflecting eerily illuminates the hole in the ice. I'm reminded by a twinge of pain the penetrating cold is invading my arthritic knees. I adjust the heater and settle back into my seat. My stare is unwavering as I watch for the mysterious shadow of an approaching pike.

Talk is a musky resides in this lake that is almost five feet long. The Sasquatch of the depths. A monstrous creature, a fossil of the past, folklore or faith, ever elusive. Sightings fashion countless conversations, stories told over beers at a nearby bar.

Time passes, the sun is setting, and reflecting light is fading. The curtain is falling, darkness over takes the hole in the ice. My adventure ends without the appearance of a pike or the ever mysterious musky but again I have embraced the great outdoors of Michigan's Upper Peninsula.

Death So Close

by Chris Kent

A sliver of moon appeared just above the silhouetted towering white pines as dusk faded to darkness. A narrow gravel road seemed luminescent in the pastel moon light as it wound among the rolling hills between the tiny 1930's mining village of Virgil and a nearby iron ore mine.

Kicking rocks down that dusty road, two nine-year-old buddies were heading home after a visit to the company store. Jimmy, blond hair hanging in his eyes, a dusty pinch brim resting on his ears. A slingshot hung from the pocket of his worn knickers. He gave his friend a sideways smile, "Come on Joey, let's go. I dare you, you're just a piker. Don't be a chicken," he flapped his arms, thumbs hooked in his striped suspenders.

"My Pop would skin me alive if I done that," Joey shuffled his leather work boots in the loose gravel, watching a cloud of ochre powder form around his ankles. The strap of his faded bib overalls hung loosely on his slumping shoulder. His feed-sack shirt was open at the collar revealing his pale freckled chest. He chewed the juicy stem of a stalk of timothy he had pulled from the tall grass on the roadside.

"Aw come on, just look in the door, we'll get outta there before anybody sees us," Jimmy pushed his friend, knocking him to the ground. Joey scrambled to his feet and the two boys darted toward a clearing off the road, disappearing into the shadows behind a small log building known as Toti's Bar.

"We're gonna be in big trouble," Joey mouthed, pulling on Jimmy's sleeve as they scurried from the road.

Evening pale left only a dim smoky glow from two small windows. A band of illumination from oil lamps hanging inside spilled out the slightly open door creating ghostlike movement on the wooden steps. The boys flattened their scrawny bodies, side by side, against the rough logs next to the door, hoping to discover the transgressions of Toti's. The saloon was a forbidden topic for boys to talk about at home, the spot the "old man" often stopped after a long day at the mine. A stopover for many miners after their grueling twelve-hour shift underground at the nearby Virgil Mine. Never spoken of by mothers, the place had a mysterious, even sinful reputation among young boys living in the company location surrounding the mine head.

Joey leaned forward, his neck straining, his face next to Jimmy's, the buckle of his bibs digging in his friend's arm. Both boys, wide eyed, staring through the narrow opening in the doorway, lamp light radiating on their faces.

An ornate walnut back bar hugged the wall, framing a cloudy mirror that reflected the faces of men seated on wooden stools. Sweat streaked faces turned red from the iron ore dust that teared their eyes and clogged their lungs as they toiled underground. Low voices intermingled in an indistinguishable drone, only to be sharply cut by the constant coughs. Effects of dust caused chronic lung disease, aggravated by the nicotine filled air.

Each sharp cough or raised voice brought a stab of fear to the spying boys in hiding outside the heavy wooden door.

Among the milling miners, near the opposite wall, was a round table marred with stains from thousands of beer glasses, cigarette burns and occasional knife carved initials. Five mismatched oak chairs, worn to an aged patina, surrounded the tabletop. The wooden plank floor under the furniture was darkened by years of muddy boots, tobacco juice and slopped beer. At the table, five grim-faced poker players reckoned the cards held in calloused hands, work shirtsleeves rolled up to expose scarred forearms, elbows resting on chair arms.

With his back against the wall, chair tilted on two legs, a tall burly driller scowled at the men across the table. Companions by day in the mine, but adversaries at the table tonight. To his left, a small man, deep furrows lining his aging face, his twisted body the result of years earlier when a mine timber collapsed nearly crushing him. A cane, whittled from a rough tree limb, leaned on the table. Next, Joe, his features barely distinguishable from the dust clinging to his face. Both elbows on the table now, hands folded enclosing his cards, covering the lower portion of his face, his narrow eyes peering suspiciously. Nearest the door, a goliath of a man, with massive arms and shoulders honed by hours swinging a mattock carving through rock. Lastly at the poker table, the dealer, hardened hands, dirt embedded around broken nails, carefully tossing card after card to each of the players, watching intently for a reaction as they formed their hand.

Working below ground created a tension ill controlled when men returned to the surface. Life was spent each day within a half-step of tragedy, death so close. Every man recalling too often the Mansfield disaster, when the ground cracked and trembled as rock and dirt between the surface and the shaft collapsed allowing the Michigamme River to pour in, filling the void, drowning twenty-seven men. Or the day the Porter Mine claimed seventeen miners who were just returning to work after lunch. Water and sand rushed into the shaft plunging men and the cage they were riding in 500 feet to the bottom of the mine. The wail of sirens or three blasts from a mine whistle were part of life in a mining town; the sound screaming the loss of a friend, brother, son, or father. A harsh reality; ore blasted, shoveled and then trammed out of the mine was frequently paid for with human souls. In this world, the value of life was diminished when measured against tons of iron ore.

An unnatural, serious mood riveted the men tonight. Emanating from hours in the mine, under hundreds of feet of rock and dirt with death as a constant companion. A narrow escape from disaster today, a brake failure on a tram. Now these five individuals were trying to evade the uncertainties of life below ground. Each man held cards dealt by another, not unlike the daily gambles they made entering the underground shafts with their lives often in other hands. To raise, hold or to fold, carefully considering the options assembled within the cards, eyes staring forward, not an indication as to what their rough hands possessed. The unsettled mood, like a cat on hot bricks, gripped the men at the table.

Breaching the almost impenetrable air, "You son-of-a-bitch," ricocheted throughout the room. A chair scraped noisily across the plank floor. One of the card players at the table folded his hand, dropping it. "What the hell you doin'? I seen that, you asshole," he slammed his fist, the table rattling. The gambler stood up, his chair clattering as it tipped over backwards. He leaned across the table resting the beefy knuckles of one hand on the tabletop, the other hand grabbing the shirt of the man on the other side of the table pulling him out of his seat, their faces within inches. Flecks of saliva flew against the miner's dusty cheeks creating tiny spots of crimson mud. "Jesus, you just about killed me in the north shaft today now you're trying to cheat me. You asshole." Shoving the man back toward his seat, sprawling him helplessly in the chair as it tilted against the wall. An inescapable tone commanded the awkward moment for men at bar. Each stared in silence at the image reflected in the clouded mirror, recognizing peril.

The two young voyeurs, hidden in the shadows, eyes fixed on the conflict at the table, gasp, held the lungful, remained motionless against the log wall. "Did you hear that?" Jimmy whispered.

Joey felt the warm sensation as a wet spot in the front of his overalls spread, his bladder involuntarily emptied. He covered his crotch with his flattened hand. "If he sees me, my old man is gonna to kill me," as tears rolled over the freckles on his cheeks and dropped to the ground.

Jimmy leaned his face close to his friend's ear, "Shut up, nobody knows we're here," then he dug his fingernails into Joey's skinny arm, leaving four crimson crescents in the pale flesh.

"Hey, who needs a beer?" the query from behind the bar pierced the atmosphere, an attempt to calm a developing tempest. Charlie, a stained white apron tied over his wool plaid shirt, reached his hand under the counter feeling for a wooden axe handle he kept for such occasions, his eyes fixed on the men at the table. He laid the club on the bar top, his fingers clenching the wood, "That's enough boys." The weapon was intended only for a circumstance beyond control, not a usual day at Toti's. However, everyone knew Charlie wouldn't hesitate if needed.

"What the hell you talkin' about, I ain't cheatin' nobody," the accused gambler straightened his work shirt and righted the chair, fanning the cards in his hand. "Don't you blame me for what happened at the mine; you're the one that didn't set the brake on that tram. Could've killed us both, you bastard. Get outta here before you're wife comes down here and drags you home."

A chorus of guffaws and snorts erupted from the men in the room.

"Ta hell I didn't set that lever, you know damn well you dunnit. Tryin' to kill me, I know it, you bastard; you go straight to hell." A steely stare knifed the atmosphere between the two poker players. For a second not a single motion around the table, every man frozen in anticipation. Again, the player pushed back his worn chair, grating against the scarred and aging white pine planks. His blue-gray eyes carving through the smoky haze signaling a threat as he glared across the table, then threw his cards on the table top. "You chicken shit son-of-a bitch."

Suddenly on his feet, pivoting, striding toward the door. His massive frame blocked the lamplight that had been escaping from the slightly open door. He shoved the door; it banged loudly against the log wall. The boys scrambled for cover behind a pile of wooden kegs that once held the distillation that fueled such rage. The boys watched as the dark figure moved toward a flivver, an aging Model A parked nearby, spinning the crank, the engine turned over. Without looking back, the man slouched into the driver's seat and drove down the road, thick red dust soon obscuring the vehicle.

"Who was that?" Joey whispered. He sat on the ground leaning against a keg, rubbing his shoulder and staring at the wet spot on the front of his trousers.

"I don't know. It was too dark; I couldn't see 'em that good. I think that old Model A belongs to Charlie, the bartender, but that wasn't Charlie. We better get out of here before somebody sees us. What you cryin' about? Jeez Joey, you pissed your pants."

"No, I didn't and shut up; I ain't cryin'. Just hurt my shoulder when that door hit me."

"Let's go, we gotta' get outta' here," gripping Joey's arm and desperately trying to get air in his lungs to speak. Just as the boys started to run from behind the kegs, a shape filled the open door. Jimmy pushed his friend to the ground, his face in the dirt. Charlie pulled the door closed, sealing in the pale lamp light leaving the boys alone in the dark.

"Let's git", whispered Jimmy, pushing Joey out of their hiding spot. "Go, Joey, hurry, faster." Suddenly dim headlights appeared over the hill lighting the gravel road, silhouetting the boys.

"Run. Don't let him see us." Diving, the boys flattened on the ground, then scuttling into the dark against the building.

The engine sound died, the car door creaked open, then abruptly slammed as a man walked toward the saloon. Shoving the door open, light streamed out illuminating the figure who had exited the car. A flicker from the nearby oil lamp reflected off the barrel of the hand gun he held. A second later a blast deafened the ears of the red-faced miners as they stared in shock, unable to believe what was happening. A player at the table slumped forward, blood slowly spread across his iron dust stained shirt, cards spilling to the floor. His hand vainly grasped at the edge of the table as he slipped to the floor. Eyes fixed in disbelief as life ebbed from his body.

The shooter spun around, took several steps out the door, disappearing on foot into the night. The boys lay breathless. Stunned and bewildered. Terrified. The deafening reverberation of the shell exploding, the faint coppery scent of the blood pooling on the table, the cordite burning their nostrils, then the eerie silence. Looking first at the sprawled figure on the floor of Toti's saloon, and then staring into the darkness where the fleeing figure vanished.

Joey mouthed, "Pop."

Chris Kent retired with her husband to the Upper Peninsula after a career in marketing and public relations in Lower Michigan. They live in a remote area, off the grid for fifteen years, with a German Shorthair, horses, bees and chickens. In this setting, where the woods, waters and sky meet, she gains daily inspiration and opportunity for creative expression. The UP, its people and places, are truly home today. Chris has had writings published in several magazines and anthologies.

8859 FATHER MARQUETTE LEAVING ST. IGNACE.

St Ignace Father Marquette leaving

Right Judgment

by Tamara Lauder

Hawaiian flowers covered her legs. They were bold but soothing, meticulously crafted, and organized with great precision according to size and color so as to not overlap, clash, or repeat themselves. Her soft, young skin provided a perfect canvas for the bright explicit colors that decorated her legs.

No one, including herself, knew how she got them, or what they were. She wasn't born with them. One Hawaiian flower appeared one morning on her upper inner thigh. She was eight. It was undetectable by others, and she didn't bring it to anyone's attention. As she got older, more flowers appeared until they were no longer discrete. They dipped below her miniskirts. They appeared each morning once she left for school and disappeared each evening before she entered the house.

She couldn't remember her mother. Nobody knew who her father was. The lame dark-skinned man with the deep, raspy voice was all she ever knew. His face was wrinkled beyond his years, yet missing the typical crow's feet due to lack of smiling and lack of sun. Each morning as she dressed for school, he would roll his long, thick, tea-colored fingernails on the Formica kitchen table as he impatiently waited for her to make their breakfast. By the end of each week, the smell of smoke and body odor was stifling as she descended the stairs, but was eventually overpowered by the greasy stench of his morning burnt bacon. She supposed they all smelled the same in the mine shaft. After all, he only had two shirts and two pairs of jeans to last him the two weeks between laundromat days, when he gave her coins to do woman's work. She, however, had numerous miniskirts—seven to be exact. She had one for every day of the week to mix and match with her three shirts.

"Get goin' now. And stay out a trouble. You hear me?"

Henry said the same thing every morning after she finished making his bacon and eating her toast. His jarring voice stole the morning silence. Each sentence he spoke ended with a ferocious cough followed by a deep gasp for air.

"And, don't slam that door!"

Cyndy said the words in unison with him, as the screen door with the broken spring slammed shut behind her.

"You come home right after school! Ya hear me? And don't be talkin' to any boys! They'll only get ya in trouble!"

Cyndy blocked out his voice, and his coughing, as she walked down the porch steps. She tried to ignore the nuances of the place, but the seeding pasture growing through the cracks in the walkway hit her knees. The raw wood revealed beneath the peeling pea green paint on the house matched the weathered unpainted porch. Cyndy offered to strip the paint, but was reminded that it was not a necessity, there was no money to replace it, and that, "it was no work for women."

As Cyndy walked to school each day, one by one the flowers appeared on her legs. School became more challenging as the flowers multiplied, but over the years, she grew accustomed to the questions, stares, and the ridicule. Cyndy just kept to herself, ignored her jesters, and did her homework. Despite their challenges, the flowers, made her feel pretty.

Each day, Cyndy went home right after school, just like Henry said, the flowers disappearing, one by one. Once home, Cyndy liked to sit on the porch, the only place that felt comfortable, safe, and devoid of ugliness on the property. Inside, the house was always dark and dingy, but especially when it lacked any decorations for the season. The kitchen held the stained and nicked Formica table top that Henry utilized for her morning wake up call. It replaced the less obtrusive broken wooden table that matched the hard wooden spindle-back chairs that wiggled at the legs and creaked when you moved. In the living room was an old eighteen inch television facing Henry's beige recliner, dirty at the headrest and worn on the arms. Next to his recliner sat an end table full of rings from his nightly can of beer. The only other place to sit was a couch covered in leather that looked like it had been harvested from a dinosaur.

It was Christmas. It was always just the two of them. It felt special though, because it was different than the routine. There were never any presents, but Henry would cook the turkey the mine gave him.

"I've got somethin' for ya," Henry said as he handed her a dusty shoe box.

"What?" Cyndy responded in disbelief.

"It's from your mother. She told me to give it to ya when you were old enough."

Cyndy could barely swallow the lump in her throat. She hadn't heard him or anyone mention her mother for years. Henry left the room. She opened the box. In it, were a tiny Bible and a letter. In a bookmarked page of the Bible was a highlighted verse.

"Do not judge by appearances, but judge with right judgment."

The letter read:

Dearest Cyndy,
I will be gone before you will remember me. Henry doesn't have much, but he vowed to take care of you. He took care of me, too.
My clothes and my Bible are all that I have to leave you, besides my love and prayers. I pray that you will always feel beautiful and that life brings you flowers.
With Love,
Your Mother,
Josie

Henry came back in to check the turkey. His raspy voice finally broke the uncomfortable silence. "She leave ya anything good?"

Cyndy stared intently at his weathered face. His usually unkempt hair was combed and slicked back with a shiny substance, and he had attempted to clean his typically black-stained hands more than ordinarily. Henry made no eye contact.

"Ya. She left me something good. Merry Christmas Henry."

Suddenly, everything felt beautiful. And, one red flower appeared.

That Morning

by Tamara Lauder

The morning breaks,
pinks, oranges, blues   paint the west
Clangs of   flagpole by night
equipment, bags, kayaks by sunrise
as the crew loads
the large sea going vessel

It was that morning
when people   young and old
standing patiently   eager
at Jansen's Fish Market and Bakery
for a cup a jo and   bakery to go

"All aboard"   the captain cries
It was that morning when
the line disperses
from Jansen's to the Queen
my place in line   next,
"coffee and a turnover please."

It was that morning
the *Isle Royal Queen IV*
departs   its overnight docking space
aligning   for suitable forward projection
Drifts   out of the quiet bay
small   but majestic
fading into the distance

It was that morning when
I fell in love
with Copper Harbor

Tamara Lauder has been a frequent visitor to the Keweenaw Peninsula for over thirty years where she spends time with family and in the outdoors. Tamara is a professional artist in the Northwoods of Wisconsin, but also has a passion for writing. She enjoys combining her writing with her artwork, and is the author and illustrator of an inspirational pictorial book. In 2019, her short story was selected for the Houghton Selected Shorts Story Contest performed at the Rozsa Center at Michigan Tech University.

My Scrap Bag

by Teresa Locknane

In the scrap bag of my life there are many pieces of cloth: memories gathered and stored throughout the years.

God tenderly holds every piece in his hand: the blue pieces of tears and sorrow to the bits of red words said in anger as well as the scraps of yellow and green joy and peace.

Each one by itself seems plain and lacking somehow, but when carefully pieced and stitched together a transformation occurs.

From my side, it appears as a jumble of seams and loose threads, but from God's point of view, a beautiful stained glass window waiting to be illuminated by the Son.

Then he softens it inside and strengthens it with a backing of faith and binds it together with his love and forgiveness.

Through the years my quilt gets dirty and torn, but he's always there to make repairs and wash it clean again until the day when he wraps it around me and takes me into his arms to be with Him forever

Teresa Locknane lives in Gwinn, Michigan, with her husband David and her two daughters. She is an avid quilter and also enjoys drawing, crafting, music, and on occasion, writing poetry. She enjoys spending her free time with her family and making quilts for family, friends, and charity.

Logging the Hurricane River

Another COVID Dream

by Ellen Lord

A white dove goes flying
far away—

Dawn is red
in my dream
and dark thoughts sink
like stones
in a deep river.
I want to go back
to the day you were singing
as the tea steeped in the cup.
But now, I stand
on the shore of a virulent sea,
and there is sorrow on the wind.
How many golden hours does death have?
I will mourn them all.

A raven comes flying
Into this day—

...after Federico Garcia Lorca

Guillotine Dream

by Ellen Lord

What I took to be a piece of chocolate
turned out to be a severed sow's ear,
petrified and shriveled in a crystal dish.
What I took to be a blazing sunrise,
turned out to be the flame-glow of a wildfire
set by vandals in my cherished forest.
And what I took to be your tears of remorse,
turned out to be an outpouring of rage
as you turned and stormed away.
It was my love-sick brain, intoxicated
with the illusion of your alluring guile
that turned out to be the homocidic finale
of my psychotic interlude.
And so it was...
my general misunderstanding of the world,
denial of naked malice, and misperception
of viral motives that became more tragic
than comic.
And those illusions precipitated my decision
to behead ... your beloved tulips.

Ellen Lord is a Michigan native. She grew up in the Upper Peninsula. Her writing has appeared in *Walloon Writers Review*, *R.K.V.R.Y. Quarterly Literary Journal*, *PSM Peninsula Poets* chapbooks and *TDAL Poets Night Out* chapbooks. She won the Landmark Books Haiku Contest in 2017 & 2019. She is a member of The Poets Society of Michigan, Freshwater Poets in Traverse City, and Charlevoices Writers' Group in Charlevoix.

Ellen is a behavioral health therapist specializing in addiction and trauma. She likes to spend time exploring the wilderness near her ancestral home in Trout Creek, Michigan.

Sumac Summer

by Becky Ross Michael

"Philip, why are you still awake?" Mom whispered. She carried a lantern to avoid the bright hallway bulb.

"Too hot," I murmured, from my spot by an open window. Four brothers snored nearby. My six sisters were quiet in their room down the hall.

"A few more minutes and back to bed," my mother warned, as she left on tiptoes.

Something outside moved from the shadows. Dr. Justin walked the path to my friend's house with his black medical bag. Was Danny sick?

The stairs squeaked, and I dove for my pillow. I ignored the need for an outhouse visit, pressed my eyes shut, and fell into a sweaty sleep.

...

The air was even warmer when the rooster crowed the next morning.

"Looks like our next-door neighbors moved out," my big brother, Harold, said at breakfast.

"No way. Danny's my best friend. He wouldn't leave without telling me."

"When I delivered their newspaper, the window shades were still closed, and their car was gone," said Harold.

"Dr. Justin was over there last night," I said. "I wonder what happened."

"I bet they didn't move," said our oldest brother, Ernie. "They probably got sick and died from poison, or something." He clutched his throat and fell to the floor with a choke.

"Don't tease," Mom said with a frown. "Danny's mother mentioned that his father had health problems. She said they might move closer to family in New York."

•••

By the end of that week, I decided Danny was gone for good. Harold reminded me it was my turn to cut the grass. I grabbed the wooden handle and gave our mower a push across the lawn. By the time I finished, the sun was high in the sky. My cheeks were on fire, and my mouth was dry as dirt.

I guzzled water at the kitchen pump and grumbled. "Why can't we ever buy soda pop from the market?"

"Treats like that cost too much for a family of thirteen," said Mom.

"Could we make more root beer?"

"That wasn't cheap, either. And we had a terrible mess in the basement when a bottle exploded."

"I have an idea for a drink," Dad said, as he walked into the room. "It's almost free and not messy to make."

"What is it?" I asked.

"Sumac ('sue mack') juice. It's been years since I made any, but I remember the steps."

"Never heard of it."

"The sumac tree's red berries can be used to make a lemon-flavored drink," said Dad. "Some people even call it sumac lemonade."

I pumped another cup of water and listened.

"The family next door has gone. No one cares if we cut berries from those sumac trees between the two houses," Dad continued.

"Guess not." Even though the neighbors had only been gone a week, I missed Danny. He'd been my best friend and could even make doing chores seem like fun.

Dad eyed the trees through the kitchen window. "We'll soak the berries in water until it's pink and lemony. Sugar or honey adds a bit of sweetness. The flavor will be strongest when the clusters turn dark red. Here in Northern Michigan, we won't see that until late summer."

A quick look at Mom told me she was okay with his idea. Hadn't my parents ever heard of poison sumac? With a gulp, I swallowed the words so they wouldn't escape from my mouth. What if Ernie was right? What if Danny's family was poisoned? I wanted to trust Dad on this. But it might make us sick, or even worse!

When I checked outside, the skinny leaves on the short, thick trees were mixed with light green flowers. I didn't see any berries.

Sleeping wasn't easy that night. I jerked awake. "Argh!" Danny and some strangers with hollow eyes and red drool on their lips visited my dreams. Could that nightmare be a sign that sumac juice might not be safe?

•••

Within a few weeks, little green berries appeared. They turned a rosier color each time I dared to peek at them. No words popped into my head to warn my parents they might be poisonous. I had to learn the facts before it was too late. Since it was summer vacation, I couldn't ask my teacher. The library was the best place to start.

"Chores are done, and I'm going for a bike ride."

"Sorry, Philip," said Mom. "You'll need to watch your younger brother and sister. I'm late for my women's meeting." The screen door slammed before I could argue.

Paul and Eunice weren't too heavy, and I could pull them to the library in our wagon. The shortest way took us past the blue water of the bay. If only we could trade places with the people who played in the waves without a care in the world.

The air was cooler inside the small, brick library. Eunice and Paul ran toward the picture books. I started my own search for adult books about trees.

"Philip Ross, I haven't seen you here in a long time," whispered the librarian after a while. "Could I help you find something?" She eyed my sister and brother.

Had they emptied all those books from the shelves?

"Ah...no, thanks. We should get going." I grabbed Eunice by the hand and Paul by the shirt. The walk back home with the wagon was even hotter, and I hadn't learned anything helpful.

Once we got in the yard, I reached to check the trees and found blood-red berries. Some clusters were even covered with white, sticky stuff. We were almost out of time. My new idea felt scary, but I had no choice. I wiped my hands across my pants and planned for the next day.

•••

I awoke early to a gray morning. After sneaking from the house, I steered my bike through quiet streets. I headed to the drugstore near the lake, where one of my older sisters had an afternoon job. While I waited by the locked door for the owner, Mr. Keiser, I peered down the road through the fog.

Teacher told us that druggists go to college for a long time. That's how they learn to make safe medicines. Mr. Keiser should also know which plants were safe. His tall body finally appeared from the fog. I ignored the lump in my throat and told him my problem. With a strange look, he motioned me inside the store.

"Aren't you one of Reverend Ross's boys?" he asked.

"Yes, sir, I'm Phil."

"Tell me all the details."

He sat on a high stool, and I began with the way Danny and his family had vanished. I described the sumac and ended with my fear that Dad didn't know the red berries were poison.

"Your worries are over," he said. "That's harmless sumac. You can tell by the red or purple clusters that point toward the sky. The sticky part you mentioned has the strongest lemon taste," he added.

"Isn't there a kind of sumac that's poison?" I asked.

"Yes, but that looks very different. It has green or white berries that hang down."

"Gee, thanks," I said in relief and stuck out my hand to shake his.

"Make sure you always check with your parents before eating anything that grows in the wild," Mr. Keiser reminded me, as I turned for the door.

I flew toward home on my bike and jumped off before the wheels stopped turning. Fat drops of dew sparkled on deep purple berries. "They're ready," I yelled, at the back door. "It's sumac juice time!"

•••

As the sun slipped lower in the sky, I sat on our wide porch with my family. Dad filled glasses with sumac juice for everyone. Mom added frosty chunks from the large block the iceman had just brought. The drink was cool, sour, and sweet on my tongue. Everybody liked it, except Eunice, who didn't like most things.

"Afternoon," said the mailman, from the bottom step. Mom traded him a glass of juice for a few envelopes. He smiled and drank it, while talking with my parents on the shaded porch.

Mom sifted through the mail as soon as he'd gone. She held up an envelope, written with ink. A cloud of worry crossed her face. "It's a letter from out East," she said and opened it. Her frown soon disappeared. "Philip, it's from Danny's mother. She says they left early that morning to beat the heat and apologizes for not saying good-bye. She'll work in her family's store while her husband recovers," said Mom, folding the page. "Time will tell, if they'll move back to Michigan."

"I'm glad they're okay," I said and turned away to hide my sadness.

"Danny sent you a note, Philip." She raised a paper written in smeared pencil.

I grabbed it and hurried to the side yard that overlooked my friend's old house and the sumac trees. Danny's story made me laugh out loud. On their way to New York, he and his mother had to change a flat tire. He described the scene so well that I pictured them in mud up to their knees as they searched for a dropped lug nut. Maybe I could think of a tale to send back?

I had a whopper of an idea. I'd write about a missing friend, fear of a poison potion and a tasty ending!

Becky Ross Michael grew up in Michigan, where she also raised a family and taught for many years. She now gardens and works on her sunny balcony in North Texas. Writing for kids and adults, her pieces appear in magazines, anthologies, and children's readers. In addition, she enjoys the challenge of working as a freelance editor. Becky's story, "Sumac Summer," is based on her father's childhood. Visit the author at platformnumber4.com

Bottom row: Paul, Eunice, Phil, Harold.
Middle row: Ernie, Rev. & Mrs. Ross; other siblings interspersed

Requiem for Ernie

by Hilton Moore

In 1953, a child's world seemed small in an isolated rural community on the rugged side of nowhere. Our nowhere was in Nelson, a small village near the Huron Mountains in the "sticks" of the Upper Peninsula of Michigan. But perhaps my painful reflection that the world was small is just a faded recollection, a grainy black-and-white memory, as my life was often beset by misery. I had polio.

When I write that the world seemed small, perhaps what I mean is constricted. It was a time when this country seemed innocent, but in truth, it wasn't small or innocent at all. America was on the cusp of violent change. By the 1960s the country would convulse, but in 1953 these endemic problems seemed far away to a young boy, much like the final destination of the seemingly endless rows of timber stacked along the railroad tracks. The land was ripening with social pathology and the inherent difficulties, and diminishing rows of pulp logs seemed to signal the end of the plentiful and idyllic life that the country knew at this time. The exhausted landscape, mostly timbered over and left bare, was dotted with fallow and deserted former homesteads. Pullulating plants intermixed with various weeds of all sorts: milkweed, sorrel, pigweed, and the like, filling the hardscrabble landscape. A change in the environment was evident to all who cared to see. Eventually the social issues, like weeds, would suck precious moisture from the formally fecund soil.

With polio, my life was hemmed in as much by social constraints as it was by the acres of summer hay that stretched far into the distance and seemed to me like penitentiary bars—though of course it was the polio that kept me imprisoned. I was fourteen and unable to play baseball with my younger, timid, and chubby friend Ernie because I wore the ubiquitous braces that were the curse of many a victim of this ravaging disease. The damn braces even made it difficult for me to navigate the stairs to my bedroom, and once there, exhausted by the climb, I would often play lonely games of solitaire until my persistent mother forced me to come down for a meal, and then the whole damn process would start again.

The infirmities of my disease left me consigned to stare longingly out the second-story window of my bedroom. The dusty and weed-infested ball diamond was across the street from our house and next to the train track, but it seemed to me a thousand miles away.

Mrs. Larsen's dilapidated house sat forlornly next to the ballfield. Bored, for hours at a time I would watch her leghorn chickens pecking at worms and bugs on the ball diamond when the neighborhood kids weren't around to throw stones at the pesky creatures.

Dr. Jonas Salk had just announced the discovery of a vaccine for polio that year, but it was too late for me. The transmission of polio was still an open question, so many families were rightfully frightened for their offspring.

Afraid Ernie would catch the virus from me, Ernie's mother instructed him not to come next door to my house, although on occasion he would slip around to my back door and let himself in. My mother was complicit in this juvenile act and didn't admonish either Ernie or me. I could sincerely understand Ernie's mother's reluctance. Though I will say, I was terribly alone. Mother felt her only son had been punished enough by God and wasn't going to inflict more pain by deliberately isolating me.

Other than Ernie's occasional visits I spent my days daydreaming, and watching fretfully as the neighborhood boys played baseball, or watching glumly as the daily trains rumbled along the right-field fence of the old baseball diamond.

Lacking much else to do in our impoverished rural area but to observe life, I became an interloper of sorts. Through my bay window spyglass I studied the nuanced world of boys, where rules and a sense of fair play were not necessarily a given. Because Ernie was chubby, he was teased mercilessly, and I sometimes felt powerless to stop the distress he must have endured. At other times, however, I remember viewing him as a comrade in arms. It was as if he, too, was a victim of an imagined war, and I wanted him to feel as tortured by an enemy as I felt abused by *my own condition*. I understand now that my need to see Ernie as a fellow victim was pathological, but at the time I was lashing out at the world and couldn't see my own failings. Now, years later, I feel a sense of shame for such a selfish vicarious need, but as a kid I felt we were brothers in pain and I often secretly gloated over his misery.

More than anything, though, we were good friends. But there was a gulf between Ernie and me that later in life I would recognize. Ernie's father was a soldier in the Marines and was stationed in Korea, a typical "grunt," my father called him. My father, who was a high school history teacher in the three-room schoolhouse in Nelson, had a dim view of the Korean Conflict, as that ugly war was euphemistically called. As a teacher, he was highly regarded in our rural village, while Ernie's dad was considered by many to be a rough character. Ernie's father shot pool and drank to excess when he came home on leave.

I was an only child, and while I *always felt wanted, I envied Ernie's neighboring house,* which was always full of frenetic activity. I mentioned my envy of Ernie's many brothers and sisters to my mother. She just rolled her eyes and winked at my father, who was camped out on his favorite leather chair in the living room. He laid down his paper, bemused. My mother smiled and ruefully noted to my father that when Ernie's dad came back, his harried wife was often left in the family way shortly after his departure. I was unsure of this adult humor and kept my best guesses to myself.

Regardless, Ernie's Catholic household had many children who roamed around the village unpenned, much like Mrs. Larsen's laying hens that scratched and pecked indiscriminately on the neighboring ballfield. After Ernie's mother's many complaints about chicken shit on her children's shoes, Mrs. Larsen reluctantly fenced the feathered offenders in her yard.

When Ernie climbed the steep stairs of our old peeling clapboard house to my second-floor bedroom, we would talk baseball and swap baseball cards. I once traded him a dog-eared Mickey Mantle card for a pristine Rocky Colavito. Ernie told me that his father had named him after a famous baseball announcer named Ernie Harwell, who broadcast his games over their old Philco radio in the early forties. Ernie's father had promised his wife that they would name their next son Ernie as a tribute to the revered announcer. Evidently she agreed, but no one was sure why. My friend Ernie had been born in 1943, when Harwell was broadcasting for the minor league team, the Atlanta Crackers. Ernie told me confidently while sitting on the edge of my bed that the Crackers won the league championship in 1946, when he was just three. His father credited Harwell's enthusiasm behind the microphone for the spectacular season the Crackers had. Ernie was rightly proud of his name.

When Ernie's father was home on leave from Korea, they listened to baseball games on their radio—when the static wasn't too bad. Ernie Harwell was a honey-mouthed announcer who called the games in a slow, southern drawl that drew the listener in like a mesmerizing séance. Ernie used to beam with pleasure when he told me of the late evening games that he and his father would listen to well into a sultry summer's night.

In 1953, the serene game of baseball was like a soothing elixir to a nation weary of wars. The misery of World War II had ended, and for all of those Americans who thought that it would be the final conflict of a troubled world, the Korean War represented just another failure of humanity—a sad addendum to history. But the game of baseball not only endured through this disquieting year, it seemed to transcend these perturbing times.

As the Conflict dragged on, Ernie's father had to go back to Korea. In my cloistered bedroom, Ernie and I listened intently to the radio as Ernie Harwell, who had now jumped ship from the Atlanta Crackers, began announcing for the New York Giants, a major league team. Just before the Fourth of July the Giants squared off against the Detroit Tigers. Harwell's voice was like butter left out on a warm day. While technically he was supposed to be announcing for the Giants, he seemed to our young ears to favor the Tigers, our underdog team.

Ernie told me that his father had written a letter to Walter O. Briggs Sr., the owner of the Tigers, suggesting that he hire Ernie Harwell as the Tigers' official announcer. My young friend Ernie showed me a crumpled letter from Mr. Briggs, Sr. that he pulled from his dirty jean pocket, which confirmed that indeed, Mr. Briggs did value Ernie's father's suggestion and thanked his father for his keen baseball instinct. I never mentioned to Ernie that Mr. Harwell had actually been hired by Walter O. Briggs, Jr., the son of the late Mr. Briggs, Sr., partly because I didn't want to ruin a good story, but more importantly, to not contradict Ernie's faith in his father's keen baseball acumen.

Some memories are like old chewing gum stuck tight under the seat of a baseball bleacher; they are a pain in the ass to extract. I remember watching from my bedroom window on early summer mornings, as Ernie played pretend baseball. Years ago it was not unusual for a portly ten-year-old with few friends to play pretend games. Maybe it is still that way; I don't know. I vividly recall one morning in mid-June, when the sun was low in the tentatively cloudy sky and the world was very quiet, the dew heavy and wet on the weed-infested ballfield—long before the local boys were up and going, and even before the morning train growled noisily past the ball diamond.

Unseen, I gazed out my open bedroom window that overlooked the ball diamond and watched Ernie at home plate. I can still hear his voice, tinged with excitement, as he jabbered excitedly to the invisible baseball crowd there to watch him play and to cheer him on. Ernie was facing the phantasm of a left-handed relief pitcher. Ernie's apparition wound up and threw a fastball as Ernie swung fiercely at the imaginary ball. Then he made a throaty yell that I could clearly hear. "It's a solid hit for the right-hander," he said excitedly, in a voice that seemed to mimic Ernie Harwell. Through my open window, I could clearly hear him shout, "It's headed for right field, and it could be a homer!" He ran as fast as his short, pudgy legs could manage, barreling around the bases, first, second, third, and then headed for home, jumping up and down on home plate, dust circling around his short, stocky frame, and yelling, "Hurrah, hurrah!" He sucked in gasps of air, exhausted by his efforts, and stood alone on home plate as if deciding what to do next. He repeated this same home run scenario several times 'till, almost painfully, he walked morosely over to the empty bleachers and sat down alone. Watching him at this most private moment, I felt as if I were intruding, but at the same time I felt compelled, drawn in by this most personal glimpse of another human being. He sat quietly on a broken bleacher and watched, as I did, the long smoking diesel train as it trundled by, filled with timber from the local sawmill and headed to the massive shipping port in Duluth, Minnesota.

Ernie sat forlornly on the bench. I recall he once had told me that he hoped to grow up to be a big league ballplayer. It occurred to me at this poignant moment that perhaps he understood on some level this was a fiction he had dreamt up and that it was never to be. Ernie was perceptive in a simple childhood way and hinted to me one day that he was saddened beyond grief at this private revelation. Looking back, it seems remarkable that Ernie knew, even at that young age, that certain dreams are out of one's reach, but he did. Ernie's insightful observation was not news to me, as I had lived with disappointment my whole life, but I had always underestimated Ernie's insights. Ironically, my own pain blocked me from feeling empathy.

Several days later, on a crisp summer morning, I watched from my bedroom window as two tall, sharply dressed Marines pulled up to Ernie's house in an official automobile and strode silently toward the porch carrying a satchel. I gazed, sickened, from my window, as I knew intuitively that it would be a sad day for everyone in our small town. The Korean Conflict had claimed one of our own. Pastor Hank Martin, Sr. delivered the eulogy; the village mourned.

The morning after Ernie's father's funeral, the sun was a clouded orb that shaded the ballfield, casting long shadows that obscured the horizon. From my bed near the window, I could see Ernie sitting alone on the bleachers, holding a Louisville Slugger bat. He had also put on a Tiger baseball uniform, complete with the long socks and cleats worn by the major leaguers. His father had given him this outfit on his last trip home. Ernie wore the familiar Tiger headgear, which he'd bought at the local hardware store. He seemed decked out to play.

He pulled himself up from the bleachers and began walking slowly toward the outfield, dragging his wooden bat behind him. When Ernie reached the right-field fence, he stopped and seemed to look back at my house, almost as if he were sensing my presence, though that seemed impossible, given the distance. He stood transfixed for a moment with a puzzled expression on his face.

Ernie then clambered over the wire fence. When he reached the railroad right of way, he paused and then walked slowly onto the tracks.

Listening and with a sense of dread, I heard the low moan of the train as it circled the bend before it headed in a straight line in the direction of the ballfield. Ernie stared down the track at the oncoming train, eyeing it warily the way a right-handed pitcher faces a left-handed slugger, the bat tucked over his shoulder in readiness. The screech of the wailing whistle and the rush of the applied air brakes was deafening as the behemoth bore down on him. Sparks of molten metal rained red from the shrieking brakes of the iron wheels, but the train kept hurtling its way toward the fragile boy. Ernie stood his ground.

Frightened that I had only my thoughts to intercede, I stood up from my bed and as quickly as my braces would allow, flung myself over to my window and shouted to the small figure squaring off with the metal monster. I desperately wanted to hold his life in my hands and try by the force of my will to compel him to move. Because of sheer distance, I knew no sound could reach him from me. "Ernie, please!" I hollered, trembling and quaking. "Ernie, get off the goddamn tracks!"

I thought I could see Ernie look toward my room. He hesitated as the train barreled down on him like an inevitability.

"PLEASE, ERNIE!" I shook my fist. "Let him be."

Though it was impossible, in my mind's eye, I could have sworn I saw him blink. Then Ernie slowly stepped off the track, leaving the bat behind only mere seconds before he would have perished. The train rushed by him with the brakes still screeching like a banshee. The engine caught the bat and blew it into pieces, scattering debris in all directions. As the train screamed by the despairing figure at the side of the tracks, Ernie slumped to his knees, and I thought I could see his shoulders sagging in what I guessed was grief and hopelessness.

I never saw or spoke to Ernie again. The following week his family moved. No one was certain where, but it was speculated that they had moved to another state where Ernie's mother originally hailed from. Perhaps the way our friendship ended was the best that anyone could possibly hope for. I mean, what could either of us have said? I will never know how his life turned out. I suppose I could try to send him a letter, but I wouldn't know where to post it, and more importantly, I wouldn't know what to write.

I spend my retirement years—naturally—watching Tiger baseball on the flat screen. Ernie Harwell has long since gone to the great ballfield in the sky, but I can still hear his melodious voice in my head. Many times in life there are bitter endings, but after all,

I didn't save Ernie's life; he did. The young lad must have wanted life more than death. I can only wonder now if he was pleased with his choice.

After Ernie moved, I asked my parents if I could have a room downstairs. This meant moving into what had been our den, but what the heck, it worked. That summer I began forcing myself to get outside, the metal and leather braces creaking and groaning from this new activity. My father and I learned to play catch together, although maybe a little awkwardly. Every now and then, I even hit the ball. I wonder what Ernie Harwell would have said about that?

Logging team with horses

Discover Hidden Campgrounds, Natural Wonders, and Waterways of the Upper Peninsula

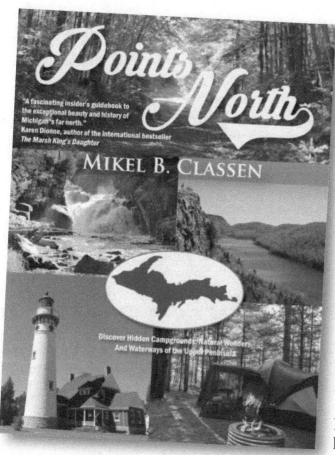

This book has been a labor of love that spans many years. The love is for Michigan's Upper Peninsula (U.P.), its places and people. I've spent many years exploring the wilderness of the U.P., and one thing has become apparent. No matter what part you find yourself in, fascinating sights are around every corner. There are parks, wilderness areas, and museums. There are ghost towns and places named after legends. There are trails to be walked and waterways to be paddled. In the U.P., life is meant to be lived to the fullest.

In this book, I've listed 40 destinations from every corner of the U.P. that have places of interest. Some reflect rich history, while others highlight natural wonders that abound across the peninsula. So many sights exist, in fact, that after a lifetime of exploration, I'm still discovering new and fascinating places that I've never seen or heard of. So, join in the adventures. The Upper Peninsula is an open book--the one that's in your hand.

"Without a doubt, Mikel B. Classen's book, *Points North*, needs to be in every library, gift shop and quality bookstore throughout the country—particularly those located in Michigan's Lower Peninsula. Not only does Classen bring alive the 'Hidden Campgrounds, Natural Wonders and Waterways of the Upper Peninsula' through his polished words, his masterful use of color photography make this book absolutely beautiful. *Points North* will long stand as a tremendous tribute to one of the most remarkable parts of our country."

—MICHAEL CARRIER author *Murder on Sugar Island*

"Mikel Classen's love for Michigan's Upper Peninsula shines from every page in *Points North*, a fascinating insider's guidebook to the exceptional beauty and history of Michigan's far north. Whether you're still in the planning stages of your trip, or you're looking back fondly on the memories you created—even if you wish merely to enjoy a virtual tour of the Upper Peninsula's natural wonders from the comfort of your armchair, you need this book."

—KAREN DIONNE, author of the international bestseller, *The Marsh King's Daughter*

paperback • hardcover • eBook
Learn more at **www.PointsNorthBooks.com**
From Modern History Press
www.ModernHistoryPress.com

Join us for epic adventures in the U.P. on land and lakes!

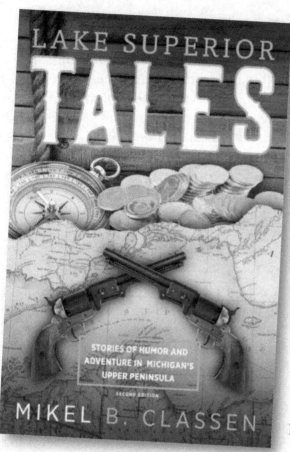

Pirates, thieves, shipwrecks, sexy women, lost gold, and adventures on the Lake Superior frontier await you! In this book, you'll sail on a ship full of gold, outwit deadly shapeshifters, battle frontier outlaws and even meet the mysterious agent that Andrew Jackson called "the meanest man" he ever knew. Packed with action, adventure, humor, and suspense, this book has something for every reader. Journey to the wilds of the Lake Superior shoreline through ten stories that span the 19th century through present day including "The Wreck of the Marie Jenny," "The Bigg Man," "Wolf Killer," and "Bullets Shine Silver in the Moonlight."

Mikel B. Classen is a longtime resident of Sault Sainte Marie in Michigan's Upper Peninsula. His intimacy of the region, the history and its culture gives this book a feel of authenticity that is rarely seen. As a writer, journalist, columnist, photographer, and editor with more than 30 years experience, his breadth of knowledge is unparalleled.

"It's clear that Mikel B. Classen knows and loves the Lake Superior area of Michigan and brings it to life in a delightful way. If you want frequent laughs, unusual characters who jump off the page, and the fruit of a highly creative mind, you've got to read this little book."

—BOB RICH, author, *Looking Through Water*

"Michigan's Upper Peninsula is a unique place in this world, and Mikel's lovely little book, *Lake Superior Tales* makes that clear. Classen has long been recognized as a leading proponent of all the wonderful attributes of the Upper Peninsula, and currently he serves as the Managing Editor of the *U.P. Reader*. So, seeing him tackle this project does not surprise me. But what I did find exciting is the electricity he captures on every page, and the energy he uses to express it.

My father was a lumberjack, moonshiner and 'gunslinger' in the U.P. a century ago, and every night he told me stories about his adventures (he was on his own from age thirteen!). Classen's *Lake Superior Tales* brings back those wonderful memories. If you like to let your imagination wander uninhibited, Mikel is the perfect tour guide. I hope this becomes a series."

—MICHAEL CARRIER author *Murder on Sugar Island*

paperback • hardcover • eBook

From Modern History Press

www.ModernHistoryPress.com

A Dog Named Bunny

by Hilton Moore

"Get your goddamn dog out of my garden. He just shit in my pea patch," old lady Larsen hollered. I shouted at Bunny, our mutt, and she came running as if her ass was on fire. She knew when to get the hell outta the neighbor lady's garden—but I always thought the darn dog didn't give a damn. If a dog can have a nemesis, old lady Larsen was surely Bunny's.

I flinch inwardly. My first lines that I write are some of the most painful to express.

I lay my pen down and roll over on my bunk. I am incarcerated in a minimum security prison; Marquette Branch, in the heart of the Upper Peninsula of Michigan. Memories engage my attention—I do not think, as much as I dwell, on the past. It's lights out time, which means the prisoners are supposed to be quiet. Low murmurs and quiet whisperings rise from the cell block. I have borrowed a thesaurus from the library and intend to use it. Some slivers of pallid moonlight filter in through the heavily barred windows, enough to write. I pause and jot down another line, aware that likely the only reader of this assigned memoir will be the overworked English teacher here in lockup. He has given our small, motley group of inmates an assignment: write a memoir, which I will make an effort to pen despite my teacher's inadequate clarity on what is required. I suppose what he wants is a collection of stories, or maybe not. Don't really know. I find his class assignments difficult, given I only finished the eighth grade before I got sent up.

I continue; it is reasonable to wonder how our family came to name their new pup, a Christmas gift in 1964, after a rabbit, but there you have it—Bunny. I suppose I could blame my lack of recall on my tender age, but I can't. As the old saying goes, "A lot of water has gone under the bridge." I suppose I should give you the family rundown so all that happened might be clearer. My older half-sister, Cassie, nineteen, was on her own and away at college. My twin brother Duane and I (Robert) were fifteen, and truly rotten teenagers. Of younger brothers, Alan was seven, William (Bill) was four, and the youngest, Hank Junior, was just a baby. All of us boys were products of my father's second marriage to Lena, our dear and devout mother who died tragically giving birth to Hank Junior. I will try not to give you too much boring personal history but feel the need to fill in the blank spaces on my notepad. Father adopted Cassie after his first wife, Delores, pregnant, committed suicide—stuck her head in a damn oven from what Cassie once told me. My mother, Lena, was my father's second wife. Despite being a minister, my father always had an eye for well-built women, which on several occasions got him in trouble with the church hierarchy.

But all of that will have to come later and isn't relevant to the story I was assigned to write. I'm twenty-four now. The point is I don't remember how Bunny got her name so the best I can do is guess. The pup, part collie and part beagle, had fluffy white ears and short stature; not sure a dog has stature, but hope you get the point. She was built close to the ground, so in our young eyes we might have seen the whelp as "bunny-like." Regrettably, because the old man is gone and given I am locked up, I rarely communicate with my brothers, so I can't inquire of the only other humans who might have a clue. Anyway, the origin of the name isn't the point of my tale; but my father's losses and his painful lie are—though strictly speaking it was to the best of my knowledge the only lie he ever told me.

My father was a man of meager means. A tall and lean parson, Pastor Hank Martin, Senior had a rural charge in the village of Nelson in the Upper Peninsula of Michigan. He was in his middle years when he married our younger and very attractive mother, Lena. Sadly, she had died in childbirth, leaving him with five young boys. I suppose with a pup, he hoped to make up for the loss the previous year. It was a "noble gesture," as they say, but the loss of a mother is such a severe psychological blow that the impact often pummels a child for an entire life. While the death of a parent is not a unique event, I mention it to frame the picture of my life and not for pity. I suppose I could just say she was dead and leave it at that, but my father's need to compensate his boys for her untimely death remains a tragic but endearing feature of his difficult life and the source of this story.

I was fifteen when we opened the Christmas box where the pup was sleeping. My younger brothers giggled with delight as the pup scampered around, growling and yipping with fervor and knocking ornaments off the tree. She managed to bust a couple of ornaments, which should have been a prophetic sign of what was to come.

As a pup, Bunny was our constant companion. The first few weeks were both a pleasure and much effort. She loved to chew and made my father angry when she attacked his lambskin slippers with a sense of abandon that could only be likened to Attila the Hun's sack of Rome. She also shredded the corner of a footstool and savaged the leg of Dad's favorite antique rocker; that and her being

stubborn about not wanting to go outside to do her business dampened my father's enthusiasm for Bunny. My brothers and I cleaned up after Bunny and tried to mollify my father, but sometimes we weren't successful.

As the pup grew in the following year, my younger brothers would wrestle and scramble about in the yard, Bunny yapping and barking and causing all kinds of ruckus, till the old lady next door would finally tire of it and pound on the parsonage door, yelling at my father to, "Shush the damn noise." I suppose the old biddy thought we were a bunch of heathens, even though our father was the lone preacher in the rural village. Mrs. Larsen's late husband had died shortly after their wedding decades before. My father had once quipped that her husband probably preferred death and damnation over living with that nasty bitch. Despite being a preacher, at times Father could be quite caustic.

My brothers and I knew Dad's personal side, which he rarely displayed publicly. His demeanor reminded me of a chameleon in that he could blend into his surroundings and purposely not be notable. My best guess is that most effective pastors are similar to the chameleon—infrequently displaying their true colors. It probably has much to do with self-preservation. Even as a young man, it was my observation that most parishioners didn't care for outspoken ministers, preferring known quantities of tepid milquetoast instead.

I should mention one more thing about old lady Larsen: she raised chickens in an outdoor coop behind her ramshackle home. Mrs. Larsen was a slender, hard-faced woman with noticeable scoliosis. She seemed content to wear hand-me-down men's trousers, with an overly long belt that dangled like an inappropriate phallic symbol; on her head, she sported a bedraggled black fedora. After many complaints by neighbors, she had fenced in her yard and garden with chicken wire to keep out the varmints and to eliminate the inevitable chicken shit deposited on the nearby ballfield where all us boys hung out. On overly warm days the smell of fresh chicken shit hung in the air. Remembering back on it, the fetid stench seemed almost sulfurous, eliciting visions of a surrealistic Xanthus storm cloud; later I would call this another portent.

Bunny proved to be an easy train, picking up the usual tricks: she sat, would lie down, beg, come when called; you know, all those various tricks that humans think are necessary, and to my best guess, dogs believe are stupid.

I don't mean to imply that Bunny was a model of a perfect pet; she had her faults. She would dig holes randomly all over our dandelion-infested yard, till the lawn looked like it had been used by the Army for mortar practice. This canine habit made it necessary to fill the damn holes every time my father forced me to mow the friggin' yard. Of course as soon as I finished mowing, Bunny, as if offended by my labor, would start digging again. This was a war that lasted her entire life.

Another one of her apparent faults was her antipathy for Ernie, the fat paperboy. He would come tearing down the sidewalk on his red Schwinn bike and just heave the newspaper into the yard, a logical maneuver to avoid Bunny's consistent charge. She would chase him the length of the lot, snapping and growling, and lunging at his pant leg. I thought this was quite fun to watch, and unbeknownst to my father, would deliberately let Bunny out of our house when I saw Ernie coming our way. I would laugh uproariously at this daily event, which I surreptitiously spied on through the parsonage window. Ernie would pedal like some kind of wailing banshee, yelling and kicking at Bunny's onslaught, and never figured out that I was the instigator.

I've heard it said that "All good things must come to an end," and this amusing trounce finally came to an abrupt halt when Bunny finally got a hold of one of Ernie's pant legs and pulled him down in a pile of boy, bike, and snarling dog, going ass-end-over-teakettle on the unyielding concrete sidewalk. Bunny refused to give up her pant leg, and Ernie, knees and elbows skinned and bleeding, finally extracted himself by unbuckling his pants and sliding out of them. At first Bunny looked quizzical, as if she might let up on the poor young buck, but in a show of defiance, she grabbed hold of his patterned boxers and with one savage rip, the boxers shredded, leaving Ernie running down the street butt naked, his penis flopping in the wind like an errant ship's lanyard.

Hearing all the commotion, my father came running, fearing a tragedy of some sort. He saw the final act and me laughing hysterically. Needless to say, he was not amused, and I was grounded for a week. While I disliked the punishment, I still think I got the better end of the deal. My father caught another round of verbal abuse that evening, but this time it was from Ernie's dad, a Marine home on leave, who cussed my father out in what I would call very foul language. Dad unhappily ponied up, paying for a new pair of boxers. After that incident, Dad made a rule that Bunny had to be inside between four and four-thirty, when Ernie made his appointed rounds. I knew better than to not follow a direct order. Although on Bunny's part, she never barked out the window or strained to mangle Ernie again. Perhaps having caught him once, the game was over with the dog convinced that she had nothing left to prove.

While my father had his share of almost comedic disasters with Bunny, he had many delightful days hunting grouse in the maple leaf fall, when trees in the local hardwood forests dripped color like so much honey. On occasion, he let me ride along, though he thought I was still too young to hunt. We would stop at likely young popple stands and let Bunny out to do her work. Though she didn't look like any bird dog I'd ever seen, she probably would have taken that observation as an insult. She helped my father get in close to a grouse and waited till the old man told her to flush—and flush she did. She'd rush in with so much enthusiasm that one time she ran over the friggin' bird, sending it head over tail till; it got its frightened equilibrium back in order. It burst skyward. Dad shot it, a clean hit. He smiled and gave Bunny a well-deserved treat.

"You're one damn good dog," he said, beaming. "What do you think, Robert?"

I nodded, impressed by my father's acumen in his choice of a dog.

I remember Dad and I were once walking a two-track, Dad carrying his old double-barrel shotgun. The overgrown trail was way back off the Baraga Plains. A late model pickup, with not a scratch on it, pulled up, and the owner leaned out the window. A fine looking English Pointer stuck its nose out, and if I hadn't known better, fixed his gaze haughtily on Bunny.

The well-dressed hunter frowned as if bemused.

"What kind of bird dog do you call it?" he said sarcastically, with an emphasis on the word "it."

Father just gazed back, straight-faced. "She is an AKC Fiffer Flusher."

"A what?"

"A Fiffer Flusher."

At this point, I wondered if this city dweller might guess that he was being put on. "Well, does your Fiffer Flusher hunt?" He gloated, holding up two grouse.

My father took off his hunting vest and dipped into the deep pocket. "Let's see." He pulled out two grouse and held them aloft. He looked back in the vest. "Oh, my gosh, I guess there is one more here. That makes three. So by my count my two-dollar dog outhunted your precious pedigreed pooch." Dad smiled politely. Without uttering another word, the cowed hunter rolled up his window and bounced along the rutted trail and out of sight.

I have often thought that life spins in concentric circles as if winding tighter, contracting—or at other times in my life, almost ironically, the rings seemed to expand outwards. Maybe the whole process depends on the whims of some unknown force. Some people call this process the will of God; some don't. As I look back, the circle that Bunny gave our family was tightening, like a watch spring over wound by the hands of fate, or by the hands of God; you can draw your own conclusions.

It was in the spring when Bunny took a liking to old lady Larsen's chickens. I should mention that Mrs. Larsen didn't like me at all. She once caught me antagonizing her hens by chucking rocks at them—which I admit I did—causing the chickens to run around squawking and raising a ruckus. As most anyone who has ever raised chickens knows, a riled chicken won't lay eggs, and Mrs. Larsen blamed the lack of eggs that week on me—which was probably accurate. On the other hand, she seemed to adore my younger brother, Alan, who she thought could do no wrong. The old hag was always giving him treats from her kitchen. Later her attachment to Alan was to cause an unintentional series of disastrous events that deeply haunts me still.

One day in early June, Bunny had evidently dug a hole under the fence, and as the old lady watched in horror out her kitchen window, tossed chickens around in the air like erratic bumper cars at a small-town carnival. Miss Larsen chased Bunny out of her yard with a broom, but not before Bunny had killed several of the old lady's prize hens. Speaking of chickens, as the old cliché goes, she was mad as a wet hen. She stomped angrily over to the parsonage and chewed out my old man, demanding we "shoot the damn dog."

By this time Bunny sat nonchalantly on the front porch, chewing on chicken feathers, her mouth covered with fresh, red chicken blood. My father, unhappily aroused from his nap, used his most calm pastoral voice to quell the old lady's anger.

"I'm very sorry, Mrs. Larsen. I will be happy to pay a fair price for the chickens. What do you think is fair?"

"I don't want your money; I want you to shoot that damn dog!" Her voice was like steel.

Dad wasn't above playing the sympathy card. "You know this dog means so much to the boys, especially since the death of their mother."

My father's conciliatory tone and his judicious use of any pity she might have felt deflated her anger like a party balloon late in the day.

I could see her visibly suck in a breath. "Well, the Leghorns are good layers, and as you know, I sell eggs to get by. So I will probably lose at least six dozen eggs till the next bantams get laying size. I think six dollars is fair for the eggs." She paused. "But there is the chicken meat to consider…"

My father winced.

"To be fair, the layers only are good for stewing, but since the damn dog killed three, I think they're worth a buck a piece, so that makes a total of nine dollars," she calculated.

Dad opened his well-worn wallet and handed her the nine dollars, which we could ill afford to lose. It wasn't lost on my father that although she was going to charge him for the dead chickens, the layers were probably going to end the day in her stewpot and she hadn't offered to give us any of the future stew.

"If this ever happens again, I'm calling the sheriff," she said, barely mollified. "I suggest you keep your chicken killer chained up."

Which in all honesty we tried, but the moment we chained up Bunny, she would howl and yip and make such a commotion that several other neighbors complained about the noise. In the end we brought her inside, which was an imperfect solution for either man or beast.

Of course, the inevitable happened. My brother Alan left the back door open, and Bunny scrambled out and made a beeline under the fence and to the chicken coop. This time Bunny killed four more chickens, and true to her threat, old lady Larsen called the sheriff.

Later that same day, there came the promised but dreadful knock on the door. Dad was expecting the sheriff, whom he knew from their passing acquaintance in the local Rotary Club.

"Hello, Pastor Hank," the hulking deputy sheriff said pleasantly. "Sorry to bother you, but your neighbor lady tells me that your dog has killed some of her chickens."

"Yes, I'm sorry to say, that's true."

"Hmm," the sheriff said. "Seems we got a problem. I . . ."

"Sheriff, can you wait a moment?" Dad interrupted.

He nodded.

"Boys, please go up to your rooms." We hesitated, wanting to know Bunny's fate. "Now," he said sternly.

My father later told us that he thought the best place for Bunny was with a local farmer, and he would find him a home. The younger boys cried at this prospect, but we knew there was no sense in arguing with his decision.

•••

Hey, Teach: Just a note. I admit that this assignment stumps me. I'm not sure I quite know exactly what you want, but I will carry on. The prison library is inadequate in many respects, but sometimes you can find a recent classic. I have been reading Michener's *Chesapeake* and was enthralled by his vivid sense of person and the scope of history. I know you have told the class that the use of cliches shows a lack of originality, but I think otherwise. To my way of thinking a well-executed cliché is the "poetry of the poorly educated," not much different than poems by Lord Byron or Wallace Stevens are to the well-educated. Indeed, most of us under-educated prisoners are blessed by the inherent poetry of clichés. I am reminded of another cliché that my memoir provoked, and that is, "Time slips by like sand in an hourglass." Perhaps, but I think that notion of time is more like the estuary that Michener described, where during the span between the ebb and flood tides, the current seems to be moving toward the sea, while at the same time seems fixed and unmoving. This seems noteworthy to me—that a river may be neither moving nor unmoving, but elements of both at the same time. I think my father was much like the estuary. While his life moved on, it was not without painful determination, and like the estuary, the mix of salt marsh and freshwater turned brackish and torpid, dark with suspended foul matter. I doubt he could have changed the outcome, which seems inevitable now. I would have wished differently for him, but his losses were too significant.

As he aged and his health declined, he visited me less and less often. He blamed his health as the reason, but I knew the pain of seeing me incarcerated was often more than he could bear. On a cold December visit, he told me he had something he needed to get off his chest. He breathed slowly, with great exertion. An unsmiling prison guard stood in the background, a constant reminder that privacy was not an option.

"Robert," he whispered hoarsely; he never called me Robbie, "I have a confession to make, one that I should have made long ago."

"What is it, Dad?"

"I lied to you boys once—about Bunny," he murmured.

"Everyone has told a lie at some point or the other, Father," I said, acutely aware of my own failures.

"That may be so, but the sin occurs when you don't confess the act," he said, pausing to wheeze. "And I believe that expiation only comes from heartfelt contrition."

"I'm not sure I understand, Dad."

"Yes, perhaps I am being too theological." He smiled and then coughed. "All this has to do with your dog." He sighed. "Yes, I know, that was a decade or more ago, but still I am bothered by the way things turned out."

"How is that, Dad? You told us you gave Bunny to a farmer—a good home, I remember you saying."

"Well, son, let me get around to the talk that the deputy sheriff had with me." He paused as if to give himself time to frame these thoughts. "The deputy said that I had to destroy the dog or give it away. But he told me bluntly that no one around Nelson would want a chicken killer. Once they get a taste of chicken blood, they never stop. 'It's pure instinct,' he'd said.

I promised I would take care of the situation." Father coughed again, holding his handkerchief to his mouth as if trying to render his admissions, like some sort of severe virus, harmless to others. "The following day when you were at school, I took Bunny out in the woods. Her eyes seem to plead, almost pathetically, as if asking for divine forgiveness and deliverance from her fate. It hurt every part of me—to end her life. I closed my eyes and I slowly pulled the trigger of the double-barrel. I shot her. Dammit, I shot her. I'm so sorry." Tears ran down his face, and I suddenly realized how much anguish he felt about Bunny's death. Now, looking back, I would describe his admission as almost a mortal wound to his soul.

"I forgive you," I said quietly, "both for what you felt was a necessary act and for the lie you told us." He *gazed* at me and reached for my hand, but we could not touch each other through the glass and steel bars that separated us.

"I guess this is where the story of Ol' Yeller ends," I told him ironically. "Don't all dog stories have a bittersweet ending?" I looked sadly at his face, the tears welled up in his eyes. "Dad, I guessed years ago that you probably had shot Bunny," I lied, partly to lessen his apparent pain. "This is not news to me, Dad. But if somehow you feel the need for my forgiveness, you have it."

"You know, son, it didn't all have to work out this way."

"I know, it was my fault," I said tentatively. "All of it. After Bunny disappeared I was so damn mad at that old bitch. Crazy mad, maybe. I have said it many times before, but the rat poison I mixed into old lady Larsen's chicken feed was meant for the damn chickens, not for her. I was too young and stupid to realize that the rat poison would make eating the chicken fatal. It never occurred to me that she would cook one of her dead laying hens. As for Alan's death—that was a tragedy that will always haunt me. How was I to know she would offer him a piece of her fried chicken?" I paused. "Not exactly the Colonel's chicken," I said, half-smiling.

Dad looked away as if in disgust at my jest. I could tell my father was not amused, but a part of me desperately needed to express some humor to lessen the deeply felt pain—both for him and for me—even if it was just unvarnished gallows humor.

Dad straightened in the hardback chair. "Robert, I will always be sorry that although you were a juvenile, you were tried as an adult. My heart will forever grieve for you. A life sentence seems so unjust." He pressed the palm of his hand against the glass, and I did the same, a touch without actually touching. I ached inside.

For a moment I was taken aback by the serenity I saw in his countenance. "Dad, I have just one request of you. You know I feel incapable of praying, but tonight when you say your prayers, besides the obvious souls, please offer up a prayer for Bunny."

He stared through the prison glass that separated us and silently nodded.

...

As I write my final paragraphs of this brief but painful memoir, my today is a tentative beginning of another series of many never-afters. In prison my days and nights slide by, as if I am incoherently speaking while neither awake nor asleep but in some state of animate existence somewhere in between.

I put pen to paper, tired, but feel impelled to finish.

That was the last year I saw my father, although on occasion, I get a letter from Cassie. My twin brother, Duane, makes an annual pilgrimage to visit me, partly out of pity I suppose, but he has a life of his own, so I truly understand. As for my other brothers, well, I guess in a sense I am dead to them.

In my father's last few visits he seemed to change, a hollowing out that was almost palpable. It was a dark, dramatic transformation that subsumed the benign man of God I knew, and instead he seemed to retreat inside himself, as if a living tomb. He died shortly after that. The warden adamantly refused my request to attend the funeral. I desperately wanted to be there, partly for my own sake and partly to make what I believed would be proper amends.

So much pain and so many deaths that my father had to endure: Cassie's mother, Delores, and his unborn child; my mother, and later, my dear brother Alan. I suppose I should also include old lady Larsen, though in some respects I don't feel sorry for her, although I am sure my father in his piousness would. In the end, my father had to face his own faltering decline. Is that not the ultimate loss, even for a man of God? Admitting to me that Bunny's death had occurred at his own hands seemed to be the final straw. It is hard to imagine that the life and death of what many would consider a mere animal could have had such profound consequences for so many human beings—but that is the case. I try to remind myself that a dog is, after all, just a dog. I will never know whether my father's significant and devastating losses or his regrettable act of shooting a living, defenseless creature of God drove him to

such utter despair. Perhaps both—I will never know. But as he aged, the shadow of death seemed to descend on him like the haunting cliché of "a hungry wounded beast." Later I suspected the severity of his losses and the very act of his deceit concerning Bunny—the covering up of his lie—unhinged his troubled mind.

He told me before he died that his sins were an affront to God, and therefore unforgivable. I tried to argue otherwise, that what he had done was insignificant and that God forgives our sins, but he was not convinced. Perhaps, in the final analysis, the reason for his sin, or anyone else's sin, doesn't matter. Sins remain what they are, human fallibilities deeply entrenched in the subconscious mind; a sickness of sorts that many believe are only purged by prayer. I will never know whether he found a sense of expiation in his final days. Regrettably, as his health failed he was unable to visit and he rarely wrote. I wonder if the state of atonement is—to use another cliché—"a fool's errand" and an unattainable illusion.

Believe me, Teach, the cell block is dark, but as always, never peaceful. I am physically and emotionally drained from this goddamn exercise. I intend to lay the pen down now and get some shut-eye. I wonder if the proverbial "silent slumber"—the last cliché that I feel impelled to write—is from a children's lullaby, don't know. I believe it speaks eloquently only to the innocent and the virtuous—and I am neither.

Hilton Everett Moore lives with his wife in Marquette, Michigan, but spends much of his time writing at his camp in the wilderness of the Upper Peninsula. After a midlife crisis, he went back to college and received a Master's Degree in Social Work. Upon graduation, he was employed in the prison system as a Clinical Social Worker. Presently, he enjoys writing and fishing in secluded brook trout streams. Unlike some effete fly-fishermen, he enjoys fishing with hook, line, and sinker and of course, a worm.

U.P. Reader is Accepting Submissions for Volume 6

The *U.P. Reader* is an annual publication that represents the cross-section of writers that are the membership of the Upper Peninsula Publishers and Authors Association. This annual anthology will be used as a vehicle to showcase and promote the writers of the Upper Peninsula. Each issue is released in paperback, hardcover, and eBook editions in early Spring following the deadline. Copies of the *U.P. Reader* will be made available to booksellers, UPPAA members, libraries, and news services. The *U.P. Reader* has received more media coverage each year since the inclusion of the Dandelion Cottage Award. We hope the *U.P. Reader* will be a great place for you to showcase original short works, too.

Submission Guidelines

- Must be a **current member of the UPPAA** to submit.

- Submissions **must be original** with no prior appearance in web or print. Submissions will be accepted for **up to 5,000 words**. Writers who submit work which has previously appeared in blog posts, web pages, eBooks, or in print will be disqualified.

- Submissions **can be any type of genre**, Fiction, Nonfiction (memoirs, history, essays, feature articles, interviews, opinion) and Poetry. These also can include photography or artwork, but author must show permission for use.

- All submissions will be **reviewed through a jury** and the submissions will be chosen through this process.

- We prefer **Microsoft Word Document** (.DOC) files only or plain text files (.TXT). Do not submit PDF files. If you have some other type of text file, please inquire.

- **Authors may include photos,** with the understanding that they will be converted to black-and-white. We reserve the right to limit the number of photos per story. Photos should be at least 300 DPI and no smaller than 2 inches on a side (i.e., 600px minimum). If the Author is not the photographer, we may ask for a simple one-page "Photo Release" form to be sent in.

The *U. P. Reader* will require first time rights in print, digital, and audio. After one year, the author may re-publish it themselves. The UPPAA retains the right to use submitted works in perpetuity. For example, we look forward to the "Best of U.P. Reader" edition to be issued for the 10th anniversary.

Publication Schedule for U.P. Reader Volume 6

- Submission deadline: Nov. 15th, 2021

- Dec 21, 2021 Jury / peer-review process begins

- Jan 15th, 2022 announcement of selected submissions

- April 1, 2022, official publication date

Send submissions to submissions@upreader.org. Be sure to put "U.P. Reader Submission" in the subject line.

Old Book

by Gretchen Preston

Photo by Karin Neumann. Used with permission

Gretchen Preston is originally from Portland, Oregon. She has a master's degree from Arizona State University in Social Work. She wrote her first book, *The Idiot Cookbook: The Complete Cookbook for the Complete Idiot* when she was 17. After moving to the U.P. 20 years ago, she wrote the *Valley Cat* series of children's chapter books. A closet poet, she has unpublished works including, "Valley Songs" and a series of love poems.

If you were a book,
I would read you from cover to cover.
Over and over,
So many times that your binding would tatter.
Then, I would repair you with chicken soup and duct tape.
And read you again
Turning your pages more gently this time.

If I were a book,
You could keep me on your bedside table
To watch over you while you sleep.
I would wait patiently for you to open and caress me,
From cover to cover, over and over.
Hidden amongst my pages you will discover humor, romance and fantasy.

When you are my book,
I promise to never bend your pages.
For your story is a part of me.
I return to you because I need an old friend
Knowing that your story holds no surprises.

When we are a book,
Our binding will be sturdy and strong.
Embracing chapters of history, adventure and grace,
We will never grow tired of our tale.
We can read each other from cover to cover,
Over and over,
Turning the pages more gently this time.

Calamity at Devil's Washtub

by Donna Searight Simons and Frank Searight

The cold, frothy waters of Lake Superior washed the sandy shore on a late, summer afternoon. A chilled wind whipped through Elizabeth's hair as she released her wavy locks from a fastidious bun. Her long skirt, billowing with the fierce wind, matched her mood. She loved the lake and its unbelievable beauty, no matter the time of year, and its ability to calm her when life seemed to be escaping from her grip.

How dare her father tell her she wasn't allowed to attend Suomi College? For pity's sake, it was 1921—she had even voted for the first time in the recent presidential election—and he acted as though it were 1821. The college had expanded its curriculum to include liberal arts, and Elizabeth was eager to try English literature courses, and perhaps go on to become a teacher, although such an ambitious goal seemed out of the question.

She carefully retraced her steps and moved toward the big lake. As sapphire blue waves crashed onto shore, she struggled to wrap her hair back into a bun. She began her short trek through the Keweenaw wilderness to the edge of the road and her home. She squeezed herself past pine trees, nearly tripping over branches and tangled roots on the ground, but was able to safely make her way to the cottage.

When she entered the tidy dwelling, Elizabeth could smell the pasties she was baking in the oven. They were nearly ready. Knowing her father expected the lodging to be cleaned to perfection, she took a rag and dusted some furniture, coming upon a picture of her parents taken years ago. Her eyes watered. Why did her mother have to run away? Did she not care her only daughter was trapped in a loveless home?

She dropped the cloth in the washtub, her stomach churning as she heard the sounds of a rattling, decrepit automobile coming to a stop next to the cottage. She had not expected her father, Henry, to come home so soon, but stood smoothing her apron as he walked into the home accompanied by a stranger.

"Girl, where have you been?" Henry demanded, looking haggard with streaks of dirt on his smudged face and tattered mining jacket.

Elizabeth stammered, "I've been making your supper."

"Don't lie to me!" he ordered, slamming his mining dinner pail on a nearby table. "The neighbors tell me how you leave every day on one of your walks."

"Perhaps our neighbors should mind their own business. I'm not a prisoner, Pa."

"Long as you live under my roof, you do as I say."

Elizabeth almost forgot the stranger until he started to squirm. He did not look like a miner and she had never seen the young man before. His face was clean and he looked comfortable, attired with crisp pants and a white shirt.

"My name is Benjamin," the stranger said, shaking her hand. "Call me Ben. My parents run a store in Eagle Harbor."

"I'm Elizabeth...Beth...and I've been to Eagle Harbor many times," she said, releasing his grip. "I don't remember meeting you before."

"I'll be graduating from the Michigan College of Mines," he said, smiling, wanting to be her friend. "In Houghton," he added.

"Are you staying for supper, Ben?" she asked, removing the apron covering her white blouse and checkered blue skirt.

He looked cautiously at her father.

"Of course," said Henry. "Why else do you think I brought him here at this hour?"

Elizabeth's eyes smarted from her father's insensitive belittlement, attempting to suppress her disdain for him, but Benjamin's brown eyes softened with empathy.

"May I help you prepare the supper?"

His comment startled her, being used to her father arranging undesirable beaus for her, but none as polite and kind as Benjamin. She was about to answer in the affirmative when Henry interrupted.

"Cooking and cleaning is women's work," he grunted. "And she's plenty good at both—when she's not sneaking off doing God knows what."

"All I did was walk to the shoreline and back," Elizabeth exclaimed, balling her fists. "I didn't do anything wrong."

Henry pointed at the dining room table. "Take a seat," he said to Benjamin. "She'll have supper ready in no time at all." He started to leave the room. "I'm gonna wash up."

The two young adults stared at each other until Elizabeth broke the silence. "Yes, please have a seat," she invited him, turning to the oven to retrieve the pasties she had made. While putting them on a cooling rack she noticed the newcomer was still standing.

"Like I said," Benjamin repeated with a smile, "I want to help."

Elizabeth exhaled a long, soothing breath and relaxed. "Setting the table will assist me."

The young undergraduate examined a few cabinets, figuring out where the plates, cups and silverware were. "I enjoy watching Lake Superior too," he acknowledged as he began to set the table. He explained, "Mind you, the scenery is great at the college too, since it's directly on Portage Lake."

Henry walked into the room, wiping his hands with a dry towel, ready for his supper. "I said you don't need to help," he barked.

"It's no trouble," said Benjamin.

"You a sissy or something, Benji?"

Benjamin stood his ground but kept himself from reacting to the crude wordage of his benefactor, restraining an intemperate response. "Not at all. I frequently assist with chores at home. My parents both run the store, so it's not unusual for my father to help my mother around the house."

Henry snorted and took a seat as Elizabeth brought the meal to the table. "Only four pasties?" he critically observed.

Elizabeth drew strength from Benjamin. If he could stand up to her father, she could, too. "I wasn't aware you were bringing a guest home for dinner, Pa. I would have made more."

"I'm eating two of them, as usual," Henry informed her, and added, "Give the other ones to Benji here and make yourself some soup."

"I won't hear of it," said Benjamin. He scooped one of the copper miner's favorite meals onto Elizabeth's plate, then took one for himself. "One is plenty for me."

Henry shrugged his shoulders, saying, "Suit yourself", and started to devour his two, loudly sipping whiskey from a shot glass with every mouthful to wash it down.

Benjamin took a bite of his meal and tried to begin a polite conversation with the young lady, hoping to smooth things over later with the abrasive, middle-aged man. "How do you make such yummy pasties, Beth?"

"The big secret," she responded, "is preparing the crust just right so it has a pleasing taste and consistency—texture is very important—then shaping it like a football and, miraculously, you have one of the tastiest meals ever prepared on planet Earth."

"I believe you. I've sampled a few. How about the ingredients you mention? Are they a secret, also?"

"Of course not, although different cooks have their own favorite combinations. My pasties always have diced potatoes and cubed meat in them, along with rutabaga,

some onion, and salt and pepper. Sometimes I vary it a bit, but when you have the combination just the way you like it, you tend to stick with it."

"I see."

"She usually doesn't cook 'em quite the way I like 'em, though," declared Henry, his bitterness spilling over the dining room table like a tidal wave. "I risk my life some days to bring up copper for rich folk." He stopped speaking long enough for Benjamin to renew eating his food, and noticed him chewing it uncertainly.

"Good, ain't it?"

"Interesting," Benjamin responded.

"Gamey," suggested Elizabeth.

"Tasty," persisted Henry, glancing from his plate and glaring at his daughter.

"Different," said Benjamin. "The meat is quite tender, but unlike other beef I've had."

Elizabeth chewed daintily. "It's bear meat."

"Is that right?" Benjamin asked.

Henry evaded his question and asked again how he liked it.

"It's just fine."

"Shot it myself and ground the meat three times so it's not as tough as you'd expect."

"Making pasties is a specialty of mine. I'm a waitress," she explained, "at a restaurant up the road from here, but I don't cook for them. I would, but they haven't asked, having their own staff for that."

"Liz here makes 'em herself. How do you like it?" he asked again.

"It's just fine."

"Daddy trapped it himself," she went on. "He also brings home deer and rabbit and sometimes a squirrel or two."

"Is that quite legal, Hank?" Benjamin asked.

"Yes, when it's in season," declared Henry.

"Which it isn't," interjected Elizabeth.

"Yes, it is," disagreed Henry, lowering his voice and covered his mouth with his hand, "if you've got traps to snare 'em with, and a gun."

"So, what is it?" Benjamin persisted, "Legal?"

"Maybe so, maybe no. All I'm sure of is the gamekeepers should learn to mind their own business. Who do they think they are?"

"People who can fine you if you break their laws," his daughter stated.

"And put you in jail if your offense is great enough," added the young man.

"Well, they better keep out of my way, is what I say."

"Pa's a poacher," Elizabeth whispered, under her breath but loud enough for the others to overhear.

"If you don't like what I bring home, then eat something else," suggested Henry with a touch of acrimony, overhearing her comment.

Benjamin smiled, making no further observation, but Henry had more to say: "Catching my own food ain't all I do. I cut timber for the logging companies when the outfit's a tad short a man, and snag whitefish or lake trout beyond the bay from time to time. Work at the mine, when I can, but getting any kind of a job there is difficult—they'll all be closed down eventually."

"Pa's work is only temporary," she explained, "when he can find work to do, but he does bring home a variety of food. There's always plenty to eat around here."

"And it's a good thing, too," Henry added, spittle and sputum of half-chewed food spilling from his mouth. "Girl, here, eats like a hog."

"I do not," disagreed the indignant young lady, dropping her fork to the plate. "Pa, why do you say such things?"

"True, ain't it?"

"No, it isn't, and you know it's not."

"Well," conceded the gruff parent, "maybe just a baby piggie."

"Pa, why don't you finish your meal and go sit outside on the porch. Drink your whiskey and smoke one of those vile cigarettes you like so much."

"Not a bad idea, Girl," Henry agreed, stuffing the rest of his meal into his mouth and scraping his plate for the last bit of crust before standing up. "I'll do it. Benji, finish your pasty and come join me outside."

Henry rose from his table, deliberately pushing his chair to the floor, then found his stash of whiskey. He went outside, slamming the door behind him.

"He's impossible," Elizabeth exclaimed, watching her father exit the small home.

"The bear meat wasn't bad," was her guest's opinion. "I rather enjoyed eating it."

"Maybe so," she agreed. "Pa certainly seems to like it, even though it's not bear season and he made an illegal kill to get it. Me, I prefer eating beef anytime, but he doesn't find a cow to steal and bring home very often."

Their meal finished, she worked about, clearing the table and stacking the dishes, while Benjamin chatted casually with his new acquaintance.

"So, you work at the restaurant, do you? I'll have to stop in when I'm in the area."

"I do, and despite what Pa might tell you, I'm a good worker. The customers—mostly tourists—seem to like me and I make fairly decent money in tips. Pa knows this, also, and he'd take it from me if he could, but I keep it hidden. I don't have enough saved yet to attend college but I have enough to make a beginning."

"There are all sorts of scholarships and such to help you along."

Elizabeth nodded and tried to direct her attention fully upon Benjamin. She enjoyed being with him and could not help but like anyone who enjoyed pasties as much as she did.

"Tell me about college," she urged.

"I enjoy it," Benjamin offered, delicately slicing a chunk from his pasty. "Half a year to go at the Michigan College of Mines. I study mining there but haven't decided yet if being a store manager would suit me better."

"I'd like to at least visit Suomi College soon."

Returning to the dining area for his matches and wiping his hands on a thread-bare towel, Henry was in time to hear her comment.

"Already told you *NO*," he reminded her. "You get married before you turn into an old maid."

Attempting to change the topic, Benjamin politely asked, "Won't the townsfolk likely believe you are shirking your parental duties?"

Henry's fist banged the table. "What do you mean?"

"Eagle Harbor is only the next town over," Benjamin explained. "Where I come from, some of the girls attend high school and then go on to higher education."

"She should stay in the kitchen making pasties. Keeps her out of mischief."

"Young women who attend college are quite respected," countered Benjamin.

"I would love to study English literature," said Elizabeth, gaining confidence with every passing moment.

"Hah," Henry offered. "When not in the kitchen, they should be at the logging camps feeding the men."

"Maybe they'd eat better food if they did," she said, defensively.

"Don't like the food I feed you here, do you? You'll take what I bring home to provide for us, and learn to like it."

"Sure, Pa. Seeing as I have no choice."

Henry was beginning to slur his words badly and helped himself to another sip of whiskey.

"So, I'm just a low-down miner, am I?" he queried, putting both hands on the table. "It's miners keeping the Keweenaw in business!"

"Ben wasn't suggesting otherwise," said Elizabeth, dabbing her mouth with a napkin. Unusually hungry, she was grateful he had given up his extra pasty to her.

"Men folk will do the talking!" growled Henry. "Keep yer mouth shut and get our dessert ready."

Benjamin could take no more of his host's harsh and insensitive words. He tossed his napkin on the table.

"I thank you both for a fine supper. Good evening."

Henry turned red. "Where do ya think you're going? I invited you here to meet my daughter."

Benjamin drew in a breath, trying to control his evolving anger. "You've done nothing but yell at Beth from the moment we walked in. She's a fine cook and homemaker, and I for one would also like to see her have the chance to attend Suomi College."

Henry retrieved another whiskey bottle, then went into his bedroom and slammed the door.

Elizabeth had kept her head down, mortified at what was taking place. She lifted her tear-streaked face and said, "I'm sorry about his behavior. Perhaps you should go now."

"I want to be your friend, Beth."

"But why? You see what it's like here, and you just met me."

"Everyone knows about your father," Benjamin said gently. "But my own parents told me who you were and contended you were nothing like him."

"It's awfully nice of you to say such things, Ben. If you're not in a hurry to leave, there's something I'd like to show you."

"Oh, what is it?"

"Let's make it a surprise, shall we?"

Once the dishes were placed in the sink to soak, they left the house and followed the wilderness trail leading to Highway 26. During their pleasant walk along the primeval forested terrain of the Keweenaw, Elizabeth explained they would follow it for a while before reaching what she wanted to show him.

Presently, pushing through shrubbery on both sides of an unmarked dirt path of dense brush, vines, and tangled roots, they came to the vastness of Lake Superior sunning itself in dying rays of light.

"Almost there," she announced, leading him onto another trail off to the right. After another couple of minutes, stepping cautiously over the rocky ground, Benjamin followed until they came to an outlook from which could be surveyed the mightiness of the Lake Superior's shoreline down below.

Down from them was a majestic geological formation of coastal conglomerate, a dark grotto familiar to most people in the area, a depression in the earth reaching down to the level of mighty Superior where it ended in a large pool of water. The tarn was both enticing and frightening, fed by the cold waters of Gitche Gumee. Shiny specs caught the fading rays of sunlight splashing and glinting in dappled light and dark in intricate patterns.

Elizabeth looked over and smiled warmly at her new acquaintance, hoping he would enjoy her special place, in her estimation the most spectacular scenic spot on the Keweenaw Peninsula—or in the entire world, for that matter. If he did, it would be one more thing they would have in common.

"Say," said Benjamin, "I haven't been here before, but I might have heard about it from several friends who mentioned it to me in the past. This isn't the Devil's Washtub, is it?"

"That's what it's called, yes," she returned, moving along the sharp, rocky projections until she reached the opening to the creation below. "It's my favorite place to come and enjoy the scenic splendors of nature at its finest.

"Now, be careful," Elizabeth cautioned as they reached the large shaft and gazed downward to see sharp-edged rocks being sprayed by the cold, surging waters of Lake Superior. "Looks as though it might have taken years of storms and crashing waves to carve the basin out, doesn't it? I come here a lot."

They stood for a time watching water sloshing within the enclosure. "Some days, the water is calm enough to go swimming, and I've even climbed down to the bottom and jumped in once in a while. At other times, though, such as this, it's best to keep a safe distance."

Benjamin's eyebrow peaked. "This could be a very dangerous place. I hope you weren't hurt."

"I wasn't, although I did struggle for a minute, and I sure wouldn't want to fall in there all the way from the top. I wanted to forget everything. Forget my horrible father and my meaningless life. I managed to climb out safely."

Suddenly, just as they were ready to leave, from behind came the sound of shifting, crunching rocks. Elizabeth's heart sank, suspecting it must be her father who she knew was familiar with the place. Not only had Henry found them, but he finally knew where she frequently came to hide from him.

"There ya are," said her father, his footing unsure and tipsy at best.

"Pa, you're drunk," accused Elizabeth. "You shouldn't come any closer."

"Don't tell me what to do," Henry said, his words slurred. His wobbly feet gave way several times as he stumbled toward them, but he managed to regain his balance.

"You're going to get hurt," Elizabeth told him, heading his way to stop him.

"I know you hide your money from me, probably up here," Henry said, slipping his way toward the basin, and chugged the last dregs of whiskey from his flask. "But you ain't going to college now or ever. You give it to me. Hear?"

He waved his flask about, teetering about the soft uneven escarpment.

"Pa, you be careful. It's a long way down."

"I'm safe enough," he insisted. "Both of you stay back; I've been on these rocks for many years—all my life—and nothing is gonna frighten me away."

"I'm going to Suomi College, Father, whether you like it or not."

"Hah! This where you conceal your valuables, Liz? Up here someplace or down there among the rocks? There must be dozens of perfect places for you to hide your stuff. I'm going down to the cauldron for a good look."

"No, Pa! No!" she insisted.

"You give it to me, hear? Don't think you can fool me for long, Girl. I'll find it cause it's mine. It's what you owe me for watching over you these last years, for feeding you, and buying you pretty outfits."

"There's nothing hidden up here or down there."

Henry made a sudden movement toward the edge.

"Pa, you get back here." She moved forward, careful not to startle him, partially restrained by Benjamin's hand.

Suddenly, Henry shaded his eyes from the speckled sunlight and raised his head, staring upwards, off into the distance.

"My GOD! What's that?" he asked, his eyes opening wider as he appeared to stare in an unbroken trance. "It can't be, *but it is*." He did not explain what he was seeing, but a look of anguish stretched the lines of his face as he took another step forward.

Elisabeth was uncertain what he saw, or thought he had seen. At first, she glimpsed nothing unusual other than the cloudy sky above Lake Superior.

"It's the Devil's Washtub, Father. You've been here often...and don't get so close."

"Not over there! Girl! Up there!"

Elizabeth looked again, upwards.

"What is it, sir?" asked Benjamin, coming up behind them.

She could give no answer.

"No, no, no!" slurred Henry, losing his balance and stumbling over the ridge into the basin below, disappearing into the swirling turmoil of the tub.

Elizabeth screamed.

Moments later his body surfaced, scrambled and splattered inside the large cavity.

Washed by the cold waters of surging Lake Superior, his face an unrecognizable scowl, he looked up at the young people with eyes glazed and unmoving.

His frantic daughter stumbled and tumbled in her hazardous haste down the projecting rocks of the rock-bound shaft, Benjamin close behind.

They reached the bottom together, breathing heavily, to find the half-submerged body. Elizabeth cried as Benjamin jumped in, fighting the turmoil of crashing waves before pulling Henry to the surface, his head gashed and bleeding. Together, they lifted him over the edge of the roiling tub, his legs and feet still dangling in the water.

Gently, they stretched the man out along the rocks, Elizabeth sobbing as feelings of fear and hatred at the man dissipated. Gently, she cradled Henry's head in her arm.

"He's dead," lamented Benjamin, releasing the vein he was touching. "But what made him jump in the first place?"

For a moment, Elizabeth wondered how she could tell him what she had observed, or imagined she had seen, before her father fell. For a moment she was unsure, but she would try.

"He didn't jump, he tripped. He appeared to be gazing up at something, but when I looked to see what held his attention, there was nothing special there—at first."

"Beth," he asserted, "you're mistaken. There's not a thing up there out of the normal."

"Of course, there's nothing up there...not now. But there was—I think—and Pa must have been looking at it when he lost his balance."

"Well, it's gone now, if it was ever there. Might have been your imagination, Beth, but who am I to decide that's all it was."

"I just don't know," she pondered.

"But it must have been just a dream, an unreal hallucination conjured in your mind, Beth," he claimed.

"Of course, it was. Don't you suppose I know that?"

"Of course, you do."

And yet, thought the young woman to herself, it was so real—so very, very real. Is it possible, she wondered, earlier people—ancient tribes—had come here, seen the same apparition, and named the rock formation so nearby, after it?

"Do you have a telephone at home?" he asked.

The young lady nodded her head, tears forming in her eyes. Benjamin gently touched her arm. "Stay with your father. I'll go for help."

Elizabeth watched as he began the arduous climb back to the top.

It was late in the evening when the sheriff and his deputy put her father's corpse into the back of their vehicle. They promised to take it to a funeral home in Eagle River, near Benjamin's store.

With a lantern in hand, Benjamin wanted to escort Elizabeth back to the cottage; however, she retraced her footsteps to the Devil's washtub. The full moon cast an eerie glow into the washtub as Elizabeth finally managed to speak.

"I presume my father coaxed you into coming here today in the hope of marrying me off."

"Not so, Beth. I saw your father leave the copper mine this afternoon and asked if I could meet you sometime....and here we are."

"A fine introduction, indeed."

Strangely, Elizabeth was not troubled by the silence descending between them, but after a few minutes was compelled to say, "My mother ran away five years ago."

"I know."

"You do?"

"She has been living in Houghton, and working as a secretary at the college where I'm a student."

Elizabeth's eyes brightened. "Really?"

"Your mother loves you, Beth. She simply didn't know how to get you away from here... from your father."

She considered his words for a moment. "I knew I must leave, sooner or later, and forge a life of my own, but my father would not have allowed me."

"He has no influence over you anymore," Benjamin observed.

"Isn't it strange," Elizabeth began and stopped.

"Strange?"

"Strange...unusual...you know?"

"What is it you're trying to say, Beth?"

"Oh, you know. The name of this place. The wild stories the college students tell about it...the devil and all, and what happened here with Father."

"You mean, the Devil's Washtub?'

"Exactly! Is what happened to him a strange coincidence or was it something— something more."

"You mean like something paranormal?"

"Precisely!"

"I wouldn't know."

"Have you ever heard of such things before?"

"I can tell you one thing: The ancient Indians who gave the treacherous place its name didn't call it the Devil's Washtub for nothing. They must have had a reason."

As the temperature dipped, Benjamin shivered. And yet, Elizabeth hadn't noticed the chill. "May I escort you home, Beth?"

Elizabeth nodded. With her father gone, she would do what she had always wanted to do for herself...go to college and earn a degree. Yes, she could do both, and much, much more. She was a determined woman.

Benjamin offered his arm to her, but she gasped.

"What's wrong?" he asked.

Elizabeth couldn't move. The brightness of the moon revealed a vision, the image of an old *something*...ancient...one of unbelievably incarnate evil, with scimitar-shaped horns growing out of its forehead.

She looked up and pointed her finger to where she had seen the vision but it was already gone. Benjamin lifted his head and studied the section Elizabeth was gazing at and after a few seconds looked back at her.

The twosome hugged, grateful for each other's company.

Donna Searight Simons and Frank Searight were a daughter and father team who collaboratively wrote "Calamity at Devil's Washtub". Frank passed away in December, and this story is dedicated to him. Both were avid Copper Country fans and usually visited there each summer. Frank's mother, Dorothy, was born and raised in Houghton. Donna is the author of *Copper Empire* while Frank has had numerous books published, including *Mystery at Copper Harbor*.

Kitch iti Kipi Big Springs

upper peninsula peace

by t. kilgore splake

◆❖◆

Ruins

holy holy holy

by t. kilgore splake

◆❖◆

wannabe writing friend
learning of my retirement
receiving monthly check
saying, "you could go anywhere"
sadly not understanding
in my upper peninsula exile
feeling comfortable with myself
poet finally home

early sunday morning
light filtering through trees
central church bell
echoing through trees
poet's shadow
alone in the forest
watching butterflies
flit and fluttering
listening to birdsongs
music for heaven
surrounded by wildflowers
sweet fragrant scents
sitting in stump
like front row pew
enjoying wilderness service

T. Kilgore Splake ("the cliffs dancer") lives in a Tamarack location old mining row house in the ghost copper mining village of Calumet in Michigan's Upper Peninsula. As an artist, Splake has become a legend in the small press literary circles for his writing and photography. His most recent book *Depot* is a modest history of the old railroad station located in Calumet. In addition there is a new eBook "splake" that was the creation of two Californian poets – Jonathan Hayes and Richard Lopez – published by Windpane press in Santa Cruz. Currently, Splake is working on a Richard Brautigan theme with a collection of poems titled *do not disturb*.

A Luxury by the Michigamme River

by Ninie G. Syarikin

A flock of birds is having a vacation
on the shoreline, one quiet summer
morning.
Sunbathing, lazing around on a carpet of
green grass.
Sitting, standing on one leg,
they were massaging their bodies
with their beaks.
Brown ducks with their bronze beaks
White geese with their pinkish-orange
nozzles
They stooped deep to reach their necks and
bellies
Spending a few seconds there scratching
twisting their necks far behind,
to reach out their backs.
Staying some moments here pecking
All of that while squeaking
Kwek kwek kwek kwek kwek kwek

They seemed to be exercising.
One crane standing straight,
lifting its chin high
while opening its wings wide
then flapping them hard.
Another crane lifting its one leg,
while opening its parallel wing
moving it slowly
and closing it down gently
then doing the same thing
to its other leg and wing
like a ballerina training on the stage

A goose rubbing its leg with its bill
Another one lifting its foot scratching its
beak
All of that under July sun

So graceful a sight it was,
with the calm rippling river
mirroring the green bush and trees
and some purple wildflowers.

Soon a raft of ducks were descending the
riverbank
Together entering the water with ease and
peace
Sailing, swimming, floating
Enjoying the cool air without chaos,
jealousy, fear, rivalry, or violence.
They swam back to the sands,
strolling on the meadow with leisure
with their behinds swinging back and forth.
Then sprawling and slouching around,
while the parakeets hopped here and there,
searching for seeds,
and three geese grazing the dried grass.

How lavish it is to freely share space and air
to breathe in.
Knowing what was stored was not going to
be robbed by greed.
Under the breeze of nature
on the bank of the Michigamme River.

Morning Moon above Norway

by Ninie G. Syarikin

Moon hanging in the dark blue sky
like a drop of Mother Pearl
a golden ball
a round cut of diamond.
Beneath me, clusters of clouds,
like floating cottons.
Then, a spread of lights twinkling,
like a spread of sparkling beads.
So calm, tranquil.

Far in the east
The bluish green and yellowish orange
are bursting out.
The sweep of brush of the Angels' fingers,
making out the gradual sunrays.
Time for the Changing of the Guards.

"Good night, Moon!
Thank you for lightening the darkness.
Sleep tight now, and sweet dreams."

"Good morning, Sun!
Thanks for taking over.
Enjoy your work today."

Ninie G. Syarikin came to the US the first time in the summer of 1987 as a young Fulbright Scholar at the George Washington University to study American literature. She then represented her home institution, the University of North Sumatra, Medan. A longtime member of the American Translators Association, she now lives in Houghton, Michigan, and works as a writer, translator, and researcher. Besides English, Ninie speaks Indonesian, Malay and Javanese, as well as being able to read the Qur'anic Arabic.

A Poetic Grief Diary in Memory of My Brother Daniel Lee Tichelaar

(January 24, 1973 – September 27, 2019)
by Tyler Tichelaar

Danny, Do You Remember?
October 3, 2019

Danny, do you remember how I constantly asked you if you remembered?

Do you remember how you would accuse me of making up things because I remembered more than you?

Do you remember when I asked if you remembered what Laura, or Nellie, or Almanzo did as we drove all the way to Walnut Grove?

Do you remember plastic blow-up bunnies on Easter morning, and how you ate too much candy and vomited all over the kneelers when we were altar boys?

Do you remember eating at the Bavarian Inn and Bonanza with Grandpa and Grandma?

Do you remember melting crayons on the metal doorstep so we could make candles?

Do you remember when we played Bible story? I was Jacob and our neighbor was my beautiful wife Rachel and you were my ugly wife Leah.

Do you remember when we were missionaries converting the Natives along some U.P. creek while Dad complained that we were scaring all the fish?

Do you remember when we lay side by side in my bed one morning while I first read to you from an Oz book?

Do you remember how when we had company, we'd have to sleep together and you would hog the sheet and blankets so I would have to tuck them beneath me?

And then you would wake me in the morning by singing "Make Someone Happy," and I told you that you'd make me happy by shutting up.

Do you remember when you rubbed mom's deodorant all over the bathroom curtains?

Or when you played Tarzan with the living room drapes and pulled them down?

Or the snow globe we tried to heat on the stove?

Do you remember being my partner in crime?

Do you remember going to movies at the Delft? I'd get Raisinets and you'd get Junior Mints.

Do you remember making stew out of rotting leaves until it stank like a witch's brew?

Danny, do you remember any of it?

I remember everything.

And now I am all alone.

A depository of a past that will always live in my mind

But can have no future.

Danny, Do You Want to Play?
November 1, 2019

Danny, do you want to play Smurfs?

Or build a sandcastle that stretches halfway across the backyard—complete with a pyramid for the pharaoh and hovels for the poor?

Do you want to go walk down the Oakridge Trail with Benji—walk until we nearly get lost, but will not care, for we are in the Winkie Country, having another adventure with Dorothy?

Will you just quit watching *I Love Lucy* and come play?

Will you play *Monopoly* with me until I own everything and you're bankrupt?

Will you build forts in the woods with me—great stately mansions—Tichelaar Court for you and Tichelaar Hall for me?

Will you spend hours with me in Grandpa's workshop, building wooden houses for the Smurfs, and temples, and wagons, and boats, and bookmobiles?

Will you come running into my room at some ungodly hour to wake me up because you can't contain your Christmas morning joy, so I can grumble and complain and secretly love every moment of it?

Will you be late again to pick me up? You always were late, and I was always mad, but not really mad—it was just my way of trying to get you to be responsible—and now I would be glad to be twice as mad if it would bring you back.

Will you just complain one more time about me playing my *Camelot* record for the umpteenth time?

Or will you come in my room once more to infuriate me by redecorating my little Christmas tree because it doesn't meet your standards?

Will you come stay with me again when I am sick and bring me a whole Smurf village from McDonald's to cheer me up?

Will you just tell me why you had to go?

I just want you back.

I want to tell you that you were my very best friend growing up.

And I always wanted you to grow old with me, so we could irritate each other to the very end. You know we would have both loved doing that.

Danny, will you believe that despite everything, I never for a moment stopped loving you?

Holiday Party
December 22, 2019

I don't want to come to your holiday party.
I don't want to celebrate with you the New Year.
I don't want to pretend
That I can be filled with goodwill and cheer.
I don't want to exchange presents;
I do not need any gifts,
Save the one that was taken too soon.

He would be the only present
I would want this year.
He would be a presence at your party
You would not know was there.
But I would feel his presence every time
Judy sang "Have Yourself a Merry Little Christmas,"
And every time I looked at your tree full of lights.
And as the New Year arrived
And you all sang "Auld Lang Syne,"
I would cry because my oldest acquaintance,
One that can never be forgotten,
Would be left behind in 2019.
I don't want to come to your holiday party.
Don't ask me. I cannot.

I Want to Wear Mourning
January 19, 2020

I want to wear mourning
So everywhere I go
Everyone will know
That my brother has died.
I want to carry a card
I can give to anyone who inquires
That explains all the details
Of his sudden, shocking death
Of how he was taken unexpectedly—
A broken foot, then a blood clot, pulmonary embolism at age forty-six,
Without warning, without any goodbye.
I am tired of explaining it over and over
To people who do not know what to say.
When they do manage to utter, "I am sorry for your loss,"
I am tired of replying, "Thank you," and, "Yes, it was a shock"
Because I don't know what else to say, but feel obligated to make them feel less uncomfortable.
I want to wear mourning to avoid all of that.

I want to wear mourning like the Victorians.
They understood death.
They lived with it more closely than we do.
They understood the agony of trying to speak of a loss
When it is still fresh.
They knew the impossibility of acting normal

When all the world has turned surreal.
Mourning clothes allowed them an out.
It warned others of their situation.
It allowed for nods of respect and expressions of sympathy
Without words.
I am tired of words.

Depression
August 31, 2020

None of the fairy tales came true.
None of the future I imagined became reality.
I always thought we'd drive each other crazy until the end
Like Lillian Gish and Bette Davis in *The Whales of August*
But August has come and gone and you did not return.
And now the anniversary draws near.
Almost a year ago I got the call.
"Dan's dead! Dan's dead!" your friend screamed to me over the phone.
I raced to your house and saw your still form and then had to tell Mom and Dad.
The shock and the tears have ended for us all now, but the pain remains.
Like your favorite Queen Victoria, I read Tennyson's *In Memoriam*, looking for comfort,
But none comes.
I read all of your favorite books—*The Wizard of Oz, Anne of Green Gables, Mary Poppins*, Beatrix Potter, Edna Ferber, *Gone with the Wind*,
Trying to hang on to a piece of you.
I still create fairy tales in my head.
You show up unexpectedly at my door.
I give you back your books, the commemorative plates, the family mementos I saved.
"Where are my clothes, my furniture, my car, the stuff I need to live?" you complain.
But then I realize you do not need them anymore.
You are not coming back.
How could you? Grandpa and Grandma and Benji never did.
I can only hope you are with them, and that you are happy.
While like Mary Shelley's Last Man I wait.
Now a Gothic Wanderer in truth.

Almost a year has passed. How many more to go?

One Year
September 27, 2020

The date comes and still I grieve,
But I find acceptance too.
I cannot spend my life wishing you were here.
For that would be no life, wishing for something that can never be.
I know you are still here in the memory of your laughter.
Alive with me as long as I live.
You frustrated me a lot in life, but far more in your going,
Yet, I forgive you.
I forgive you and let you go.
If it is meant to be, I will see you again someday.
Meanwhile, I will go forward and live my life, not for you but for me.
For that is what you would want.
I will do the things I always wished we had done together that now never can be.
I will celebrate each day I have and share it with you.
But I will do so because I wish to live life fully, not because I must live for you.
I will be grateful for the years we had together, a closeness two *only* brothers only can share.
And I will accept that now that era has passed.
I could not treasure it so much if it were not over.
I will love you always, and I will continue to live.
Until the day I hear your laughter again.

TYLER R. TICHELAAR is the author of twenty-one books including *When Teddy Came to Town, Haunted Marquette*, and *The Marquette Trilogy*. His latest book is *Kawbawgam*, a biography of Ojibwa chief, Charles Kawbawgam. Tyler is also a professional editor and the owner of Superior Book Productions. Visit him at www.Marquette-Fiction.com.

Waves

by Brandy Thomas

The initial waves crash over you like the gales of November.
Waves 40 feet high pulling you down
And smashing you to pieces against the shore of your loss.

The initial waves crash over you like the gales of November.
Waves 40 feet high pulling you down and smashing you
To pieces against the shore of your loss.

You know the storm is coming and you prepare as best you can,
Hoping to emerge bruised and battered but not broken.

Over time the storm weakens, and the waves slowly subside
Leaving you exhausted, drained, but on the way to healing
Till the grief becomes a gentle lapping
At the shores of your heart.

Brandy Thomas is a freelance editor who lives and works in Marquette, MI. She edits across the publishing spectrum but specializes in adult science fiction and fantasy as well as children's books. In addition to editing the written word, she is also an audiobook narrator and editor. For more information about Brandy please visit www.ThomasEditing.com.

My First Kayak Trip

by Donna Winters

Before you jump to conclusions, let me say my first kayak trip was not a long and challenging water journey. However, it *was* notable in unexpected ways.

Back in July 2005, about two years after my husband and I moved from Lower Michigan to a home on the Garden Peninsula, my sister and her family from Texas came up to vacation in a rental cottage near us. They brought kayaks, a son-in-law, a grandson, and other family members. I had been eyeing their kayaks with interest when my sister, Patte, and her son-in-law, Shawn, invited me to take a paddle over to Snail Shell Harbor, about a mile away, where Fayette Historic Townsite is located.

After giving me about five minutes of paddling instruction, Shawn held the Necky Manitou recreational kayak steady and I climbed in. Shawn and Patte stepped into a two-person fishing kayak and led the way toward Snail Shell Harbor. The water and wind were calm and the sun was sinking in a clear sky, making the journey pleasant both physically and visually. By the time we rounded the buoy outside the harbor, the sun, which had become a huge red globe, had sunk below the horizon, leaving a pleasant afterglow.

If you've never approached Snail Shell Harbor by water, the sight is breathtaking. A two-hundred-foot-high limestone bluff rises on the left side of the harbor while a series of pylons from nineteenth-century docks marks the right side, eventually giving way to a modern dock where current-day boat-ers tie up. Straight ahead are the historic buildings that constituted the iron smelting company town at Fayette, active from 1867 to 1891. The smelting furnaces that rise fifty-four feet into the air, the molding houses extending out from either side, the company store and warehouse, and the town hall are all positioned to face visitors who approach by water. Nearby are the reconstruction of a laborer's log cabin, the historic Shelton House Hotel, the Superintendent's House, and managers' homes built in salt-box style.

By the time we arrived, most of the human visitors had gone home or to their campsites and a doe had wandered into the community from the nearby woods. Such intrusions of nature are always mesmerizing, and we watched avidly from our kayaks as the doe ambled in front of the furnace and then turned up into the village, crossing gravel roads with graceful movements until she disappeared from view.

With the deer show over, we turned our kayaks around to head out of the harbor. Sunlight faded as we rounded the buoy on our return trip. Within moments, a spectacular light show rose in the sky. Beams of pink and gold radiated upward from the horizon. Never had I seen such colors following a sunset, and I instinctively knew this was a sight to remember. It was truly heaven-sent. But the wonder of the evening sky didn't end there.

As dusk faded into darkness, a huge full moon, brilliant white, hung above the trees and lay down a shimmering path of light that streamed from shore. As we neared the beach in front of our destination, that path lit our way, leading exactly to our landing place. Just above the beach, a small light blinked on and off. My husband, worried we might not find our way home, was working the on-off switch of a flashlight. Little did he know an even greater path of light had shown us the way.

The evening was magical—transcendent. In my twelve years on the Garden Peninsula, I never did see another sunset to equal that glorious night of my first kayak trip.

Donna Winters has been a published writer since 1985 and is the author of the Great Lakes Romances® series. She has over twenty titles in print and has been published by Thomas Nelson Publishers, Zondervan Publishing House, Guideposts, Chalfont House, and Bigwater Publishing LLC. Learn more about her and her books at amazon.com/author/donnawinters

Loggers in the woods

U.P. Reader — Volume #3 (2019)

Featuring

"The Purloined Pasty" and "The Amorous Spotted Slug" by Larry Buege

"Grand Island for a Grand Time" by Mikel B. Classen

"#2 Pencils" by Deborah K. Frontiera

"The Rolls K'Nardly"

"Seeds of Change" and "The Lovers, the Dreamers,and Me" by Amy Klco

"The Best Trout I Never Ate" and "Pirates, Gypsies and Lumberjacks" by David Lehto

"Cut Me" and "The Demise of Christian Vicar" by Sharon Kennedy

"Warmth" by Bobby Mack

"Welcome to Texas, Heikki Lunta!" by Becky Ross Michael

"Aiding and Abetting" By T. Sanders

"Three Roads" by Donna Searight Simons and Frank Searight

"Trouble with Terrans" by Emma Locknane

"Stellae" by Lucy Woods

"Free" by Kaitlin Ambuehl

"becoming zen" and "good life" by T. Kilgore Splake

"Catching Flies by Aric Sundquist"

"You Are Beautiful" and "The Snake Charmer" by Ninie G. Syarikin

"Summer of the Yellow Jackets" by Tyler R. Tichelaar

Ask your local bookseller or visit www.UPReader.org to order

ISBN 978-1-61599-447-2

U.P. Reader — Volume #4 (2020)

Ask your local bookseller or visit www.UPReader.org to order

ISBN 978-1-61599-508-0

Karen Dionne Interview – The Wicked Sister

with Victor R. Volkman

Editor's Note: the following interview was recorded live on Zoom with host Victor R. Volkman and guest Karen Dionne on July 25th, 2020. It was a lively give-and-take and I hope you will enjoy it as much in print as we did live. If you missed the UPPAA Spring Conference 2019 in Marquette, you may wish to consult U.P. Reader #4 (2020) for a transcript of Karen Dionne's plenary address entitled "What I Learned from Writing My Breakout Book."

Victor: We have Karen Dionne on the line. She was of course the author of *The Marsh King's Daughter*, an amazing bestseller. I don't know how many countries it's in, but twenty-five languages. I'm going to say at least forty countries. As Karen was mentioning before we started rolling the tape, she had to cancel her book tour in the UP for reasons everybody understands, but we will have bookplates for her available at Snowbound Books in Marquette and Falling Rock in Munising. It's just a cool little sticker with her actual signature on that you can fix to the inside of your book just as if it had been signed in person. The Wicked Sister is going on sale August 4th, so I'm pretty sure I'm the only one in the room who's read it. We're going to have a little discussion about some of the themes of the book and I've structured it so we won't get into spoiler territory. I hope you find it interesting.

We'll also be talking about the process of writing itself and the creative decisions that Karen has made along the way. In addition to the recent book she's written, she has a deep history with the writing community specifically the Backspace organization, which was a huge help to many people online, and organized those conferences in New York. She's also a member of the International Thriller Writers where she served as managing editor of their publication and on the board of directors. She's really involved in the author community and it's just amazing to be in touch with someone who's really giving back to help people get started in their careers.

Let's get into *The Wicked Sister*! I've got a basic synopsis which brings us to the start of the story which involves Rachel Cunningham as our protagonist. She's been locked away in a psychiatric facility for fifteen years. Originally she was committed by her guardians and then she's voluntarily recommitted herself as an adult because she is dead certain that she is the one who caused her parents' deaths. But a surprise visitor brings a revelation to find out that she is not responsible, and of course she wants to return to her home and the so-called scene of the crime which is a log cabin in a remote area of Michigan's Upper Peninsula.

That's a basic sourcing from where we're going to start. Karen, when we last spoke, it was June 5th, 2019, and you had just turned in the manuscript for *The Wicked Sister*. It might have been after an all-night writing session. I'm not sure. Tell us about what happens after you submitted the book to the publisher. How does that work?

Karen Dionne: Yeah. Well, that was a very memorable day because I was late with the manuscript and then my publisher had given me an extension, but that Saturday that I keynoted at the conference, that was the hard and fast deadline. I had to turn it in that day no matter what or I was in deep trouble. And so I had been touring several places through the western end of the UP. My daughter was with me to do the driving. I was working on my laptop in the car. Each morning I was getting up earlier and earlier.

So the morning of the keynote, I got up at 4:00 a.m. and I worked solid from 4:00 until 9:00 when it was due. I never budged from that hotel chair which was very hard chair. I sent it off, went over to the UPPAA Spring Conference, and then later in the afternoon I just crashed in the hotel room for several hours. So what happened after that was my editor, of course, read the manuscript very quickly because of the time frame, because it had been overdue. It takes a year to get a novel accepted by the editor onto bookstore shelves, so we were in a hurry for it.

So he read it; he gave me some comments. I quickly reworked the comments. He was happy with it. And so we had what's called a final manuscript by about the middle of July. And then after that, everything was out of my hands. Then the publisher had the manuscript copy edited and of course, I gave input on the copy edits. The art department started working on a cover for the book. And all of these internal things. There was the sales team that had an early read and they determined what they were going to do for marketing and started trying to create buzz for the book. All that happens behind the scenes when you're published with a major, major publisher like that. That day was a very, very special day. I will never forget it.

Victor: That's great....is it basically one galley that comes back later and you get a chance to redline it?

Karen Dionne: Well, when the copy edits come back, an author still has a chance to make fairly substantial changes, but once you get what are called *page proofs*, that's where the manuscript pages have been typeset exactly as they will appear in the book. Then any changes that the author makes, if you make substantive changes, you have to pay for that book to be re-typeset.

There are a couple of opportunities for the author to make adjustments if a sentence doesn't sit right or you thought of a detail that needed to be added. But even pretty far along in the process, one of my foreign publishers, I think it was in Sweden, the translator noted what was really an actual mistake that none of the copy editors had caught in the US edition. And so I wrote to my editor and I said, "Ah, can we fix this? Is there time to fix this?" And it was right before the books had actually gone to the printer and he said, "Yes, there is time to fix it." It was a small change but it was an important one.

So there are a lot of eyes on the book which I'm grateful for because as an author, you can't catch everything. It really helps to have other people making sure that the book is accurate internally and accurate to its setting, and history, and surroundings as well.

Victor: Yeah, I totally agree with you on that. I've just finished my 40th audiobook recording and in almost every one, the narrator finds a mistake. In the last one, the detective met a witness twice for the first time, but anyway, that stuff happens. Okay, you mentioned before that the movie rights have been acquired and casting was going on. Can you bring us up to date on that and do you have any input as to the teleplay?

Karen Dionne: Yeah. It's super exciting that *The Marsh King's Daughter* has been optioned for film. That's something that I never dreamed might happen, to be honest. As I was writing the book, I was writing a book. I wasn't thinking in terms of movies. I know some authors do. Sometimes they're imagining an actor and actress as the character as they are writing. I did not. So it was a big surprise to me when there was film interest for the story.

Since that time, we've had four directors and two actresses attached to the project. So early on, my agent told me, don't get excited. It's Hollywood, it's very volatile. Until they actually make the movie, anything can change, and I've certainly seen some of that happen. Where we stand right now, the production company is still very much behind the movie. They just asked for an extension of the option because the COVID-19 shutdowns have affected everything drastically there. I have not heard any word on when they might start shooting. There is an A-list actress attached and I can't tell you.

It's not my news to share, but I think people would be pretty excited. So I'm hoping that Hollywood will start to open up soon and things might get moving again. I've been told, not specifically with regard to my story, but in general that in Hollywood, the first movies to get back into production would be ones with a small cast that take place outdoors.

Victor: Great. I'd like to shift into full *Wicked Sister* mode here and I understand that you've been agonizing over an excerpt to read. Are you ready to do that?

Karen Dionne: I did. I'm going to read from the opening because it really, I think, sets the stage for the book.

Victor: I agree.

Karen Dionne: Thank you. So as Victor said, the basic story is that my character, Rachel Cunningham, grows up in this beautiful log cabin. It's south east of Marquette. It's fictitious, but it's on a piece of property that's very isolated. It's 4,000 acres that have been in the family for generations and her parents are wildlife biologists. She follows her mother and father around in the woods. Her mother studies black bears. Rachel feels a very strong connection to black bears in the story. But the novel does not open with her happily following her mother in the woods on her rounds. She's in the mental hospital because she believes she's responsible for that tragic shooting accident that took her parents lives when she was eleven.

So this is how the story begins in her voice. Rachel says, "Sometimes when I close my eyes, there is a rifle in my hands. My hands are small, my fingers are pudgy. I'm eleven years old. There's nothing special about this particular rifle, nothing to distinguish it from any other Remington except that this is the rifle that killed my mother."

"In my vision, I am standing over my mother. The rifle is pointing at her chest. Her mouth is open and her eyes are closed. Her chest is red. My father runs into the front hallway. Rachel, he screams when he sees me. He drops to his knees, gathers my mother in his arms, looks up at me. His expression, an unfamiliar jumble of shock and horror. He rocks my mother for a long time as if she is a baby, as if she is alive. At last, he lays her gently on the worn parquet floor and gets slowly to his feet. He takes the rifle from my trembling hands and looks at me with a sorrow greater than I can comprehend and turns the rifle on himself."

"'Not so,' says the golden orb spider from the middle of her web in the corner of my room where the cleaners never sweep. 'Your father killed your mother and then he killed himself.' I don't understand why the spider is lying. Spiders normally tell the truth. How do you know? I can't resist asking. She wasn't there when my parents died, I was."

"The spider regards me solemnly from eight shiny eyes. 'I know,' she says. 'We all know.' Her spiderlings skitter about the edges of the web, as insubstantial as dust motes, and nod to me. I want to tell the spider that she is wrong, that I know better than anyone what happened the day my parents died and I understand the consequences of my childhood crime better than she ever will because I've been living with them for fifteen years."

"Once you've taken someone's life it breaks you, shatters you into so many infinitesimal pieces that no one and nothing can put you together again. Ask any drunk driver who killed a pedestrian. Any hunter who thought the friend or brother-in-law he shot was a deer. Anyone who held a loaded rifle when she was too young to anticipate what was about to happen."

"My therapists say I'm suffering from complicated grief disorder and promise I'll get better in time. My therapists are wrong. I'm getting worse. I can't sleep and when I do, I have nightmares. I get frequent headaches and my stomach hurts all the time. I used to think constantly about killing myself until I realized that living in a mental hospital for the rest of my life is the greater punishment. I eat, I sleep, I read. I watch TV, I go outside. I breathe the warm summer air, feel the sun on my skin, listen to the birds chirp and the insects hum, watch the flowers bloom and the leaves turn and the snow fall and through it all always, always in the front of my mind and deep in my heart burns this terrible truth."

"I am the reason my parents will never see, smell, taste, laugh or love again. My parents are dead because of me. The police ruled my parents' death a murder-suicide perpetrated by my father. All the news reports I've been able to find, agreed. Peter James Cunningham, age forty-five murdered his wife, Jennifer Marie Cunningham, age forty-three for undetermined reasons and then turned the rifle on himself."

"Some speculate that I saw my father shoot my mother and that's why I ran away, others that I found my parents bodies and this is what sent me over the edge. I would have told them that I was responsible if I had been able to speak. When I came out of my catatonia three weeks later, I made sure that everyone who would listen knew what I had done. But to this day, no one believes me, not even the spider."

Victor: Thank you for that. That was a great reading. You've got a great reading voice.

Karen Dionne: Thank you, thank you.

Victor: That just gives us several enigmas that pull me along I have to keep reading, I have to find out what's going on! That is just awesome. All right let's talk a little bit about bears in your story. It's not in the excerpt, but it's a theme all the way through the book. The bears are both a source of danger and comfort to the characters. For example, Rachel has a stuffed bear and of course there's an extremely rare albino bear that she befriends. On the other hand, the bears are a constant potential threat to the family as they're studying them. Bears also play a pivotal role at the end of the story. And you even have a lot of detail on the Oswald Bear Ranch. Do you yourself have a personal fascination or a story about bears that you can share with us?

Karen Dionne: Well, when my husband and I lived in the UP, we moved from the Detroit area as a young married couple in the early 1970s as part of the Back to the Land movement and we built a little cabin while we lived in a tent and carried water from the stream and sampled wild foods. So I had not had any direct contact with bears, I could have. There was one day when I was heading for an old apple orchard behind our house, where there were some blackberries. I was going to pick those blackberries and some chokecherries and make jelly.

My infant daughter was on my back in a backpack. And walking down the road, I came upon a pile of bear dung and it wasn't too fresh so I wasn't too worried. I kept going, but the piles just kept getting fresher and fresher. I decided that running from a bear with my baby on my back; this was probably not a good idea. So I turned around and went home.

But I think what has fascinated me about bears is for one thing, black bears are Michigan's largest predator, and it felt right to feature them in the book. But I wanted to feature them not as something to fear, but as a creature to be respected. And so I did visit Oswald's Bear Ranch to do research and I talked to Dean Oswald quite a little bit and learned a lot about what it's like to care for bears. I badly wanted to go inside one of the enclosures with him, but his liability insurance wouldn't allow it. So I had to just stand outside. It's probably just as well. I like bears. So it was a pleasure to me to give Rachel this particular love for bears as well, because it's always fun when your characters share something in common with yourself.

Victor: Yeah. The white bear is a character in the story and it's fascinating to have a little bit of an animal companion. Let's segue over to fairy tales, which seemed to be a big influence for you. In this book, you've cited *Rapunzel, Hansel and Gretel, Cinderella, Snow White, Sleeping Beauty, The Willow-Wren, Red Riding Hood, Robin Hood of the Twelve Huntsmen*, and there's probably more I missed and of course *The Marsh King's Daughter*. How do you see these ancient tales impacting us centuries later?

Karen Dionne: Yeah. I think many readers cut their teeth on fairy tales. Show of hands who read fairy tales when you were little? All the hands go up, right?

Victor: Right!

Karen Dionne: And I was no exception. I've got my childhood fairytale books on the shelf behind me here and I think I read them, these are the unabridged versions and I read them when I was maybe eight or nine. But the language is so lush, for one thing, and then I think the other appeal of fairy tales that makes them so timeless is, generally speaking, at the end, justice is served. So the protagonist of the fairy tale, it ends happily ever after, right? And the bad character gets their comeuppance, generally speaking. There are exceptions, of course. And I think that pattern of storytelling is something that just really strikes a chord with us, no matter what generation we are.

Victor: Cool. That's nice to see that that kind of tradition sort of carried forward. Let's talk about the setting a little bit. More so than *The Marsh King's Daughter*, this book seems to paint a vibrant picture of the UP with its natural resources and history. In *The Marsh King's Daughter*, at least to me, the UP seems to be primarily a harsh and bleak climate of extreme cold and in the summer extreme heat and everything.

Karen Dionne: And with extreme bugs.

Victor: Extreme bugs. In this book, you go out of your way to explain some of the background with iron mining and so on. I'll just read a short passage if you don't mind.

Karen Dionne: Yeah, yeah.

Victor: "Our cliff is part of the Marquette iron range, one of three iron rich mountain ranges in the western UP. Most of the cities on this end of the UP were founded due to mining. Marquette, Ironwood, Iron River, Ishpeming, Negaunee and some depend on mining to this day. Peter's grandfather likes to show off a copper nugget the size of a baseball that he claims was found on our property, and things of that nature." Was this a conscious choice for this book to go further into geographic details?

Karen Dionne: It was and that's interesting that you spotted that in the reading because the reaction to *The Marsh King's Daughter* as was mentioned, it's been translated in twenty-five languages and so it's been published in a lot of countries around the world. Many people write to me and say that they're fascinated by the Upper Peninsula. Some even plan trips here. I don't know if that happened or not but they claim that the book inspired them to go and visit the UP.

But I realized that all readers in those other places knew about the Upper Peninsula was what I put in the book, right? And so I thought well, okay, if people are that fascinated with the Upper Peninsula, I'm fascinated. I'm going to sneak in a little more of the history and the geography of the area. So that was definitely something that was in my mind including those details.

Victor: That's cool. That's a nice little, sort of Easter egg for the reader. This is kind of related—you seem to have a great appreciation for the beauty of the natural world. Is that something that you grew up with?

Karen Dionne: I actually grew up I guess you'd say in the city or in the suburbs. My family moved to the Detroit area from Ohio when I was eight and I grew up in Grosse Pointe Woods. So you would think that's pretty far from the woods and then the natural world. But my family always went camping and I loved it. I loved exploring the sand dunes and the woods. And even as a child, I would collect the little pine cones and my mother tells a story about apparently I discovered tent caterpillars and I thought they were the coolest thing ever. And brought a whole bottle back to the campsite.

Victor: Oh my god.

Karen Dionne: So I think that's where the initial love of the natural world came from. And as I said, my husband I moved to the Upper Peninsula in the early 1970s because we wanted to be closer to nature all the time. And we lived in the Upper Peninsula for thirty years. So it just speaks to me. Everybody has their preferences, but I have sometimes said if you were to show me ten pictures of places that I could live from the most congested like New York City to gradually the least congested like a mountaintop in Tibet, well, I would pick the mountain top into that. There's just something about the emptiness and the natural world that really speaks to me. And so I love the Upper Peninsula and it's been a joy to write two characters who also love the natural world.

Interestingly in the third book that I'm working now is set in Grand Marais and Lake Superior features largely in this third story, but I'm writing it from the point of view of someone who moves up from the Detroit area, so she doesn't know anything about the area. And so it's all first impressions, right? She's never seen a great lake before because she was a city kid. So I'm having fun with that, basically going back to that first year that we were in the UP and everything was fresh and new.

Victor: That's great. I love it. Everyone loves a fish out of water story. It's the basis for a lot of series television. I've got one more locale question so let's get to that. The story takes place on the family resort about forty-five miles from Marquette. That reminded me of a famous naturalist wildlife photographer George Shiras III. His family retreat was called Whitefish Lake which is now a state park in sort of the same area. Was the estate in the story modeled after any kind of real life retreat?

Karen Dionne: I did not know about that when I created my little world. I knew I was going to set the book in the forest and *The Marsh King's Daughter* takes place in the marshland, in the Tahquamenon River Valley. And I wanted something that was the opposite. So in *The Marsh King's Daughter*, Helena lives in complete isolation and just basically a ramshackle old house. So what's the opposite? A beautiful mansion. And also, when my husband I lived in the Upper Peninsula for a lot of years, we did furniture upholstery.

So I've been in some of these beautiful log cabins as a tradesman. And so I wanted to set it... The nice part about fiction is you can create it however you like. So I give this log cabin a copper roof and stained glass windows. It's really over the top because it's fiction. You can make it up how you want. Later, I realized that Marquette has *Granot Loma* which is like the largest log cabin in the world. And so, I used some of the pictures from that as I was imagining the interior in *The Wicked Sister*. [Ed. Note: Granot Loma is a 26,000 square foot log cabin situated on 415 acres just north of Marquette]

But was that setting inspired by them? No. But there are shades of that. When I heard about the estate that you're talking about, I almost felt like, "Well, yes, okay. I was on the right track when I made up mine."

Victor: Yeah. The descriptions of the log cabin are so vivid, I feel like it really puts me in the room.

Karen Dionne: Nice. Thanks.

Victor: So I love that part. Let's talk a little bit into the characterization. To me, this seems to be strongly a women's story. At least five of the major characters are women, and the male characters are all somewhat tangential, and even the father figure, Peter

Cunningham, seems to be weak. Is that an intentional choice?

Karen Dionne: I do tend to push the less important characters way in the background. I've noticed that. In *The Marsh King's Daughter*, of course, the story was all about Helena's relationship with her father, The Marsh King. And her mother is so beaten down and so ignored by the father and by Helena then too, because that's what she learns, that in the story she doesn't even have a name. So I figured this time, I'm doing pretty good. At least Rachel's father gets a name in this story.

Victor: I love stories about powerful women.

Karen Dionne: And this is called *The Wicked Sister*. Obviously, Rachel has a sister and so the core of this story is their relationship. Rachel's mother also tells her half of the story in the past and she too has a sister. I had two sisters. So that's why it's a little female heavy, I think.

Victor: Let's get a little bit into the psychology of one of the characters, Diana, the psychopathic child. The psychopathic child is a recurring theme over a lot of literature and film. I'm thinking of William March's *The Bad Seed*. Why do you think that is and what does that say about believing that people are basically good or at least born with a *tabula rasa*? Any thoughts on that.

Karen Dionne: My thoughts differ a little bit. I knew that Rachel's sister was going to be a psychopath and that's not really a spoiler. You guys will figure that out pretty early on if you read the novel. I knew that that's what she would be, but I wanted to depict her realistically. It isn't like in the movies where a psychopath just goes around killing people because they apparently enjoy killing. The more that I read about true psychopaths, they don't enjoy killing, they don't get pleasure from it, but they will kill if it somehow serves their purpose. So in the case of Diana, I wanted to show the tragedy of a family who has a deeply disturbed child because I knew a family that adopted three siblings and the two younger siblings did very well in the new environment, but the older sibling, he had some serious issues. And he was vio-lent towards his younger brother and sister and eventually at the age of twelve, they had to institutionalize him. And to me that's like a *Sophie's Choice* sort of thing. How as a parent do you make this decision? You love your children. You love all of them. To send one away for the sake of the other two?

So that's the core question that I'm working with in telling the story in the past from Rachel's mother's point of view. She knows that her daughter has, you would say, violent tendencies or she's unrestrained. And she doesn't show any care and empathy. At what point does the parent say, "This is out of our control. We can't handle this." Obviously, because they end up dead, she waited too long. But that's one of the things that I wanted to depict in the story was just the dilemma for the parent of a child who has severe issues like that and what it's like to deal with that.

Victor: Yeah, that's a fascinating thread to follow in there. I found it interesting that the psychiatrist says and I'll quote, "It is important to understand that her condition is not your fault, no more than if Diana had been born with any other non-heritable birth defect."

Karen Dionne: Yeah. So in my research, most psychologists say that psychopathy can't be diagnosed in children until like the age of eighteen. But there are a few, and a growing number, who feel that they can diagnose it in children as young as three, four, five. So these tendencies do show themselves and sadly in the early parts of the book, most of the incidents that I have Diana be involved in are true. Other children have really done those things. So I won't get specific as to what they are, but it's a real issue, a real problem that shows itself early.

Victor: Right. So that answered that question. Diana seems to follow the classic route where people on the road to becoming serial killers have a path of desensitization. They start out by hurting maybe frogs or small animals and moving up the scale to people. Is this something that you found as a pattern in your research?

Karen Dionne: Yeah, I don't see it that way and this is probably a good time to explain. I've already mentioned that Rachel's parents and of course her sister Diana, too, they're wildlife biologists. So when Diana, even as a child, let's say dissects an animal, she's not doing it out of cruelty, she's doing it as a scientist would. She's thinking, "Well, I want to know what's inside." So the things that she does are basically like a scientific experiment, but without that filter of, "Wait a minute. I'm killing this other creature unnecessarily or whatever else it might be."

So like I say, it's a more cerebral than an emotional thing with her. So I don't see it as so much as escalating as just her life is one big experiment trying to understand the world, and it might involve harming something or someone.

Victor: Got it. It's like an extreme detachment. That's very interesting.

Karen Dionne: Yes, right. That's right.

Victor: Let's talk a little bit more about the character development. I first ran into the idea of an unreliable narrator in some old film noir movies where things are told from one person's point of view and then there's like a huge shift and then you think, "Well, maybe that's not right." Well, it's a literary tradition that mixes reality with delusion or fantasy. Is Rachel an example of an unreliable narrator do you think, or does she really have the ability to communicate with the spiders and so on?

Karen Dionne: I'm leaving the final call on that to the reader.

Victor: Somehow, I knew you would.

Karen Dionne: Yes, yes. The thing is we've all known of people who have such a strong connection, usually not to all animals, but one particular one, that's where the idea of a horse whisper or these people who are so connected to lions or tigers that they can just interact with them in amazing ways. So I'm thinking of that. However, Rachel has had severe trauma as a child and she made no effort to get better for a lot of years. So maybe it's all in her head and that's going to be up to the reader to make up their mind.

Victor: Well, that's always good to leave some things open ended. In terms of the writing process, I was really hooked by the

way that you managed to interweave chapters in two different settings and each one ended up on a cliffhanger especially towards the end of the book. That must have been difficult. Did you have a way to work that out?

Karen Dionne: Cliffhangers are fun especially if you're writing suspense or thrillers or psychological suspense because you carefully bring the reader to this moment and then you don't let them have the resolution yet. And so when you're interweaving two storylines, past and present in this case, it makes it even more powerful because not only do you break the chapter at this climactic moment and not give the answer in the next chapter that would have been sequential, you go to the other character and you make the reader wait another chapter before they get the continuation of that. So it's something that I actually find easy to do and it's fun. I'm a very nice person in real life but I guess I do like to manipulate my readers. So what can I say?

Victor: Certainly makes it hard to put it down because you want to get back to that thing. Let's talk about firearms, which are a huge part of this book. Each character has their own relationship, as it were, to firearms and rifles in particular. I'll just read a brief passage. "And yes, as it happens, I do know quite a lot about rifles. As I said on my grandfather's lap, he taught me each rifle's name and what it was used for, .22 long rifles for small game, Winchesters and Remingtons for medium game, larger rifles for wolf and deer all the way up to the Mannlicher-Schoenaur big bore capable of bringing down a rhino. Did you use guns growing up or at any point?

Karen Dionne: I've never touched a gun in my life. So those parts of my novels obviously have to be researched. Going back to *The Marsh King's Daughter*, this is a family that lives off the grid. So of course they do hunting and fishing. And so I had to watch a lot of really ugly YouTube videos of skinning animals. And I would go to discussion forums to get the language for shooting and hunting because you can read an article about hunting and there's a remove. But if you hear people talking about it on discussion forums, you can pick up the tone of the language that they use.

So I was very intimidated to write my first scene where Helena kills her first deer at the age of six. It happens in the winter because they have no respect for hunting laws. And I could easily write her walking across the frozen marsh and what the air feels like and imagining the fish below her and a crow cawing. All of that was fine. But to actually hold a gun and what it feels like to shoot it and then set it here, that I know nothing about.

But I wrote the scene and when my writing partner at that time found out that I did not hunt, she had her husband who does hunt read it and he gave it a "thumbs up". So I was happy about that. And I think it's funny because much later after *The Marsh King's Daughter* published, I was contacted by a DM at Facebook from an author who I don't know personally and he writes what I call boy books, military shoot 'em up, this sort of thing.

He told me that he was reading and enjoying *The Marsh King's Daughter* and he said he doesn't usually tell people this, but he said he's been an avid hunter all his life and he said when he read the scene where Helena is learning to track and where she shoots her first deer, he said, "I knew you were a hunter too."

Victor: You really pulled it off then.

Karen Dionne: I did, I did. I did not give away my secret; I guess I just did now. So if he's watching, sorry about that. So it's more by necessity, and the reason guns factor so heavily in *The Wicked Sister*, I was inspired by an incident that had happened a long time ago, but it just always stuck with me which was a shooting accident that involved a toddler and the toddler was sitting in his car seat behind his mother in the car and he found a loaded handgun in her purse, shot and killed her.

Like I say, it always stuck with me and I thought: what would it be like for that person. As they grow up, at some point, this little boy was going to find out what he did. How could you make that part of who you are? How do you come to terms with that

and go forward even? And so that's what I wanted to explore. The core question that's driving Rachel is how did she get past this terrible accident that she thinks she's responsible for?

And so, of course, you know with that, guns are going to feature largely. And I postulate that the hunting lodge, or the lodge where they grow up, was a former hunting lodge and so, yes, there's a lot of taxidermy there. And there was a gun room. Obviously, when Diana's parents moved there, they cleared out of all the guns, but that doesn't quite take care of it for them. I don't think there'll be guns in the next book, but we'll see. Maybe there will be.

Victor: I have a couple questions that were emailed in from Ann Dallman. They relate more to the process of writing and being successful, so let me just run through those. Ann says, "I'm a self-published author. What would you suggest as the next step to take to get into mainstream publishing? I've spoken to some people who told me that agents, publishers, et cetera, aren't willing to work with self-published authors to get them out into the mainstream. And I'm curious to find out if that's really true." Do you have an opinion?

Karen Dionne: My opinion, no, that's not true. It all comes down to the writing. When I was organizing writer's conferences, I knew a lot of literary agents. I know fewer now, but they're all looking for that next thing, that thing that gets them excited. It's all about the writing. So your publishing history doesn't matter. In my case for *The Marsh King's Daughter*, my early novels were published by a mainstream publisher, traditional publisher, but they didn't do particularly well.

And anyone who's looking, any editor who wants to acquire a book can look at the author's track record and see what their past history is. That's why some authors might change their name at that point. They want to start their career fresh again without a history. However, my agent said that wasn't necessary in my case because the writing was so good that it would overcome that past history where the books only did so-so.

So that would be the case for a self-published author, too. It's not a negative. It's nothing that's going to count against you. Everything comes down to the words on the page. So by all means, if you think your book, the one that you're working on now, is going to be the kind that would get publishers excited and would reach a wide audience, absolutely, query agents. And you don't even have to tell them you self-publish. They're not interested in your history, they just want to read the book and find out if they fall in love with it or not.

Victor: That's great to hear. That's very encouraging. I mean, you've got a big publisher behind you. So maybe you don't have an answer for this, but what are some cost-effective ways that you can think of to promote a novel?

Karen Dionne: A lot of people think that having a publisher behind you means that the author doesn't have to do anything. I do get a lot of support, but yes, I do a lot on my own. The author is the one who knows their book the best, right? And so I'll suggest ideas for articles to my publicist and it's true that I have the assistance of the publicist in placing these articles, but I still write them like a personal essay, that kind of thing.

That's a really broad question. It's really kind of hard to narrow it down, but I'm a big believer in not putting a lot of money into the promotion. I would rather put my time in writing than invest in the cost. I've heard good things in regards to Facebook ads, but it's such an individual thing. Why don't we leave that to Carolyn Howard-Johnson. She knows more about that than I do.

Victor: Well, thanks for that. She had another question. She wanted to know if there were any specific managers or publishers that you could recommend who would be willing to work with self-published authors.

Karen Dionne: Well, again. The fact of having been previously self-published, that is inconsequential. The best resource that I know of for finding agents is a website called agentquery.com. So it's one word run together, agentquery.com. That has a database of agents and you can do a search on them by topic, by project interest. They keep it current and they're legitimate agents who are making sales and not going to take advantage of a newer author.

You want to narrow your search, yes, but at the same time you want to cast a broad net because writing is so subjective and what one agent likes, another might not. So you just have to keep the faith in your project and query a lot of agents until you find that one who just loves what you wrote and then you're on your way.

Craig Brockman: The only other one was, just because your book is so interesting in the format of in relation to the UP. When I tried to agent my book, I got pushed back because it was too regional. And I think maybe they're just being polite, but that's okay. I've had super acceptance as far as people from out of the area and stuff that have really liked it and enjoy it, just like your book to getting to know the UP. Not from my perspective, but from your perspective, I'd really like to know what your experience was trying to break down the door trying to get stuff out there from the UP?

Karen Dionne: My novels that got me my agent, I've been with my literary agent for twenty-one years. They were not initially set in the Upper Peninsula. I've always liked exotic places. So my first novel was set in Antarctica and the next one was set at Chaitén Volcano in Northern Patagonia, Chile. I only came to set the book, *The Marsh King's Daughter,* in the Upper Peninsula, because the character came to me in the night and it just flowed and it seemed like the right story to happen in the Upper Peninsula.

But my agent didn't pitch it as a book set in the Upper Peninsula. At heart, *The Marsh King's Daughter* is a father-daughter story. While certainly, it's a major part of the book, the book would not be the same if it was set anywhere else. I don't think initially that was part of his pitch and, "Oh, cool, it's set in Michigan's Upper Peninsula." Probably not.

He was talking about other aspects of the story. So if you think the regional aspect was a turn off, maybe just don't emphasize that in the query and shift it to the characters because it's really the characters that matter in the end anyway. If you want to mention that yours is... I'm assuming yours is set in the Upper Peninsula also?

Craig Brockman: Hey, author Karen Dionne has had great success with her book set in the UP.

Victor: Thanks, Craig. Do we have anything else from our studio audience?

Brandi: No one else has written or raised their hand.

Victor: Okay. All right. Well, thank you, Karen, for taking out an hour of your day on a beautiful Saturday in the middle of summer. I can't thank you enough and it's been a lot of fun to talk to you again and hear what you're up to and I cannot wait to see your third book set in Grand Marais.

Karen Dionne: Okay, it's fine. Well, I really appreciate the opportunity to talk to you and I know that this was part of my keynote that I gave a year ago, but I just would like to re-emphasize that the two main things that I have learned from my experience, because I've been writing seriously for twenty years and *The Marsh King's Daughter*, which was my breakout book, was my fourth published novel, and now of course it's going on from there.

So the two main things I want to emphasize is if you're an aspiring writer, keep at it. Don't quit. There were a lot of times when over that twenty-year period before *The Marsh King's Daughter*, I thought well, maybe what I've had is as good as it's going to get. Maybe that's all I'm going to do. And I had a couple books published and mass market paperback, yay. That was really fantastic. But I didn't quit. I kept writing, and look at what has happened since? So that is my number one takeaway.

And then the number two takeaway is if you've been writing for a while and you're not seeing the results that you would like either from querying or maybe you're published with a small publisher and you'd like to step up to a big publisher, don't be afraid to change what you write. Just because a person starts writing in a particular genre, in

a particular way, doesn't mean that's where your strengths lie.

My early books were not bad books, but the psychological suspense that I write now, quality wise, they're a huge step up from what I was writing before. So if I hadn't been willing to change what I'd been doing and try some writing techniques that were new to me, like handling a dual story line, I had never done that in my early books. Using flashbacks and how you incorporate past and present and all of these different things that I had to learn how to use those techniques in order to tell the stories that I wanted to tell. But in the process, I discovered that I was a better writer than I realized.

So that would be my other thing. Don't be afraid to try something new. Don't think that just because, "Oh, I've been writing this mystery series for three years and of course I'm going to write mysteries." Consider changing it and you might find a strength in an area that you didn't realize that you had. So I hope that overall, the conversation has been encouraging and, yeah, I look forward to seeing your names on the New York Times Bestseller list.

Victor: Oh, that's so sweet. Great. I can't think of a better way to wrap this up. Again, thank you on behalf of the whole UPPAA board and everyone. We wish you every success with *The Wicked Sister* launching August 4th in bookstores around the world.

Karen Dionne: Thank you so much for having me.

Victor R. Volkman has served on the UP-PAA Board since 2009. He is the owner of Loving Healing Press, Inc. in Ann Arbor, Michigan, which specializes in publishing empowering books which redefine what is possible for healing mind and spirit. LHP has published more than 250 titles including those of Modern History Press, which tells stories of conflict and the struggle for identity in modern times. He received a BS in Computer Science from Michigan Technological University in Houghton, MI.

Memoir as a Healing Tool

by T. Marie Bertineau

◆❖◆

Natalie Carolyn Photography

Memoir writing has the ability to act as a therapeutic aid; a balm on the ache of a bleak past. In this transcript from the UPPAA 2020 Fall Conference, T. Marie Bertineau, author of the recently released memoir, *The Mason House*, discusses her memoir journey. You'll learn what brought her to the keyboard—and kept her there—and how keystrokes contributed to a positive outcome. She'll discuss steps needed to open oneself up to writing in this genre and what you might expect along the way. Other topics include identifying when you're ready to take on your project, the importance of uninhibited writer's flow, ways to later hone that writing to create story, and how you might at last promote emotional healing through greater understanding of your past.

Bertineau was born in Michigan's Keweenaw. She is of Ojibwe/French Canadian/Cornish descent and is a member of the Keweenaw Bay Indian Community of the L'Anse Reservation, migizi odoodeman. Her work has appeared online with Minnesota's Carver County Arts Consortium; in *Mino Miikana*, a publication of the Native Justice Coalition and Waub Ajijaak Press; in UPPAA's own ***U.P. Reader*** and is slated to be anthologized with the Chanhassen Writers Group of Minnesota. Her debut, *The Mason House*, was released by Lanternfish Press in September 2020. Married and the mother of two, Bertineau makes her home in the Upper Peninsula.

•••

Thank you, Victor, and thank you all for taking time to sit with me this evening for the next hour or so to talk about memoir writing. I've been thinking about how best to present this information, and I realized that over the past several weeks, UPPAA has had a number of outstanding presentations, each packed with useful and timely material, much of it focused on techniques and how-tos; all the nuts and bolts of not only the craft itself, but also of the industry. With that in mind, I thought I might scale back a

Cover design by Kimberly Glyder

little and just talk about emotion, because memoir is all about emotion.

Now, I've always considered myself a fiction writer, but somehow, I created a memoir a few years ago that was picked up by a small press with a big heart. It was just released three weeks ago, and it's called *The Mason House*. The book focuses quite a bit on my childhood in the UP. I spent a lot of time in a fading mining town called Mason, which is located in Houghton County along M26. Perhaps some of you are familiar with that particular town. The book began as a tribute to my Cornish gramma, but the end result was much more than I ever expected, not only for myself, but also for my family—both immediate and extended. In my experience, memoir turned out to be healing for many of us, so that's why I'm here tonight. We're going to talk about my journey and see how it could

apply to something that you might feel a need to do.

There are many different reasons to write memoir; you don't have to write just because you're struggling with pain or trauma. You can write memoir about happiness, dreams that you've realized, careers, relationships, life changes, etc. Any of those, you name it, there is probably a memoir out there about it. But we're here tonight to talk specifically about healing memoirs, about processing emotional pain or trauma through memoir writing, which is what I did with *The Mason House*.

The Early Years

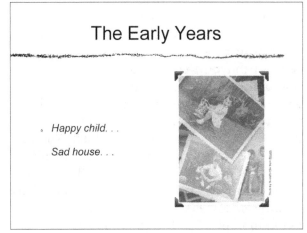

I like to call this slide a memoirist is born, and here's why.

I was born in Upper Michigan and of course my family was very involved with mining—or rather, my ancestors were involved with mining. However, by the time I was born, the mines were closing and all the jobs were disappearing. There was a lot of poverty in the Keweenaw, and my family was no different. We faced declining socioeconomic conditions, and we were caught up in that. That was on my biological father's side of the situation. On my mother's side, the Indigenous side of my family, we were still reeling in the aftermath of forced assimilation. There was the trauma of residential schools, loss of cultural practices, loss of original language, loss of religious practices, and the loss of medicinal practices known to us throughout generations. All of that historic trauma was still thundering through. So, we had all that to contend with as well.

Also, we had an interracial marriage. My father was French Canadian and Cornish; my mother was Ojibwe. Though for the most part that was accepted, there were still a few instances where it was not, so that was an additional stress. And finally, a wave of health traumas impacted my family resulting in three deaths very close together. All of this combined in my early childhood and led to alcohol dependence in my home, a loss of stability and, unfortunately, a pattern of domestic violence. These were just some of the challenges my siblings and I faced as children.

Yet, despite all that, I was a fairly happy child. They say children are resilient and that must be fact, because I was doing pretty well until I was about ten years old, when trauma struck yet again. As a child, it seemed maybe I could handle the dysfunction of my homelife, because I had a place to go. The home in this slide is the original Mason house. This photo was taken in the early 2000s, I believe, long after I had left. You can see it's deteriorating quite a bit. That was my gramma's house, where I spent all my weekends, all my school breaks, and most of my summers. My last memory of my gramma living took place in the room on the front left side, just beyond that window.

Girl Interrupted

◦ *Beginning is easy; continuing, hard. . .*

Japanese Proverb

That home was my happy place. And this isn't a spoiler for anyone who might one day read the book, but my gramma suddenly died when I was ten. For me, that is when the seeds of memoir were sowed. I didn't

know that yet, and it would take some forty years for me to figure it out, but that's when it happened. Gramma's death was an immense trauma for me. Her house was my refuge and her death shattered me. It was the first time I was old enough to understand what death meant—that I wasn't going to have her in my life anymore—and I felt so alone. I had all that grief I needed to process, but I didn't have a healthy setting for that. As soon as my gramma died, my life became even more chaotic, so I never had a chance to work through the stages of grief.

I'm sure a lot of you are familiar with those grief stages, but just briefly we'll go through them. First, we have denial and isolation, which are natural coping mechanisms: you receive bad news, it's too much for you to take in, and you shut down. Then, you may experience an anger phase, which some say is actually beneficial, because if you're spinning out in denial, isolation, and anger—even though it can be ugly—it is a way for you to reconnect with reality. Then, there is a bargaining phase, which many of us do through conversation with a higher power while trying to bargain our way out of the situation. Depression comes when you finally come to terms with what has occurred. You may be in a space where you're thinking, *yes, this is real, this is happening to me,* and now you're looking at how you are going to spend the rest of your life. People can get stuck in depression for a long time. I was stuck in depression myself. I was a *functioning* depressive for most of

Five Stages of Grief

◦ *Denial and isolation*

◦ *Anger*

◦ *Bargaining*

◦ *Depression*

◦ *Acceptance*

Elisabeth Kubler-Ross
American-Swiss Psychiatrist

my life, but I was depressed. Then the final stage is acceptance. I tend to view acceptance as one of those French film endings. They say Americans like their films to end happily, or at least satisfactorily. They don't want to leave the theater with a sad ending. The French are very different; they go for realism in their film endings, and I think acceptance in the grief stage can be a bit like the French films—it's usually not a happy, yellow-brick-road kind of ending. You simply learn to accept what has happened to you and find new ways to go on with your life.

The Inciting Incident

Despite whatever happens to us along our journey, life goes on, right? You'll still experience new jobs, marriages, ups and downs; life is a cycle that doesn't end as long as our hearts are still beating. Now, let's say that somewhere along this endless cycle—which you've probably grown accustomed to and take comfort in—something happens. For those of us familiar with fiction writing and plotting, you know that an inciting incident is the event that sets the whole story in motion. It's the kickoff to whatever your story is going to be. For me, this wasn't the kickoff to my *original* grief—the childhood grief I carried all those years. It was the kickoff that brought it all back to the surface some forty years later. This incident occurred five years ago. It came about when I separated from a long-term job that I enjoyed; however, the job was physically demanding, and my health was suffering. I just couldn't do it anymore, and I had to resign. I had a lot of grief about that, because I liked my work. And I was getting older. I was worried about my health. My job prospects were, of course, lower at that age and with my health concerns. I was starting to feel helpless, questioning my self-worth, wondering what I was going to do, how would I contribute to my family's income...all of that came up, and it was a scary place for me.

I must have been vulnerable at this point, because it was then that all the grief from my childhood came back to me. Now what was I going to do? Here I was with all this grief

and this feeling of being overwhelmed. What do I do with it all? It was a challenge. Thankfully, by that point in my life, I had learned some coping skills. I decided that I didn't want to give in to those feelings of despair or depression or anxiety about what was going on. I wanted to turn that around—I didn't want to shut down, I didn't want to isolate or deny what I was feeling. I'd been doing that my whole life. So, I made a different choice. I chose to channel all those emotions into writing, which had been a hobby (and actually, at one point, a career choice). I had enjoyed writing throughout my life, and I had always wanted to pay tribute to my gramma through writing, so I decided that I was going to write a story about her. That's what led to *The Mason House*, which is a memoir whose main themes turned out to be grief and loss.

Setting the Stage

> ## Setting the Stage
>
> - A peaceful place to write
> - Solitude
> - Time
> - Music
> - Tangible guides

Here is how that journey looked for me when I set out. The first thing I decided to do was turn it into a job. I established a home office—a peaceful place to write, which oddly enough turned out to be in the center of my living room. We had a great room, which was a kitchen, dining, and living room combined, and so in front of the fireplace, I set up a small desk with my computer. I could see all the birds in the trees on one side of the house and the comings and goings of the neighborhood out front. And that was a nice, safe space for me, because I could think about the past on the left, but if I felt unsafe, I still had the reality and security on the right.

I also had a lot of solitude during that time, which was priceless for writing. My kids were grown; my son was in late high school, so he was gone all day, my daughter was out of the house by then, and my husband worked in an office. He would leave at 8 o'clock, and I would kiss him goodbye, grab my cup of coffee, and off I would go to my computer. Usually, I sat there about four hours a day, but sometimes it would be way late into the afternoon. There were a few times that when my husband arrived home from work, I was still sitting there. I was usually in my pajamas, too—I rarely got out of my pajamas while I was writing.

Another thing that helped me stimulate that writing mindset was music. My family was so musical. Music was such a huge part of our childhood, and so for me, playing the music that I recalled from my childhood was an excellent vehicle to get back into that emotion and into those memories. Something else I thought was helpful was use of tangible guides, items that I had picked up that were familiar to me from my gramma's yard: pinecones, sticks, acorns...whatever I could find that felt like the Mason house, I'd pick up and store in a little baggie beside my keyboard.

Writer's Flow

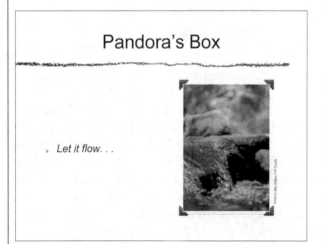

Pandora's Box

Let it flow. . .

Once I had all this going, and I was sitting down each day, I quickly developed a habit of writing. It was nice, because I felt like I was getting somewhere. I was moving ahead, emotion was flowing out onto the page, and I felt

good about it. I'd say this photo of this brook best represents how my writing flowed in those days. It was a bit timid and gentle, particularly in the early months. Some people might sit at the keyboard, and this might look like Tahquamenon Falls or Niagara or something. It all depends on what you've got going on in there and how free you are to let that out.

I might take a moment here to tell you something about flow. Usually, when you're writing memoir, it involves other people, and you may worry about writing about them. Memoirist Sharon Harrigan says in her article, "How to and (Especially) How Not to Write About Family:" *One way to invite writer's block is to imagine the people you are writing about looking over your shoulder.* You don't want to do that. Write whatever comes out. Don't censor yourself. Don't be afraid to say what's on your mind or in your heart. Don't worry about the thoughts or feelings of others *at this point*. You just want to write. Memoir is *your* perspective of what happened to you as a child or during that trauma or whatever it is you're writing about.

Oftentimes, things that go on in our lives involve others to an uncomfortable degree. There will be time later to go back and address how much or how little you're going to say about others in your story. But as you start out, you just want to write. You want to give in to the emotion and the memory and write everything you can. Thinking too much about the opinions of others will hinder your writing. You want to avoid that in your first draft. I think that's why, too, when you're writing memoir, the space you create for yourself is so important. You want it to be private, because you don't want anyone else to come upon your writing before you're ready to release it. Just know that. Protect it, but be free with it for *yourself*.

Also, as a disclaimer, I *did* worry excessively about the feelings of others because of the alcoholism in my family. When I first started writing, I avoided that topic. It took me a long time to loosen up and write *that* story. As you step into it yourself, know that if you think about it too much, it may create a roadblock for you.

Processing Emotion

When you're processing emotion, you'll find there will be times when the writing journey will not be easy. As a matter of fact, there are going to be many times that you—just like me—question why you're even doing it. If you're poking those bruises in your soul, you'll know it. You'll know you're writing memoir, because it becomes very real. It's connecting with somewhere *inside* and that's what you want it to do; that's what memoir is about. Remember that and be gentle on yourself. When I was writing sensitive scenes, many times I had to do self-care. Whatever you do, have a tea, take a bath, pet the dog, go for a walk...whatever you do to comfort yourself, you'll need to do while you're writing memoir.

One of the emotions you're going to struggle with is anger. Anger is the second phase of grief, so if you're processing grief, you're going to have some anger. That's going to happen, so just know that it's okay and don't be afraid of it. Don't be ashamed. But know this: Good memoir writing isn't about the anger. It's not about getting back at any*one* or any*thing*. It's not about revenge. A good, healing memoir is about the discovery of empathy and compassion and understanding. It's about the *understanding* and new perspective. And it's about sharing *that* with others, not the anger. You're sharing the new perspective you gained by writing about it and figuring out how it all fits together and how it affected your life and how you moved on. That's important to remember when you write memoir, especially where anger is involved.

Author and writing coach Marion Roach Smith had this to say about revenge and anger in memoir writing:

> Instead, while writing about the hideous aspects of life, you should attempt to teach us something about the behavior of those involved, about your behavior, about all human behavior. Let us into your story by shedding light on our own dilemmas, fears, happiness, or wide-eyed wonder.

So, if you're writing about things and you start to feel anger building—you start to taste the bitterness of it—take a break. I had to take a months-long break once because of this bubble of anger that welled up inside of me. I saw it in my writing. It turned dark and spiteful, and I didn't want that in my story. I'd made a commitment to myself that my story wasn't going to be about that, so I had to disengage. If you are someone who naturally processes emotion through writing, and you have anger arise while writing memoir, try taking it to another piece of work. When you're feeling better, come back to your memoir. And I'm not saying you're not going to have *any* anger in your memoir, because there should be—it's a natural human emotion—but don't make anger the *theme* of your memoir.

Okay. This next one, for me, was a big one: Sadness. I was not prepared at all for the level of sadness I felt while I was writing my memoir. Things that I wrote about, the way that I went about it...I don't know. Perhaps it was the sensory details. But it all brought it back to me so strongly. It felt real, like I was living it. I was missing all the things that I lost, the things I had longed for my whole life. All of it was right there, and I felt so sad. Memoir writing brings back those memories. It brings them back to the surface. If you're doing it well, you'll be able to feel it, touch it, and smell it. It will be a visceral experience for you. If you don't experience that while writing your memoir, try focusing more on the sensory details, because it will happen for you with time and practice.

Make History Come Alive

Understanding the Past

◦ *Connecting the puzzle pieces of life through chronology and mature perspective. . .*

When you write memoir, you don't want it to be dull or lifeless. You want to make it come to life on the page. Use the elements of fiction. You have character, setting, style, theme, plot, and point of view (which should be first person, and memoir is written predominantly in past tense). These are your friends when you're working on memoir. It's very much like writing fiction, except you're not making up the story. All these elements make your story come alive. They bring your characters to life. There's presence when you use them. There's sensory input not only for you, but also for your readers. They are living your life with you, and that's what you're trying to accomplish with memoir. You're inviting the reader to live those memories, to live this story with you. You're saying, *Come with me on this journey. Take my hand. Come see what happened to me. Maybe my story will help you.*

Understanding the Past

"The best memoirs have been written by those who have allowed enough distance between their lived experience and the writing about it."

~ Diana Raab, PhD
Writing for bliss

At the same time you're doing all this for your reader, guess what? Here's what's happening for you: You're learning to see your life and your loved ones in a whole new way. You're coming to an entirely new understanding of the past, and that's such an amazing and transformative process. That is exactly what memoir writing is about, and you'll definitely know it when you hit that mark, because you'll feel it. There's such clarity there. That's probably one of the greatest gifts to processing grief or trauma through memoir, particularly when you have allowed enough space between the trauma and the writing—

you get to finish your puzzle. All the sands of time sift into order and the distance adds clarity.

I'd like to share a passage from *Writing for Bliss : A Seven-Step Plan for Telling Your Story and Transforming Your Life* by Diana Raab, PhD. Victor Volkman, president of UP-PAA, shared this book with me last spring, and it's an excellent resource if you're thinking about taking on a project such as this—not just for writing a memoir specifically, but any memoir-type writing to help you with whatever healing that you might seek:

The best memoirs have been written by those who have allowed enough distance between their lived experience and the writing about it. This distance provides a much appreciated additional perspective...when an individual writes about an experience, especially in the form of memoir, it offers the opportunity to give a new meaning to that lived experience by understanding it through the present day lens.

So, you're looking back and seeing things differently, and that's important for memoir writing.

Lessons Learned

With all this understanding on the horizon, hopefully you're going to learn some lessons. First, learning to forgive. Maybe you hold some forgiveness somewhere that you've been unable to offer. A lot of that is going to come from understanding, and that's what happened for me. I can't say myself— and that's in my book—that I reached the point of complete forgiveness for some of the things that occurred in my past, but I was able to understand from a point of empathy, and I think that helped heal relationships.

Another lesson is acceptance. That is the final phase of grief, right? If you reach the point where you're thinking, *Oh yes! I get it now. I understand!* you should be at the final phase of processing your grief—a good place to be. You see the whole picture from that distance. You see all the cogs and gears that went into your grief story. It's very much like coming out of a thick wood after having been lost for years and years. You can look back, you can see what you've been through, and see that you've survived. You're still here, you're in one piece (for the most part). It's such a transcendent experience, looking back with understanding. It sets you on a whole new path emotionally.

A Manuscript Develops

Now, once you reach that point of understanding, you should have a manuscript. I should say here that there are many different ways of memoir writing. You don't have to publish what you write: you can write for yourself, you can write for family, you don't even have to do a memoir per se, you can journal, write essays, fiction, poetry, stream of consciousness, any form that helps you process emotion. I specifically knew that I wanted to try to publish my book as a tribute to my gramma, so that's how I went about my process, and what I'll talk about here.

Once you get the first draft down, you now have a beginning, a middle, and an end. You may feel a shift in your purpose at this point. You've processed, you've transcribed, you've narrated your story on paper or on the screen as the case may be, and now your job isn't so much about that healing work anymore. You've done that. You've done the hard part. Hopefully, you're finding that you have new purpose now, and it's sitting there in a bundle in front of you. It's your manuscript. You might be feeling refreshed and ready to put all that difficult, painful work behind you and start with a new focus, which is editing and working to bring your book to market.

Where Do We Go from Here?

○ *Editing love, loss, legacy. . .*

When I first looked at this slide I thought, *Oh! That sounds cold. How do we take all that we just went through and edit it?* How do you edit *real* love and loss? Real, personal love and loss? But I found that it wasn't so hard for me to do, and I think here's why: I had spent a good year with my story, and I guess the acceptance I had come upon allowed me to now view all that emotion more as story. I wasn't so connected to it in a *sad* way. I had processed that, and so I could take it separately and say, *Okay, how am I going to shape this?* How are other people going to perceive this? How am I going to bring my readers into this story and make it something relatable to them?

What I had to do—and eventually what you'll need to do—was go through and find the deeper meanings, find the themes. Are you hitting those points? Take a step back to recognize plot—there is a plot there—and that will help you sequence your story better. Then, it's a matter of combing through your manuscript, word by word, to painstakingly work to improve your phrasing, tone, imagery, pace, and dialogue. All that has to shine before you start to query or before you decide to self-publish—whatever your goal is. This process of editing can easily take longer than writing the original draft.

This is where you also begin to parse those scenes or secrets or dialogue that you were uncomfortable revealing in your first draft. Remember when we talked about that, avoiding censorship? Well, now you get to become the censor again. How much of that do you need to get your story across? Does the scene contribute to forwarding your story? If it doesn't contribute, if it's just there for the shock value or if it's something you just really needed to get out, cut it. You wouldn't believe how many powerful scenes I was able to take out of my story and still not affect the overall story. I would've thought it would because those scenes were so big in my mind and in my memory, but it didn't. *This* is the time when you start doing that. You start thinking about the other people and what you want to say and how you are going to address it.

When I wrote my first draft of *The Mason House*, I was an emotional wreck. I would write a scene or a chapter and then I would leave it overnight. Then, the next morning, I would get up, print it, and read it aloud. There was no one home, so I could read it with all the inflection and animation needed. Almost every time I did that, I would sob, because it had been so long since I was in my gramma's house or felt like I was in her house. It had been a long time since I had thought so closely about her mannerisms or her phrases or what she felt like, all of it. I hadn't thought about it for so many years, and so including that in the memoir brought her to life for me. Many of the scenes in her home were very emotional in my memory, and it made me emotional to read. I didn't know how I was ever going to edit my work when each time I read it I cried. But by the time I got through all my edits, I felt a lot better. I didn't feel like I was sad anymore. I honestly sometimes felt happy reading it—or perhaps just content in my space—because I was in such a different place now. I would always miss my gramma, but I felt like I had finally connected the dots, and that's how my memoir helped me.

In closing, I think the most important thing about writing a painful memoir is when you can step back, edit your story, tweak it, mold it, whatever you need to do to create it, but when you can step back and see your story for story itself, that's a sign that healing has taken place. And that's what happened for me.

1 Harrigan, S. (2020, June 9). How to and (Especially) How Not to Write About Family. https://www.janefriedman.com/

2 Roach Smith, M. (2011, Sept. 20). Don't Write a Memoir to Get Revenge. https://www.janefriedman.com/

3 Raab, D., (2017). Writing for Bliss: A Seven-Step Plan for Telling Your Story and Transforming Your Life. (First Edition). Loving Healing Press.

Houghton, Mich., Loading Copper

Loading copper ingots, Houghton

U.P. Publishers & Authors Association Announces 2nd Annual U.P. Notable Books List

MARQUETTE, MI (January 25, 2021)— the **Upper Peninsula Publishers & Authors Association** (UPPAA) announces the 2nd Annual U.P. Notable Books List this week. UPPAA Publications Chair **Mikel Classen** (Sault Ste. Marie) initiated the effort as a response to the lack of representation of U.P. writers in other Michigan state literary circles. Classen said, "Traditionally, recognition of Michigan books has been dominated by the university presses downstate and we would like to take this opportunity to highlight literature that focuses closer to home for us."

Evelyn Gathu, Director of the Crystal Falls District Community Library, has just teamed up with UPPAA to co-sponsor the **U.P. Notable Book Club**. The club is available to any U.P. resident and features monthly Zoom meetups with national bestselling authors including **Karen Dionne** (*The Marsh King's Daughter*). Members borrow the books from their local libraries or purchase at local stores prior to discussions. Please visit **www. UPNotable.com** for all the latest news!

To build this second annual list, UPPAA consulted with Upper Michigan booksellers, book reviewers, writers, and publishers to winnow down the notable books to a bare ten titles. You can find reviews of many of these books on the **UP Book Review** (www. UPBookReview.com). It must be emphasized that the list is unranked, each title deserves equal merit as U.P. Notable Book. These ten books have been deemed essential reading for every U.P. lover and we highly recommend you ask your local librarian or booksellers for them today!

1. *Kawbawgam: The Chief, The Legend, The Man* by Tyler Tichelaar (Marquette Fiction, 2020)
2. *World War II Conscientious Objectors: Germfask, Michigan the Alcatraz Camp* by Jane Kopecky (2020)
3. *Eden Waits: A Novel Based on the True Story of Michigan's Utopian Community, Hiawatha Colony* by Maryka Biaggio (Milford House, 2019)
4. *In the Night of Memory* by Linda LeGarde (UMN Press, 2020)
5. *Houghton: Birthplace of Professional Hockey* by William J. Sproule (2019)
6. *Michigan Flora: Upper Peninsula, 2nd Ed.* By Steve W. Chadde (Orchard Innovations, 2019)
7. *Dead of November: A Novel of Lake Superior* by Craig Brockman (Curve of the Earth, 2020)
8. *I Spy... Isle Royale,* by Susanna Ausema (Isle Royale and Keweenaw Parks Association, 2019)
9. *Points North* by Mikel B. Classen (Modern History Press, 2018)
10. *Women of the Copper Country: A Novel* by Mary Doria Russel (Atria Books, 2020)

Established in 1998 to support authors and publishers who live in or write about Michigan's Upper Peninsula, UPPAA is a Michigan nonprofit association with more than 100 members, many of whose books are featured on the organization's website at www.uppaa. org. UPPAA welcomes membership and participation from anyone with a UP connection who is interested in writing.

Young U.P. Author Section

UPPAA is extremely pleased to announce the winners of the 4th Annual Dandelion Cottage Contest that celebrates the creative writing of the U.P.'s newest generation of writers! Each winner will take home a cash prize, a commemorative medallion, and a hardcover edition of the *U.P. Reader* in which their submission appears. Additionally, the winner of the Senior Division will have their name inscribed on the traveling trophy which will reside in their school in the coming year. Starting in 2019, we inaugurated two divisions for the contest: Senior (grades 9-12) and Junior (grades 5-8).

This year's participants came from 13 different schools around the U.P. Some schools submitted up to 4 entries from their students. The judges would like to thank each and every student who submitted their work. There were so many great entries in each division that the judges had a difficult time whittling down the list to just three winners for the Senior division and one winner for the Junior division.

Junior Division Winner

• **Annabell Dankert**, Grade 5 (Rudyard Elementary) for "The Dagger of the Eagle's Eye"

Senior Division Winners

• **First Place: Kyra Holmgren**, Grade 12 (Negaunee High School) for "The Treasured Flower"
• **Second Place: Nicholas Painter**, Grade 10 (Whitefish Township Community Schools) for "The Imposter Among Us"
• **Third Place: Walter Dennis**, Grade 10 (Lake Linden-Hubbell High School) for "Ash"

Participating Schools (in alphabetical order)

Marquette County
• Bothwell Middle School, Marquette
• Duke Academy, Marquette
• Gladstone Middle School

- Gwinn High School
- North Star Academy, Marquette
- Joseph K. Lumsden Bahweting Anishnabe PSA
- Negaunee High School

Chippewa County
- Rudyard Elementary
- Soo Theatre, Sault Ste. Marie
- Whitefish Township Community Schools

Houghton County
- Copper Country Christian School
- Dollar Bay/Tamarack City
- Lake Linden-Hubbell High School

Official Dandelion Cottage Contest Rules

- Each teacher may nominate up to two short stories to represent their school.
- Home-school co-ops representing more than ten students will be treated as a school.

- Home-schooled students not affiliated with a local school or co-op may submit directly to the contest.

- Maximum length: 5,000 words.

- Authors must attend or be home-schooled in an Upper Peninsula School District.

- Teachers, parents, and others may offer suggestions and comments, but all writing must be the work of the author. In the real literary world, editors will offer suggestions. This is to be a learning experience.

- Short stories must be submitted electronically in MS Word (preferred) or PDF format by February 1st each year

- First place winner in the high school division will receive $250.

MUNESING HARBOR LAKE SUPERIOR.
W.J.Morgan & Co.Li

Engraving munising harbor trade card

- Second place winner will receive $100.

- Third place winner will receive $50.

- Winning school will receive a trophy for display during the coming year.

- Only one prize ($150) will be awarded for the best middle-school entry.

- Authors will retain the copyright to their work, but UPPAA reserves first publishing rights for eighteen months after submission. Winning entries will be published in the annual U.P. Reader

- For more information please visit www. DandelionCottage.org or write to LS-Buege@aol.com

The Dagger of the Eagle's Eye

by Annabell Dankert (1st Place, Jr. Division)

◆❖◆

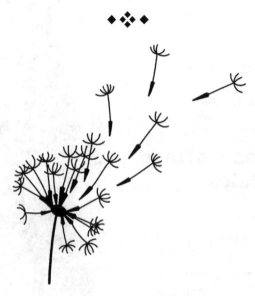

Long, long ago, in a time of knights and dragons, there was a small village. In that small village there was a small cottage. In that small cottage there was a young girl, and her name was Roonie. She had strawberry-blonde hair, deep blue eyes, and a very unusual dream. She wanted to be a knight! Back then, girls weren't allowed to be knights, but that didn't stop her.

One day, when Roonie was doing her chores, she heard a strange noise. It sounded like humming. It was coming from an old, dusty chest. "Great-grandfather's chest!" Roonie exclaimed. Slowly she started to open it.

"Ah! Bless me! Another Sedwick!" a voice boomed. Roonie jumped. A map rose from the chest. "Oh, You look much like your great-grandfather, Roonie!"

"You know me?" Roonie asked, now wondering why she was talking to a map.

The map said, "Hello great-granddaughter of Sir Howard the Third. You are about to go on a great journey. It will make you what you've always wanted to be: a knight," the map said with a sigh.

"How? I'll be all alone? Who even are you?" Roonie said, head full of questions.

"I am a making of man and magic, and the will of your great-grandfather brought me to this world," the map explained. "And you will not be alone. For on your journey, you will meet a young girl, with hair as red as a rose, eyes as green as a tree, and a heart as big as the sea. She is one, of many, to help you." With that final word, the map flew out the window.

"No! Come back! Don't go!" Roonie yelled. Before she realized what she was doing, she flung herself out the window. "Ahhhhh!" Roonie screamed. Thinking quickly, she reached out to a nearby branch. She grabbed it and held on to that flimsy branch for dear life. Five feet off the ground, Roonie decided to let go, but before she had the chance the branch broke and she fell on her behind.

"Ouch...." Roonie groaned. She could see the map in the distance. Swiftly, getting to her feet she ran after it.

The map flew through town. Nobody seemed to see it or care about it. Nobody, but a girl who looked to be about Roonie's age. As the girl bent over to pick it up, Roonie yelled, "Don't touch it! It's mine!" The girl looked up, startled.

"Oh I'm sorry. I didn't see you drop it," the girl said, handing her the map. When Roonie looked up at her she noticed that the girl had hair as red as roses, and eyes the color of trees.

"I'm Roonie. I am leaving this village. I could use some company. Will you join me?" The girl looked stunned, but eventually managed a nod. Roonie realized something. "I never got your name." The girl stopped in her tracks.

Slowly looking up she said, "Loonie. My name is Loonie."

•••

After 30 minutes of walking in silence, Roonie finally asked, "Where are you from, Loonie?"

"A village in the far north," Loonie replied.

"Oh," Roonie said. They didn't say another word to each other until they came to Map Lord's Maps.

"Do you think we need a map? I know the forest pretty well. Wait where are we even going?" Loonie asked.

"Well I have a magical map that can tell us…" Roonie began. But before she could explain Loonie stopped midstep. Roonie looked to see what distracted her.

"What is it?" Roonie asked. Roonie then saw that she wasn't looking for something, she was looking *at* someone! There, leaning against the shop, hidden in the shadows, was a boy. He had thick black hair, blue eyes, and had been looking right at Loonie with a smile. He started to walk right toward them. Loonie was turning pink as he came over.

"Hello. I'm Seth. Who may you be?"

"This is Roonie, and I'm Loonie," Loonie said awkwardly.

Seth smiled.

"Roonie and Loonie, nice to meet you." As he was getting ready to shake their hands, four men came out of the shop across the street. One of them pointed at Seth, the other three ran toward him.

"We should probably get going," Seth said, grabbing Loonie's wrist. They weren't sure what else to do, so they ran through town.

As they started to run, the guards slipped, as though they just stepped on invisible ice. Before Roonie could think too much about it, they came to the kingdom gate.

"This might take a second," Seth said. He moved his right arm to the left then right, then he did the same with his left hand. Roonie knew what he was doing, but it was impossible! *Wizards died out 70 years ago!* Roonie thought. Yet it seemed like the gate was getting thinner and thinner until, suddenly, there was a gap big enough for a teenager to slip through.

"Seth! You're…. You… You're a wizard?" Loonie stuttered. Just then the four men caught up with them.

"The King will be happy to have the last wizard as a prisoner," the fat guard said.

"Go, go, go! In Fox Tail Woods!" Roonie yelled.

They stumbled through the opening and ran like their lives depended on it, because Seth's did. No one ever dared to enter Fox Tail Woods, but it was the only place where they would be safe.

Now with the guards gone, their worries behind them, their adventure began.

•••

"I suppose I should explain some things," Seth said, trying to catch his breath. The trio had been running for an hour before they found a clearing where they could stop and rest for the night.

"So you are a wizard?" Loonie asked, raising an eyebrow.

"Yeah. I guess I can tell you now: I'm a wizard."

Still catching their breath Roonie asked, "Why were you following us? Why were those men chasing you?"

"Well, I had a good feeling about you two." Seth shrugged. "Those men have been hunting the wizards for four years. I'm the last one. No others but me," Seth explained, looking down.

"Ah that may not be true! There are many more than just you!" the map boomed from Roonie's backpack.

"Ahhhh!" Loonie and Seth yelled.

The map flew up into the air and said, "Tis true! In town I saw seven wizards!"

"Why is there a flying, talking map in your bag, Roonie?" Seth asked, with eyes wide. All Loonie could do was nod.

"Seth, Loonie this is my great grandfather's, Sir Howard the Third's, map. It's a creation of man and magic brought here by the will of my great-grandfather. I'm stuck with it," Roonie said trying to calm her friends down.

"Stuck with me? You chose to jump out a window to follow me! You're stuck with me?" the map grumbled, flying back into the bag.

"The important thing is, we're here now. So, do either of you know how to survive in the wild?" Roonie yelled to make herself heard over the stream of questions being thrown at her.

No one heard her over the scream a few yards away. Roonie stumbled back looking for something to defend themselves with. She found a large stick. Seth knew it wouldn't be enough to help them, so he snapped his fingers and the stick turned into a golden sword, and Loonie was suddenly holding a bronze dagger. Roonie was astonished. For being only fourteen, Seth was amazing at magic. On the handle of her sword was a silver eagle. On Loonie's dagger was a golden bear.

Slowly they headed toward the scream. As they crept through the woods, an ember fox darted out from behind a tree. Roonie stopped to stare at it. The fox was so elegant. The longer she stared, the more entranced she became. Something was odd about this fox.

They heard the scream again. Quickly, Roonie snapped to attention. They ran to where they heard the scream. Seconds later they were face to face with a girl, who had to be 12 or 13 years old. She was on the ground writhing in pain. She had chocolate color skin, big brown eyes, and a thick black mop of hair. She stared at them, pleading with her eyes. Her leg was gushing blood. Something had bit her. Seth made a bandage appear. He was going to put it over her leg when the clouds shifted, and the moon appeared.

The injured girl let out a loud scream. Ears sprouted from her head, claws grew from her hands, and a tail perked up. The girl got a deadly look in her eyes. Roonie understood now why the fox they crossed paths with just a moment ago was so enchanting: it was a werefox. Roonie was putting the pieces together, like a puzzle in her mind. This girl had been bitten by the werefox, and she was hungry.

•••

The werefox, who was a girl just seconds before, let out a blood-chilling yelp. Before anyone could do anything, the werefox lunged for Roonie. As quickly as she could, Roonie dived out of the way, but not before the warefox's claws caught on Roonie's bag and ripped it open. The werefox stumbled, then fell. Roonie unsheathed her sword and was prepared to drive the sword into the creature's heart, when a cloud drifted over the moon. The creature was a girl once again, and had a horrified look on her face. Seth rushed over to her, wrapping the bandage around her leg. Giving her a hand, he helped her to her feet.

"I'm Seth. Are you OK?" he asked.

"I am Scarlet. No, I don't think I'm OK. One minute I was running from guards, the next I was attacked by a rabid fox."

"I'm Roonie, and that's Loonie. Why are you running from guards?" Roonie asked.

"I stole something," Scarlet admitted. "I didn't really steal it — it belonged to my great-grandfather, so I just took what should have been mine in the first place," Scarlet said, showing a silver dagger.

"The Dagger of the Eagle's Eye! I've read about its curse!" Loonie said.

"A curse only to its enemies. A single scratch can kill you," Scarlet said.

"We need to get back to camp. We'll move on in the morning," Roonie said, searching the ground to see if anything had fallen from her backpack.

As they walked through the woods, Scarlet asked, "What happened after the fox attack? I just don't remember."

Glancing at one another, wondering if they should tell her, Seth questioned her. "You mean you don't remember? Anything about..." he paused, looking for help.

"Scarlet, there is a reason this is called Fox Tail woods. You were bitten by a werefox. You turned into one and attacked us," Loonie said cautiously, trying to keep her calm.

No one spoke. Not until Scarlet shouted, "Sweet!" Everyone was shocked by this, but were relieved that she took the news so well.

When they finally reached camp they were quite ready to rest. Loonie and Seth practically collapsed. Only Roonie and Scarlet were still awake.

"Scarlet, how did you break into the castle where the dagger was?" Roonie whispered, so she wouldn't wake the others.

"I was gifted the same way my great-grandfather was. He was a spy. He was the only one who could get in and out of castles undetected," Scarlet responded. Roonie had more questions, but she fell asleep before she could ask them.

•••

The morning sun rose, and Roonie rose with it. On her way to collect firewood Roonie heard a small voice. The voice was singing. The voice was calm and smooth. It made Roonie walk towards it like she was under a spell.

"Come now child, don't be scared, you don't make enemies everywhere! Come and see just how cruel and mean people can be. Open your eyes and take my hand. I'll be your guide throughout the land."

Roonie was fixated on the sound. She followed it — drawn to it — getting closer and closer until a pixie was visible. The pixie had dark black hair, and a dress made out of what looked like dead flower petals. The pixie did not seem startled at all by Roonie's presence.

"Come child. Sit with me." The pixie had to be, at most, six inches tall. "I am Beatrix, get your friends! I will take you all somewhere safe." But before the pixie could start her song again, Roonie heard screaming back at their campsite. Without hesitation, Roonie ran as fast as she could back to camp.

"Wait! Don't go that way! STOP!" Beatrix yelled behind her. Forcing herself to resist the voice, Roonie rushed to the campsite. She saw Seth and Scarlet tied up to a tree, and Loonie trapped in a net. They were surrounded by pixies.

•••

"Owasya Owasya!" The fairies were circling Seth, Loonie, and Scarlet when Roonie got there. Roonie was shocked. What happened? A second ago she was talking to a pixie, now they were attacking her friends?

Before she could reach for her sword a net came down around her. The net was made of thorns. All she could do was give a cry of pain.

"Ha!" a pixie laughed. "We just wanted the werefox's knife! But the last wizard, too? We got the gold now!"

The pixies continued their chant, "Owasya, Owasya!"

"What are you doing?!?!" Seth screamed.

"Oh nothing. Just absorbing your power," another pixie said.

"Why? People love you! They look up to you!" Loonie asked.

"It's not love we want! It's fear! Fear of millions!!" a boy pixie said, "The sun will set in a few hours. Until then you'll..." but his words were cut short by an arrow flying out of a tree. It demolished him.

An elf with golden blond curly hair, deep blue eyes, and a big smirk on her face swung down from the tree and landed next to Roonie. With a sword in her hand, she cut the net keeping Roonie pinned. Once Roonie was out, the elf shot an arrow at the rope that tied Loonie's net to a tree. The arrow went right through the net, causing Loonie to drop to the ground. The net immediately fell apart.

"She's trying to save them! Don't let the wizard get away! Start the chant!" a pixie demanded.

"Owasya. Owasya," the pixies started their chant again. A yellow light burst from Seth's mouth and eyes. Scarlet began to transform into a werefox. That's why the pixies needed a full moon. so that Scarlet was at her most powerful.

"Darn it!" the elf said, pulling back arrows. The elf had ten arrows for her bow. Aiming at the swarm of pixies, she shot. The arrows destroyed at least 60 pixies. She shot three more groups of ten arrows. The last few pixies fled into the woods.

The elf cut the rope that bound Seth and Scarlet. Scarlet collapsed to the ground and passed out. Seth managed enough strength to say, "Just... taking a... little... rest. Thanks." Then he passed out too.

Flipping back her hair, the elf turned to Roonie and Loonie, "You have your hands full, I see. I'm Cala, Searcher of the Lost Order."

"The Lost Order? You mean..." Loonie trailed off.

"Wizards, yeah." Cala said. "I'm searching for the last group of wizards. The elves used to worship them. They were leaders. Ever since they vanished, elves have sent seven children to locate them. I'm one of them. We need our leaders back. We need to make sure that they are safe from the people who took them," Cala said with a deep sigh.

"We should get moving," Cala said, as she hoisted Seth on her shoulder. Roonie had Scarlet on hers. Loonie had her dagger out of its sheath, just in case the pixies came back.

They continued on their journey believing all was well. But that feeling would end in just a few minutes.

•••

As they were walking, a strange sound could be heard. It sounded like a thousand birds. It was getting closer.

"Let's get some cover," Cala suggested, nodding to some bushes. Before they could move, a shadow flew over them. The shadow resembled a giant bird. Turning around they saw that the bird was a ten-foot tall condor, with talons as large as Roonie's sword, and it was heading straight toward them!

Roonie could not see. There was so much movement; so much noise. She heard Loonie scream. Then, there was silence. Roonie looked up. She saw Loonie and Scarlet, looking pale. At first, Roonie was relieved, because it seemed the bird hadn't done any damage, but soon it became clear that all was not well.

"It took them!" yelled Loonie. "It took Cala and Seth!" They didn't know at the time, but the condor was taking their new friends somewhere. To *someone*. Although she could no longer see the bird, Roonie could hear the screams from a mile away.

•••

In the Condor's talons, all that Cala could see were trees and more trees, and an enormous castle in the distance. Before she could grab an arrow her bow slipped from her grip. She watched her only form of defense fall to the ground below.

The giant bird released them outside the castle where seven guards waited for them. "Get moving you two!" said the small guard with a deep voice. Four guards, one on each side, grabbed their arms and walked them into the castle. They took them to the throne room where a princess sat waiting for them.

"Well, well, well. If it isn't the brat who stole the most powerful weapon in the world. So where is it? Where is the Dagger of the Eagle's Eye?" she asked, rudely. Seth glanced at Cala. She seemed just as confused as he was. Suddenly he remembered: *Scarlet's dagger! What did she call it?* he thought. Cala, however, looked like she could kill the princess in front of her.

"What are you talking about? Why did you bring us here?" she yelled.

"Hmm. That doesn't sound like an answer to *my* question. Maybe a trip to the dungeon will help you think." A smirk grew on the princess's face. Guards rushed towards the bewildered pair. "Put them in Spike Eel Cell," the princess commanded. They tried to dodge out of the way but the guards were fast and dragged them to the dungeon.

Not sure of their fate, they could only hope that their friends would come to save them.

•••

As they were being led to the dungeon, they could have sworn that the guards were shaking. Before they knew what was happening, they were tossed into a pool full of dark water surrounded by bars.

"Welcome to Spike Eel Cell. Have a nice swim," the guard smirked, slamming the cell door.

Trying to swim out of the pool, Cala felt something brush her leg. She looked down and let out a shriek. An eel was circling her. The eel was at least five feet long. It had grayish-blue scales. What scared her the most was the fact that it had sharp spikes buzzing with electricity. Seth saw it too and was frozen with fear.

"We have to get out of here," Cala said. All Seth could do was nod. As if a lightbulb lit up in her head, Cala got an idea.

"That way!" she cried, pointing. "Swim that way! I'll swim this way!"

Seth understood what she was trying to do. The eel couldn't follow them both. The question was, though, who would it follow?

Seth began to swim. Then he swam faster, until the spike eel was no longer behind him. Quickly, he jumped onto the bars of the cell lifting his legs out of the water. Cala was swimming towards him, with the eel at her heels. She jumped for the bars, but not before the eel got a good zap on her leg. Seth caught her in mid jump. Her leg was shaking.

Seth took a deep breath. "Take my hand," said Seth, extending his arm. Cala grabbed hold of it, though she wasn't sure why. Before she knew it Seth muttered a few mixed up words. The wall became a doorway.

Outside they saw Roonie, Loonie and Scarlet trying to climb the castle walls. They nearly fell off it when they heard them calling their names.

Roonie was overjoyed to see Cala and Seth running towards them. "You guys are alright!!" she shouted.

Cala asked, "How did you guys get here so fast?"

"That's a story for another time," Roonie replied mysteriously.

"Uh, I hate to break up the happy reunion, but we need to stop the princess. I think she's after Scarlet and her dagger," Cala said while pointing at the castle. "I don't think she'll stop at anything to get the Dagger of the Eagle's Eye."

•••

Scarlet led the way to the castle, everyone careful to follow her steps. When she darted around a corner, everyone else did too. They did this until they got to the throne room. The only one in the room was the princess. She sat up abruptly.

"Who dares to enter my throne room?!" she shrieked. Scarlet made her way to the throne, revealing the dagger.

When the princess saw the dagger, she sneered, "You! You...You thief! Guards! Guards!" Twenty-five guards marched into the room. When they saw Ronan pointing at the group of teenagers, they flew into action. Taking out their swords they charged at them.

Barely having time to prepare their weapons, Seth shot fireballs from his fingertips, sending the guards tumbling backwards. With that minor delay, the team whipped out their weapons, and engaged in battle with the guards. It was five to one, but they had a wizard, an elf, a master thief and two brave girls. The battle had begun.

Two guards charged towards Scarlet, but Scarlet being a master of stealth, easily dodged the attacks. Out of nowhere, Scarlet whipped out the dagger and drove it into one of the men's armor. Luckily, the soldier's armor was so thick, that it didn't touch his skin. It did, however, send him running from the throne room, thinking that it had.

Loonie and Roonie were back to back, Roonie blocking as many swords as she could. Loonie was throwing her dagger at soldier after soldier. Whenever it missed, due to it's magic powers, it would always come back to her like a boomerang. The dagger hit the guard in the shoulder, causing him to collapse onto the ground.

Seth and Cala were fighting close together. Cala, even without her bow, was a very good fighter. She was throwing kicks and punches. Seth could feel her presence behind him. He wondered if it was suddenly hot in the throne room, or if he was imagining it. They were drawn closer together — now back-to-back. Seth saw a tooth fall to the ground, and a guard clutch his mouth. Cala had knocked his tooth out. Seth knew at that moment that he was standing back-to-back with the coolest woman on the planet.

The princess kicked Scarlet in the gut. Scarlet, bent over in pain, let the dagger drop to the floor with a clatter. Roonie, and the rest of the squad, heard the most horrifying laugh they had ever heard. When they turned at the evil sound, they saw Scarlet on the ground, clutching her stomach, and the princess holding the dagger.

Roonie, Loonie, Seth and Cala ran towards the princess in a fit of rage. A guard grabbed Loonie. Roonie ran back to help free her. She drew her sword, and swung it at the man's leg just as she heard a different blade fly through the air...

•••

"NO!" Seth yelled, running towards Cala. The Dagger of the Eagle's Eye was flying through the air, right towards Cala's heart. Seth had never run so fast, but it felt like he was running in slow motion. Cala couldn't get out of the way fast enough. She was prepared to die right there, but the dagger never hit her.

Seth was on the ground. Blade in his heart. Scarlet, rising slowly to her feet, saw Seth. Her kind heart was filled with anger and hate.

A voice in her head encouraged Scarlet to go to the dagger. She went over to Cala who was bending over Seth, the guards now gone. Roonie and Loonie were trying to do something. Anything. Scarlet marched over to them. They all looked up at her. She bent over Seth. Cala, with tears in her eyes, was heartbroken. One of Cala's tears fell on his head. Gold spun around him. He coughed. Then opened his eyes.

Roonie and Loonie were shocked. So was Seth.

"H... How?" he stammered.

Cala thought she knew the answer, "Elves have a unique gift. I...I can heal." Without thinking he pulled her in for a kiss. Scarlet wasn't interested in that, though. Reaching down she pulled the dagger out of Seth's chest.

"Ahhh!" Seth yelped. The princess was scowling on the throne when Scarlet walked up. She grabbed the princess by the throat and hoisted her up on the wall.

"Scarlet!! What are you doing?!" Roonie yelled.

"What I should have done a long time ago." Scarlet sneered, spinning the dagger in her hand. "She came to my village when I was a young child to claim it as her own. She took my parents, and all the village leaders, and

killed them. It's time to make up for that." She pulled back the dagger.

"Scarlet, please!! Stop! I know it must be hard. I have no idea what you have been through!" Loonie pleaded. "But trust me, it will get better! You have us now! You will never be alone again!"

Scarlet, on the verge of tears, dropped the dagger. Together they fled the castle before Scarlet could change her mind. They took a condor to the mountainside, where they prepared to say goodbye, and go their separate ways. Seth and Cala were off on a quest to search the world for the last wizards, trying to bring back the lost nation. Scarlet, Loonie, and Roonie were determined to continue Roonie's original mission.

"We'll see each other again... right?" Seth said, holding out his hand. Loonie placed her hand on Seth's. Roonie, Cala, and Scarlett did the same. Seth, still clutching his wound, waved his hand over their joined hands. Bands appeared on their wrists like tattoos. Roonie looked at hers. It showed them all, right there, in that exact moment.

"They'll help us see each other when we miss each other," Seth said. With those final words, he hopped on the condor, Cala right behind him. They took off toward the mountain — the place where they would first look for the wizards.

"Ah. Well, that was fun. Now, if you listen to me, and stay focused, we have to head due north before the world ends," the map suggested, interrupting the moment.

Annabell Dankert is a fifth grade student at Rudyard Elementary (Chippewa County). She spends her days reading, writing, and drawing. She can often be found reading two or three books at a time, and writing two or three stories at a time. She even keeps a notebook by her bed so she can write down story ideas as they come to her. Annabell loves being outside and all things animals, including training her dog, Nikki. Annabell enjoys going fishing and camping with her family, and has a compliment for everyone she comes in contact with.

The Treasured Flower

by Kyra Holmgren (1st Place, Sr. Divison)

◆❖◆

It was a quiet May morning, and the sun had just begun to rise and make the dewdrops glisten. A tabby cat lay on the grass, watching the butterflies with mild interest. The cat's owner sat nearby. Armed with thick gardening gloves and pruning shears, she was tackling an unruly oleander bush. Loose strands of blonde hair had escaped from her braid and fell in her face, and the knees of her jeans were covered in dirt. She was deep in thought, and so she was startled by the slam of a door. The cause of the racket, a young girl in pajamas, strode over to the bush.

"Audrey, what are ya doing out here?" she asked, her voice still husky from sleep.

"Working. What does it look like?" Audrey responded, never looking up from the bush she was pruning.

"Well I know that! But I just thought you'd be in the greenhouse, looking at that one flower. The Chef's Barkspur?"

"It's the Baker's Larkspur. And I would be, but have you been in there recently? They're all dead." Audrey punctuated this with an aggressive snip from her pruning shears, and grimaced at the result. The girl seemed just as oblivious as ever to her sister's mood.

"Really? Aw, that sucks. Hey, there's Pebble!"

"Oh no..." she knew how this would end.

"Hey, what's that supposed to mean? I was looking all over for Pebble, but I couldn't find him! How could you hide my best friend from me? He was probably lonely!"

"Edith. Pebble doesn't like you," she stated dryly.

"No, he does too like me! Watch!" Edith strode over to the cat, whose relaxing nap in the sunlight was interrupted by a set of arms snatching him up. As she held the cat tightly to her chest, he yelped and tried to struggle free from her arms. After a scuffle between the two, the cat freed itself and leapt to the ground. With a huff, it padded over to Audrey and meowed, as if he were complaining.

Audrey looked over her shoulder. "You know, he's going to bite you if you keep doing that."

"Whatever! C'mon inside with me, Dad's making pancakes!"

Audrey sighed and slowly stood up, squinting as the sunlight hit her eyes, showcasing the freckles spread on her face like freshly sown seeds. Dusting the dirt off her pants, she followed Edith to the door, with Pebble in tow. When she got to the door, she found Edith waiting there, with a sheepish smile on her face.

"I might've... uh... locked the door when I came out..."

Shaking her head, Audrey removed a key from her carabiner on her belt and opened the door. "I'll never understand how you keep doing that," she mumbled, as Edith happily bounced inside. They were greeted with the sweet smell of pancakes, and Audrey's stomach growled in response.

"Hey girls! Could one of you grab the syrup for me?"

"Sure, I'll get it." Audrey strode over to the pantry and reached for the syrup on the top shelf. Unfortunately, she didn't see Edith's eyes and eyebrows scrunched in determination, and when Edith charged over to the pantry and smashed into her, she was not prepared, and she promptly fell on her butt.

"Hey! What are you doing?" Audrey yelped in surprise.

"I want to get the syrup! Get out of my way!"

"No, you're too short. God, you're annoying," she said after rolling her eyes.

"Dad! She's being mean to me!" whined Edith.

"Get moving, Thumbelina," Audrey ordered.

"No! I'm getting it!" Edith said, defiance filling her voice. The tone of the conversation had quickly shifted, similar to how a cloudy day quickly becomes a thunderstorm. Audrey let out a huff, and they wordlessly had a staring match, neither of them relenting. They were those plants that never seem to perk up no matter how much water you give them; stubborn and sour. Edith smirked, and you could practically feel Audrey's patience snap like a rubber band. Audrey marched forward and shoved Edith out of the way, with a little more force than was necessary. Immediately, and predictably, Edith began to protest.

"Dad! Dad! Did you see that? Audrey pushed me on purpose! She hurt me!" Edith was using the classic theatrics known to younger siblings.

"Don't be overdramatic. I hardly touched you," Audrey responded, the classic older sibling response that would conveniently absolve herself of blame.

Their father sighed, "Clearly, neither of you are morning people. Edith, stop antagonizing your sister. Audrey, be nice."

The girls exchanged one last glare at each other before settling at the dining table. As soon as Audrey set the syrup down, Edith immediately grabbed the bottle and drenched her pancakes, draining half the bottle and letting syrup run down the sides in the process. She evilly grinned, waiting for Audrey's reaction, but was disappointed when she was ignored. For all that trouble, she was only rewarded with an eye twitch, and now her pancakes were islands in a sea of syrup.

Audrey was careful not to show it, but internally she smirked at her younger sister dejectedly picking at her syrup with a side of pancakes. She turned to her father, who was intently reading the newspaper laid out under his plate. Deciding not to comment on the few droplets of syrup on his shirt, she asked: "So, Dad. What's your plans for today?"

He looked up at her, and she wondered how it was possible to get syrup on your glasses. She was even more impressed by the fact that he didn't even seem to notice it, and for their entire conversation, she had to pretend that one of his dirt brown eyes didn't look covered in syrup. Rather than dwell on this, she simply decided to imagine that he had heterochromia, just for today.

"Hmm, well, I was going to examine that plant Edith found the other day. So, I'll probably be in the lab, although I have a meeting with the park ranger today as well."

"Oooh, are you guys going to be outside?"

"No, we're just going to be discussing wildfires, seeing how it's that time of year again. Safety precautions, warning signs, all that boring crap."

"Oh... so you're not hiking around today?" she said, miserably failing to keep the disappointment out of her voice.

"No... but you know, Audrey, you're a young woman now. I bet you don't even need my supervision anymore."

"That is true..."

"Hmm. Maybe I should make you take your sister. I'm not sure I trust her to be unsupervised yet," he suggested.

"HEY! You can trust me! I'm mature for my age!" Edith squawked, indignant at the notion that she was just a little kid.

He laughed, "Haha, I'll just let you two decide." Her father got up to leave, but before he left, he paused and turned to Audrey. "Also, make sure you wash the dishes." After hearing Audrey's groan and Edith's snicker, he added to his request. "Edith, you dry them," With that, he turned and shut the door gently behind himself.

Audrey's chair screeched on the floor as she got up. She carried all the dishes to the sink, except for Edith's. She was still sitting in her chair, pouting. "C'mon Edith, Dad said you have to help." She looked over to her younger sister. "And could you put away the syrup too? Whatever's left of it, anyways."

Edith didn't respond, but Audrey could hear a chair being dragged across the kitchen in the direction of the pantry. She struggled to not laugh at Edith's stomping footsteps drawing closer, and at how violently Edith grabbed a towel. However, when she applied the same violence to the glass plates, Audrey became a little concerned.

"Sheesh, be careful. I don't want to have to clean up glass," she warned.

"Hmmph, if you're going to be bossy about it, then maybe you should do it yourself," Edith retorted, although her movements slowed, seemingly taking her older sister's advice.

"I'm not the one forcing you to do this, but whatever." They worked in silence after that, Audrey reluctantly scrubbing the dishes and Edith putting little effort into actually drying them. When they were almost finished, Audrey looked over to her, and hesitated before asking her question.

"Hey, Edith? Will you come into the woods with me?"

"Why should I? You're being mean to me, and I don't really feel like it."

"Wha— you were the one who started that! But never mind, would you please just come with me?"

Edith sighed. "Ah, sure. I was just messing with ya anyway. I know you're scared of the woods."

"Where on earth did you get that idea? I'm not scared!" Audrey protested.

"Sure, you aren't. It's not like you're scared of the bears, or cougars, or wolves. And I know you don't worry about getting lost or injured when you're alone. All by yourself. Nobody there to help. Juuuust you. Yep. I bet you're not scared at all," Edith said, quite sarcastically.

"I—" Audrey started to defend herself, before realizing how useless that would be. Damn it, why did her little sister have to be so good at making observations? She's as watchful as Pebble when he spots a mouse. "You are so annoying. C'mon, let's go. And put down the cat, he's not coming with us."

"Aww..."

And so, two hours later, they found themselves tromping through dry moss patches and swatting at the mosquitos swarming around them. Audrey didn't seem to mind, her thoughts occupied by identifying the flora around them. Edith, sweating and bored, did seem to mind. Edith tried to bear it, but she was not a fan of heat, boredom, or mosquitos. The unholy combination finally got to her, and she cried out in exasperation.

"Uggghhh! I'm so tired of this! When can we go back in?" she almost sobbed as another mosquito landed on her.

Audrey sighed. "Fine, we'll head back in a while. I just want to see what's up here." "It's probably just more stupid moss. Man, I'll never get what's up with you and plants. Same with dad too. You guys are like, obsessed," she complained.

"I'm sorry we appreciate the beauty of life, Edith," Audrey retorted, matching her sister's earlier sarcasm.

"Wow, Audrey, you sure did get off—"

"Edith," Audrey interrupted.

"What?" Edith replied, annoyed at the interruption. She was about to complain about it, until she noticed that Audrey had stopped in her tracks. "Audrey?"

Wordlessly, Audrey stepped forward and leaned down, her hand gently cupping a small blue flower. She studied it intensely for a moment, before turning to her sister with a smile. "Edith, come look."

She approached Audrey, and crouched down so she could peer down at the dark blue flowers in her sister's cupped palm. They were a bit dry, but they were still unmistakable. Edith gasped, "Is that the..."

"Delphinium bakeri. Commonly known as the baker's larkspur," Audrey finished Edith's sentence. "I can't believe we stumbled across this. And look around us, Edith, there's more! Do you know how rare these are now? If we take this back to the lab, we could save the species!" Audrey's eyes were practically glowing with excitement.

"Woah... honestly, I don't really care about plants but that's kinda neat."

"Saving a whole species from extinction is 'kinda neat'?"

"Excuse me, but I'm not a plant nerd! I'm trying here!"

Audrey ignored that last statement. "Hmm... I don't have the materials to transplant these flowers. We'll have to head back and tell dad."

"Finally!" Edith exclaimed with relief, not even hesitating for a second before turning around and starting the march back home.

•••

The humidity of the greenhouse was getting to be a bit unbearable; especially accompanied by the heat of June. Audrey wiped her sleeve across her brow. She had just come to check on the flowers she'd found a few weeks ago; she hadn't meant to stay so long. But something about being surrounded by all these healthy little flowers, so endangered that it'd be a miracle if they didn't go extinct, filled her with a sense of euphoria. It was as if a flower inside her had just started to bloom. And in this environment, the flowers were thriving. They had stopped blooming due to the season change, but their stems were a lively green and moist to the touch. Audrey had even taken the opportunity to plant some outside, and although that had been a bit self-indulgent, the flowers thrived under the constant maintenance outside as well.

Audrey stood up and walked to the door leading outside of the greenhouse. She looked out the window to see her father eating lunch in the garden, and she suddenly noticed the familiar pangs of hunger that always overcame her after getting lost in her work. She stepped out the door, and took one last glance at the lush greenery. Her eyes held onto the sight of the baker's larkspur for a moment longer, and she smiled to herself before joining her father.

"Well, hello, Audrey. Glad to see you're still alive. You were in there so long, I was beginning to worry," he teased.

"Yeah, yeah. I'm fine. Starving, though," Audrey replied. She pulled out a chair and sat down across from him. "Boy, the sky is awfully hazy today," she observed.

"Mm, that's just the perks of living in California, I suppose. It's such a surprising sight, given the time of year." He took a sip of his coffee. "Go ahead, take a sandwich. I don't want to see you get hangry."

"I'm not hangry! Ugh, I wish you'd stop saying that!"

"Oh dear. I spoke too soon," he mumbled under his breath. He spoke up to reply to her. "Oh, I'm sorry, sweetie. But still, you should eat."

"Fine." she said, before angrily snatching a sandwich and taking an aggressive bite from it. She munched in silence while he drank his coffee and admired the garden.

"Wow, those daylilies really do look nice next to the orchids. Although, I must admit, I'm fond of the pitcher plants as well." He took a sip, and paused. "Of course, my personal favorite has to be the baker's larkspur. It's a miracle that you were able to even find some, much less rehabilitate them. I'm proud of you, ya know."

Audrey looked up from her sandwich. "Oh... thanks!" she responded awkwardly. She looked out past the garden, at a worn-down dirt trail leading into the forest. "Hey dad, could we take a walk today?"

"Well, that sandwich certainly seems to have fixed your attitude. And of course, I'll come, seeing as I'm not very busy today." He rose from his chair and looked at her expectantly.

"Oh, now? Okay." Audrey got up too, taking a sip of water and wiping her mouth off. The two of them entered the woods, the sound of their footsteps accompanied by the trees rustling in the strong wind.

"So," her father cleared his throat. "How are you?"

"Oh, I'm fine. You?"

"Ah, same ol, same ol. But really, how are you? You seem to be doing much better lately, but a while ago, you seemed to be in a bit of a funk."

"Did I?"

"Yes, you did. Your sister would not stop complaining about how you were ignoring her, and you didn't seem as talkative as your usual self."

"Oh. Yeah, I guess I kinda was. I think I was just kinda bored, with nothing exciting happening and not many people I could talk to. It gets a little lonely out here, with nobody but you guys around. I wasn't making much progress with the larkspur either. But once I found the flowers, it gave me some motivation, and it didn't seem impossible to save them. Now, I have something to work toward."

"That's good. You know, I worry about you sometimes."

Just before she could reply to him, she was interrupted by a wail, and turned around, letting out a small gasp of surprise as she saw her sister running towards them.

"Audrey! Dad!" Edith shouted, tears rolling down her face. In her arms, Pebble lay trapped, looking frazzled from being held close to Edith for so long.

"Edith! What is it?" he demanded.

"There's a fire! And it's getting way too close to the house! What do we do?"

"We have to go, now!" he ordered. "Edith, Audrey, let's go."

"Dad! What about the larkspur?"

"Audrey, I'm sorry, but we have to leave it!"

"No, I can't abandon it! The species will go extinct if that fire gets to it!"

"Forget about the damn plant! Our lives are more important."

Audrey was conflicted. She looked frantically from her father and Edith's concerned faces, back to the direction of the greenhouse. She hesitated, but before she could

think, her feet had already made the decision. She turned and sprinted away from her family, and toward the fire.

"Audrey, no!" Edith cried out.

"Get back here right now, it's too dangerous!" he commanded, but she was already out of sight. He started to follow her, but stopped in his tracks, and turned to Edith, whose eyes were wide and tear-filled. He grimaced as he turned around, grabbed Edith's small hand, and ran, dragging her along with him out of the woods, in the opposite direction from Audrey.

•••

Audrey panted as she ran. She was exhausted, but she was filled with determination, like a newborn turtle struggling to reach the water. She was so close! A rabbit darted out from the brush beside her, but she paid it no mind. Her legs felt like lead, and her lungs were protesting, but despite the danger, a stubborn desire to save that plant had ignited in her, and nothing could snuff it out. She coughed from the smoke; it was getting harder and harder to breathe. Smoke filled her vision, and she could see an orange glow in the distance. She decided to keep her eyes on her feet, and when the trail beneath her started to look familiar, she looked up and gasped.

The garden was ablaze, and the table she'd shared with her father less than two hours ago was quickly becoming ash. So were most of the flowers in the garden, and the ones still alive didn't have much time left. The sight of the garden caught in angry, unforgiving flames made her feel like someone had just stabbed her. She had spent countless hours of her childhood in this garden, and now it was burning before her very eyes. Waves of heat washed over her, and with desperation, she looked to the greenhouse, hidden in smoke. A small, candle flicker of hope ignited within her, and she quickly formulated the best route to get there. She started to run, before hearing a loud crash behind her and another wave of heat. Audrey spared a glance behind her, and realized a flaming tree had fallen right where she was standing only a minute ago. Shit, that could've hit her. A pang of fear sprung up in her chest and threatened to overtake her, but she pushed it down. It was far too late for her to turn back now, and Audrey had a mission.

She reached the door, and growled in frustration when the door wouldn't budge. Frantically, she ripped her carabiner of keys off her waist, and rapidly sorted through them, looking for the right one. Finding the greenhouse key, she slammed it in the keyhole, and marched inside. She almost passed out from the heat; she hadn't even considered how warm the greenhouse would be with a blazing fire surrounding it. Grabbing a few small pots, she raced to the flowers she'd worked so hard to save. Seeing those tiny green stems still unharmed, she allowed herself a sigh of relief. Audrey was thankful; if the flowers were already ablaze, her hopes would've been crushed and she would've endangered herself for nothing. She slung her backpack off her back, unzipped it, and grabbed the trowel she always kept inside. She started transplanting the flowers, with the speed of a rabbit and the caution of a tortoise. Once she was satisfied with the flowers she'd potted, she nestled them in her bag, positioning them so they would be the least jarred by her escape from the fire.

The fire was creeping in the greenhouse now, and her back was hot. She needed to get out, now. She looked to the window, and she hurled the trowel in her hand with the most strength she could muster. The glass shattered, letting more smoke pour in, and she darted to the window. She crawled out, not even noticing her hands bleeding from the shards. She ran away from the house, but a sickening feeling in her gut stopped her, and she paused to cough. Audrey was somewhat regretting her decision now; how was she going to make it out of the fire?

As she stared down the road, she squinted. The smoke looked... weird. A few moments later, she realized that it was a light, and it was coming closer to her. She almost sobbed in relief when she saw her dad's familiar red pickup truck approaching, its one still functioning headlight illuminating the smoke. Oh, thank god, she was going to be saved!

It rumbled to a stop beside her, and she just had time to leap in and slam the door before the truck did a U-turn, tires squealing on the old, worn out pavement. Her father looked at her through the rearview mirror, and just shook his head, although the look on his face was one more of relief than anger. In the passenger seat sat Edith, and she turned around to look at her older sister.

"Audrey..." she started, and then smirked. "I got shotgun." With apparently nothing else to say, she turned back in her seat and stared out the window. Unfortunately, this comment broke the ice, and allowed her dad to begin his lecture.

"Audrey, what the hell were you thinking? You could've gotten killed!" he said.

"I'm really sorry, Dad. That was pretty stupid of me," Audrey apologized. He didn't seem to hear her, and continued his rant.

"I'm serious, Audrey, do you know how dangerous that was? Do you know what could've happened?"

"I'm sorry for worrying you, Dad. But I got the flower!"

"That's great and all, but I'm just glad you're okay. Don't pull any more stupid shit like that, okay?" he requested.

"Okay!" she agreed. They all sat in silence after that, her father driving, Edith looking out the window, and Audrey lost in thought. She snapped out of her thoughts when she realized she should check on the flowers. She quietly zipped the backpack open, and took a look inside. Some of the dirt had spilled in her bag, but she smiled when she saw her beloved plants sitting safely in the pots. She reached in the bag and held them so the truck wouldn't jostle them. It wasn't long until the motion of the truck rocked her to sleep, her hand still cradling the flowers.

Kyra Holmgren is a senior at Negaunee High School. Her hobbies include reading, writing, and playing video games. Kyra's favorite reading genres are fantasy and young adult. She has three dogs, and she loves to dote on them. She also enjoys spending time outdoors, although she's not very fond of the cold.

The Imposter Among Us

by Nicholas Painter (2nd Place, Sr. Division)

◆❖◆

"AAAAAAAAHHHHHHHH!"

A scream pierced the air throughout the station, waking Blue from a deep sleep. He looked around to see the rest of the crew sitting up in their beds, also woken by the noise.

"What was that!?" exclaimed Red, who slept in the bed next to Blue.

"It sounded like someone screaming," Blue replied.

"I know that but who screamed?" Red asked.

"I have a feeling it was Pink," Green said, "Look, her bed is empty!" he pointed to her bed.

Everyone looked to where he was pointing to see that was true, the bed was empty. They all looked around to see if anyone else was missing. Her bed was the only empty one. Blue, Red, Green, Yellow, and Brown were all in the room. So, what happened?

"OK, I think we should go look for her," Yellow said. "I'll head up to cams, the rest of you look around the halls."

"Sounds like as good of a plan as any to me," Blue said as he hopped out of his bed. The rest of the crew also got up and they went their separate ways. Blue looked around the hall calling out for Pink every few seconds. When he rounded the corner he found her, but not in a way he would have liked to. She was lying on the ground, or at least half of her was. Her torso was missing and only a single bone stuck out above her waistband.

"AHH! Guys! I found her!"

The rest of the crew ran to Blue to see what made him scream, and they all saw Pink's corpse lying in the center of the hall. They just stared, mouths open, at what they saw.

"OK," commented Brown, "Not to state the obvious, but if Pink's dead, that means one of us killed her. We all have the alibi that we were all in the living quarters, sleeping at the time we heard her scream. Did anyone see anything suspicious?" The crew all shook their heads. Just then, the ventilation system kicked on, causing a chill to run across the group, but it gave Blue an idea.

"The killer could have used the ventilation system to make a quick getaway to the quarters," he said.

"Sounds like you know what you're talking about, Blue!" exclaimed Red as he backed away. "Are you the one who killed Pink? For all we know, she was alive when you found her, you could have killed her and then called for us!"

"Red, there is no reason to start pointing fingers yet," Green remarked. "We are all very upset about this. Yellow, did you see anything on cams?"

"Nothing, but it seems that the cams won't record anymore." Yellow replied. "They only show live feed, almost like someone cut the wires leading to the recorder."

"We have to find the killer," Brown commanded. "If anyone would like to confess, we could get this over with. But if not, this whole crew could fall apart."

The whole crew stayed silent. Blue looked around, Red was studying him, Brown was looking from person to person, Green looked worried, Yellow was looking at the ground. "If no one is going to say anything," barked Brown, "then we are just going to have to wait till someone fesses up."

They all headed back to the living quarters to get ready for all the work they had to do. Blue looked at his list of things to do and saw something out of the corner of his eye, a vent cover on the wall next to Red's bed.

"You just wanted me dead, didn't you Red!" Blue shouted. "There is a vent right next to your bed, it would have been super easy for you to just calmly make your way back after murdering Pink! I made the connection of the vent so you accused me to make sure I couldn't figure out it was you! Well, now we know who the killer truly is!"

"Is it true Red?" asked Green, "Did you kill Pink?"

"W-what!?" Red took a step back. "No! I wouldn't kill anyone! Least of all Pink! She was my cousin!"

"Then justify why you are the one who first started accusing others," demanded Yellow, "And this!" She picked up a screwdriver covered with blood from the floor next to Red's bed. "Since we have no place to lock him up, I vote we throw Red off of the ship to prevent any more killings!"

"All in favor?" Brown asked.

Yellow, Blue, and Brown raised their hands. "Green? What about you?"

"I... I don't know! We are sentencing a man to death! He won't last ten seconds out in space!" He thinks for a moment. "Fine... I vote to throw him..."

"What!? Guys! I'm your friend! I wouldn't kill anyone! Please! Don't kill me!"

They all grabbed him and hauled him off to the storage room where the airlock was.

"Any last words, Red?" Blue asked.

"Nothing..." they set him on the ground inside the airlock, and flipped the switch. A large door came down and sealed off the airlock from the rest of the storage. A single tear fell from Red's downcast face. The outer door quickly opened and Red flew out into space.

"Now that the killer has been kicked out of the station," Brown said, "We can work on our tasks for today."

"Someone is going to have to pick up Pink and Red's tasks," Green commented.

"I'll take Red's," Yellow said, "Who wants Pink's?"

"I'll take hers," Brown replied.

So the crew headed off to do their tasks, but not before a siren sounded, indicating that the oxygen system had been remotely shut down. The siren started counting down till the crew runs completely out of oxygen.

60, 59, 58...

"Quick, someone needs to head down to the Oxygen room to fix the system and get us more air!" Brown shouted over the sirens.

"I'll head down there," Blue volunteered. He ran off in the direction of the Oxygen room. When he reached the room, he input the code written next to the keypad. He then made his way off to administration to input a second code but was stopped dead in his tracks when he saw Brown's head lying on the table in the center of the room.

"B-Brown! No!" Blue screamed.

5, 4, 3, 2, 1. Oxygen depleted, please input code...

Blue focused and input the code into the keypad, and the sirens stopped screaming.

Oxygen restored.

Now that the disaster was over, he shifted focus over to the head on the table just as Green ran into the room.

"Blue! What Hap..." Green started and then saw the head on the table. "BROWN! Blue! You killed Brown! How could you!?"

"What! Me? I came in here to turn on the oxygen and found his head on the table!"

"Likely story, but you are the only person in here! You just didn't have time to hide in the vent!" Green sprinted out of the room and screamed "YELLOW! HELP!" Blue sat down in one of the chairs and tried to think of who the killer could be. Could it be Green? Or was it Yellow? But he knew one thing for sure. Red wasn't the one who killed pink.

A dark shadow crossed into the doorway and crept its way forward, unnoticed by Blue. A large gap opened up in the thing's face, exposing rows of sharp teeth. Blue looked up in time to see the mouth open and rolled out of the way just as a large spiked tongue shot out of it.

"NO!" a scratchy voice screamed. "Get back here, you idiot!" It twisted toward Blue as he ran out of the room, and straight into Green, who stumbled over onto the floor.

"Now you're knocking me over?" Green scolded Blue. "What is wron— OH MY GOD!"

Blue helped Green stand up and they ran down the hall. Gunshots started going off behind them. Blue looked back to see the large black figure had morphed into Yellow. But Yellow was running faster than either of the boys could dream of going.

"Quick," Blue whispered, "into storage, let's try to get her into the airlock!" They ran into the airlock and she stopped at the door.

"You think you can fool me?" she said, in a voice that seemed to be a mixture of her original voice and a beast's. "You two are so stupid!" She slammed her hand on the button on the wall, causing the airlock door to shut, but before the door could shut, Green made his way out of the door, but Blue was unable to make it out and the rear door opened, sucking Blue out into space.

Emergency Oxygen Supply Activated. Time remaining: 10 minutes.

Blue floated through space but he saw something out of the corner of his eye: Red's body, helmet removed, head missing. It looked like he took life into his own hands and didn't wait for his emergency oxygen to run out. Blue thought about doing the same but decided if he waited, Green might be able to let him back in. He tried to swim through space to get to the airlock door and banged on the door.

Emergency Oxygen Supply Depleted. Time remaining: 30 seconds.

The big door opened and he swam in to see the window covered in blood and a shadow with its hand on the button on the wall. The big door shut behind him and the blood-covered door opened and Blue saw a pair of yellow boots standing in front of him. As the door opened, Yellow's body fell into the airlock, and Green stood above her, with his hand outstretched, offering to help Blue stand up.

"Thanks man," Blue said, "How did you kill her?"

"Who said she was the only one?" Green replied, and the last thing Blue saw was Green's spiked tongue right before it shot through his head.

Nicholas Painter is a 10th grader at Whitefish Twp Community School in Paradise. He loves to read and almost always has a book within arm's reach. Nicholas enjoys school, especially math and science. He participates in Drama and loves performing in plays, both during the school year and in the summer at the Erickson Center for the Arts in Curtis.

Ash

by Walter Dennis (3rd Place, Sr. Division)

◆❖◆

•••

Of course! Just my luck! I get lost in the woods and decide to stay in some random abandoned hotel, that by the way is totally not creepy at all, and now I can hear footsteps coming down the hallway. Drawing closer and closer to my room. Perfect. Just perfect. Hunting me down. *Stomp... stomp... stomp...* Then they pause. I don't breathe. A long creak echoes through the building as an ancient door swings up. I peek out of my bed. My door is still closed. I let out all the air I didn't even realize I was holding in.

Then the footsteps start again. This time closer and closer, until they stop at my door. I cover myself with the old bed sheets and push myself deeper into the bed. Another creak, and this time it is my door. I don't move a muscle. *Please, please, please just go away. Please don't notice me.*

The sound of something breathing heavily fills my room. Then it takes a step into my room. *It's over.* I peek my head out from under the covers. A dark silhouette of a person is standing in the doorway of my room. I can make out long black hair and tattered clothes. Then she looks directly at me, with her empty, lifeless eyes, and starts sprinting toward me.

It all started when I had decided to go on a hunting trip alone in the woods. I didn't plan on being away from home for too long though, because I still had a big research project for work that I needed to have done in a few days, and I still hadn't finished it yet. It was unusual for me to not have finished all my work by now, but I was so distracted with the beginning of hunting season that I couldn't focus on it. So I eventually gave in. In and out. I'd be gone for a day, and If I was lucky, I'd come home with a deer, but not everything went to plan.

It was a foggy and moist day. Not perfect for hunting, but it would do. I set up my little deer blind in the usual spot, right at the end of the blueberry trail. Then I waited, and waited, and waited some more. Nothing ever happened. Then I heard splat... splat... splat. It was starting to rain. *Welp... I guess I better call it there. Don't want to get poured on.*

I zipped up my bright orange jacket, put my hood up, slung my backpack around my shoulder, and packed up my blind. I started down the blueberry trail, heading toward my pickup truck waiting for me on the side of the road. Then it started to really rain, and after the rain came the thick fog. I continued to follow the trail, until it abruptly stopped. *What? The trail can't just disappear. I've been on this trail plenty of times, I can't be lost. If I remember correctly the trail should be right through these trees.*

On the other side of the trees was something that I had never seen before. A small clearing gave way to a giant, abandoned building. It seemed to resemble an old hotel. Faded white siding lined with big windows, some boarded up. As I stared in awe at the giant building in front of me, I spotted the door. A fancy glass double-door that appeared to be in perfect condition.

I sprinted over to the door, as thunder struck the sky above me. I set my hand on the metal handle and pushed inward, halfway expecting to have to force the door open, but to my surprise it opened with ease. The interior looked perfectly fine. *Weird.* This definitely was some kind of a hotel though. The room that I had just walked into resembled a hotel lobby.

A living room area was to my right, filled with furniture covered with white sheets. A big brick fireplace sat mounted on the wall, looking like it hadn't been used in years. A desk was to my left, complete with a small bell and an old-looking computer. *Surely this place hasn't seen any customers in a very long time.*

Well, might as well make sure that nobody is here. I walked over to the bell and tapped the top. Ding! I waited and listened. Nothing.

"Hello! Is anybody here?" I yelled into the dark room.

No response again.

Guess I'm alone. I'll just wait out the storm here. Hopefully It's over soon, I still need to finish my project for work. I don't want to just wait around in the lobby though, maybe I'll do some exploring. Surely there's some interesting things in an abandoned hotel. I pulled my flashlight out of my backpack, and checked my watch. 6:47 P.M. *Wow! The time really flew by!*

I clicked my flashlight on and turned to the right. Straight down the hallway. It almost looked like something was moving in the darkness at the end of the hallway, but I was sure it was nothing. Then I started walking down the hallway, getting ever more eager to explore.

That's it, I guess. I had made my way back to the lobby where I'd started. It turned out that this was pretty much a normal hotel, filled with rooms to stay in. It had everything a normal hotel would have: a pool that appeared to have been emptied a long time ago, a few small meeting rooms, laundry rooms, and even a master suite. All the rooms were left unlocked too!

I looked down at my watch. 9:05 P.M. *Holy crap! Where did all the time go? Hopefully It's done raining.* I walked up to the front door and peered outside. The storm was definitely still going strong, and it wasn't showing any signs of slowing down soon. It was getting darker and darker, and a creepy fog was starting to roll in.

You know, maybe the power is still turned on out here. I don't want to just sit alone in a dark lobby. There must be some kind of master breaker box or something around here. Probably in the basement... I better get home soon. I still need to finish my work.

My flashlight lit up once again as I flipped the switch. I just took a second to reflect as my light illuminated the dark hallway in front of me. *This is crazy.* I did spot a staircase heading down at the end of the hallway when I explored the place, I'm sure that's where I would turn on the power.

I slowly crept down the hallway until I made it to the staircase. I took one step down, then paused. A shiver ran through my body. *It's getting cold. I wonder what Jill and Lucas are doing right now. Hopefully they're not worried that I'm not home yet.*

A wooden door greeted me at the bottom of the steps. I opened it and stepped into the basement. It was frigid. I looked around with my flashlight. It was pitch black down here. The basement was a huge concrete room filled with machinery and furniture covered with more white sheets. *This is super creepy. All I need to do is find the main breaker.*

I illuminated the walls with my flashlight until I spotted a big important-looking breaker on the wall. I walked over to it. Then I heard a sound. It sounded like a footstep. I opened the door to the breaker. Another footstep. Shivers went through my body. *Is somebody here?*

The breaker was filled with switches, each switch labeled with a room number. *There must be a main switch right?* Step... Step... Step. The sound was happening more and more often now. It sounded like it was behind me. Step. Step. Step.

I spotted it: the switch labeled "main." Louder now. Step. Step. I switched it on. There was a loud buzz, then everything came on. I spun around, partially thinking that something would be behind me. Waiting, but there was nothing.

I returned back to the lobby, turning on all the lights on the way. I looked out the door again. Still storming. I checked my watch, I was getting tired. 10:03 P.M. *How about I just stay the night here. I'm sure I can finish the project tomorrow morning.*

I dug for my phone in my backpack and eventually found it. No service. *I'm sure my wife and son are fine too. I just gotta finish that project. How about I sleep in the suite. Nice change of scenery for the night.* I walked down the hallway toward the suite.

When I got there I opened the door and flipped on the lights. Everything looked so nice. *If only someone renovated this place, It would honestly be really nice.*

I used the bathroom, and surprisingly the toilet flushed. *Weird. Everything still seems like it's in perfect condition. Whatever. This whole place is weird. Hopefully I can get out of here and finish my project soon.* The rain tapped on the roof as I pushed myself into the fancy-looking bed. *It's so comfy.* I shut my eyes as I heard a distant strike of thunder outside.

I suddenly awoke to the sound of footsteps coming down the hallway toward my room. Then I heard a click as the power went out again. I bolted upright. The footsteps continued toward me. Then they suddenly stopped, as a door creaked open. Luckily it wasn't my door. Then they started again. Heading towards my door again. I held my breath.

Then my door popped open. I saw a silhouette of what looked like a young girl. I was in shock. She had long black hair and tattered old clothes. Then she started sprinting at me, as a terrible scream escaped her mouth. I braced for impact. I held up my fists to block her. Then she faded away... *Am I dreaming...* Then I fainted.

Everything was black. Then a soft but somehow raspy voice filled my head.

"You're not my mom"

"What?"

"Who are you?"

"What is happening? Is this some kind of weird lucid dream? I can think and hear, but I see nothing."

"I can hear your thoughts... Who are you? You're not supposed to be here."

Then I pushed myself to talk, instead of just think, "H-Hey. I'm Grayson. I'm sorry, I got lost in the woods and thought that this was abandoned."

"Abandoned?" She seemed surprised.

Then neither of us said anything. Just the darkness was there.

This must be a dream. Why do I have to go through all this just to get back to my work?

"You're not dreaming. This is real," she said.

"Who are you and what is happening?"

"I'm Ash.... I'm looking for my mom and you're not my mom."

"What happened to your mom?"

"I woke up one day and she was gone. Everyone was gone. We were just staying here for the weekend. Now I am just trying to find her again. I miss her very much. She is the most important thing to me in this entire world."

"This hotel looks like it's been abandoned for a very long time..." I mumbled, "Do you live here?"

"I guess you could say that. Ever since I woke up I just kind of have been here. I've never left. I haven't eaten or slept in days. I just want to see my mom again."

Then I saw her in the distance of the darkness. The girl from the hallway. Her head was tilted at an angle as she stared at me.

I bolted up in my bed again. I was breathing heavily. I peered out the window of my room. It was pitch black out my window. *I have to get out of here.* I grabbed my backpack and the folded-up deer blind, and made a break for the hallway. All the lights were back on. I ran to the lobby and pushed open the door, and stepped into nothing. Into black.

Literally nothing. Just black. Then there was a thud as the door back into the hotel vanished in the darkness, and I heard her again.

"You almost escaped," she said in a calm, yet unsettling voice.

What is happening? I want nothing to do with this.

"Back to the topic," she sneered, "What do you know about my mom?"

This girl is crazy. "Nothing." *I relaxed myself. If I can't escape this dream then so be it.*

"You must know something. She was only here a few days ago."

"A few days ago? This hotel looks years abandoned," I responded.

"Years? It can't be," she snickered.

"I have a question for you. Do you know what year it is?"

"Uhhhh... yes, It's 1910."

1910...

"It's 2025."

"It can't be."

Neither of us said anything.

Then she spoke up, "Do you have a family?"

This was definitely a weird dream.

"Ye-Yes," I stammered, "I have a son named Lucas, and my wife, Jill."

"Where are they?"

"They are at home. I got lost in the woods."

"So you're like me? You just want to see your family again?"

This is getting seriously weird.

I interrupted, "Are you a ghost?"

"No..."

"Well... you said you don't eat or sleep, and you seem to think that we are still in the 1900s... What is the last thing that you remember?"

"My mom tucked me into bed at the hotel... and that's it.... Wait. No. Yes. Hmmm... Now that I think of it I also remember people, hearing faint yelling as I went to sleep, but that's it. I've felt so alone and empty since then."

"I hate to break this to you, but I'm pretty sure that was over one hundred years ago," I said.

"Y-know... Let me think about this.." her voice cut off, "All I want to do is see my family, and if all you're telling me is true then why am I still here."

"I don't know." I murmured.

Then neither of us said anything for a long time.

"I miss my family," she said suddenly.

I didn't respond.

I sat in the darkness for a long time, thinking about my family. *What would I do If this was real, and I was in her position? Would my own family miss me? I barely see Lucas nowadays, I am always working. I wish I could spend more time with him and Jill. Don't be silly. This can't happen in real life. Ghosts aren't real.* I pinched myself, and I felt it. *What?* Then I shut my eyes for a second, and fell asleep.

•••

When I awoke I was back at home. Sunlight shone through the windows. I yawned as I grabbed my phone from the nightstand. The reminder that I had set sat on my home screen. "Research Project due in Three Days."

I looked over to the other side of the bed. It was empty. Jill must've gotten up already. Suddenly, I remembered the crazy dream I had. *Was that a message? I sure do wish I spent more time with my family. It was a wakeup call.*

I stumbled into the kitchen and spotted Jill sitting at the kitchen table, reading the newspaper.

"Good morning honey!" she said excitedly.

"Good morning!" I responded.

"Me and Lucas were about to go on a walk to the park. He asked if you could come with, but I told him that you had work to do."

"I'll come!" I responded.

"I'm sure he'll be excited." She laughed.

I spent the rest of the day with my family, and didn't even think about my work. *The dream really was a message.* Once it was late, and Lucas was put to bed, I figured I'd better check my email. There's always something going on with the newspaper company. Never a slow news day around here.

The first email was from my boss. "How's your research going? You're doing it on the myth about the hotel in the woods where the murder happened, right?"

Walter Dennis is a sophomore at Lake Linden-Hubbell High School. He enjoys spending time in the woods of Michigan's Upper Peninsula; whether that's on a bike, a 4-wheeler, or even on a walk. He loves to explore and take the road less traveled. Besides that, Walter enjoys hobbies such as swimming, reading, and writing.

Help Sell
The U.P. Reader!

◆❖◆

The popularity of the *U.P. Reader* is growing, but we need it to grow more.

Help us sell the *U.P. Reader* by selling the Reader alongside your other books. The *U.P. Reader* at its wholesale price allows those who wish to carry it to make a nice profit on the sales. Bookstores and individuals can all benefit from helping the U.P. Reader grow.

If you have writing that has been published in the *U.P. Reader*, you should be selling copies of the Reader alongside your other work. This not only helps get exposure for your writing but for all the others that were accepted alongside yours. Part of the mission of the *U.P. Reader* is to get the many voices of the writers of the UPPAA in a single publication so that readers would have a place to find and sample the incredible talent that makes up the authors and poets of the Upper Peninsula.

Taking a few Readers to an event can make the difference in selling. Those who have been selling the U.P. Reader have seen good sales and considerable interest in the publication from readers and customers. Many customers ask the seller if they have a piece in the book to sign it. As the U.P. Reader is helping you as a writer, you can be helping the *U.P. Reader.*

Do you have local booksellers in your area? Encourage them to stock the *U.P. Reader.* Bookstores that are selling the Reader are seeing brisk sales. Many of the bookstores have restocked their issues several times and are saying how much they enjoy them. They are profitable and returnable. The *U.P. Reader* is a win-win situation for bookstores.

Take a copy of the U.P. Reader to your child's English or Language Arts teacher. The Dandelion Cottage Award is open to all children in U.P. schools and homeschool. There is never a fee to participate!

Back issues of the *U.P. Reader* are also still available. They can still be ordered right alongside the new issue and can be combined to sell as a set. There are many who still haven't discovered the *U.P. Reader* yet, and a package set is a nice way to introduce them to the joys of reading a *Reader.* These can still be purchased wholesale just like the current issue.

There are hardcover versions of the *U.P. Reader* as well. These are beautiful bound versions of the *U.P. Reader* that are a wonderful keepsake for the real *U.P. Reader* fan. Again, these can be ordered wholesale and sold right alongside the paperback versions.

To order, go to UPReader.org/publications on the web and put in your order. Contributing authors will be emailed a discount code and their orders will be discounted to the wholesale price (50% Off!).

Please help us, help you make the *U.P. Reader* a success!

Come join
UPPAA Online!

The UPPAA maintains an online presence on several social media areas. To get the most out of your UPPAA membership, be sure to visit, "like," and share these destinations and posts whenever possible!

Web Sites

- **www.UPPAA.org**: learn about meetings, publicity opportunities, publicize your own author events, add your book to the catalog page, read newsletter archive.
- **www.UPReader.org**: complete details about deadlines, submission guidelines, how to place a print advertisement, where to buy U.P. Reader locally, and more.

Facebook Pages

- **UPPAA**: www.facebook.com/UPSISU/ —OR—type in **@UPSISU** into the Facebook "search" bar
- **UP Reader**: www.facebook.com/upreaders/ —OR— type in **@UPreader** into the Facebook "search" bar

Twitter

- Message to **@UP_Authors** or visit https://twitter.com/UP_Authors

Comprehensive Index of U.P. Reader Volumes 1 through 5

◆❖◆

CPSIA information can be obtained
at www.ICGtesting.com
Printed in the USA
BVHW062304230421
605732BV00014B/2473